HIGH RISE STORIES

HIGH RISE STORIES

VOICES FROM CHICAGO PUBLIC HOUSING

COMPILED AND EDITED BY
AUDREY PETTY

FOREWORD BY
ALEX KOTLOWITZ

Assistant editor
CRYSTAL THOMAS

Research editor
ALEX CARP

Advising editor
PETER ORNER

VOICE OF WITNESS

Additional interviewers
MICHAEL BURNS, SHAVAHN DORRIS-JEFFERSON, JOYCE LEE,
JILL PETTY, ERIC TANYAVUTTI, CRYSTAL THOMAS, AVA ZELIGSON

Transcribers
LYANNE ALFARO, GIOVAN ALONZI, CHARLOTTE CROWE, NICK DEBOER,
IAN DELANEY, YANNIC DOSENBACH, SAUNDRA DOUGHERTY,
HANNAH DOYLE, AZRA HALILOVIC, NATHANIEL LASH, MEGAN ROBERTS,
ANN SZEKELY, TED TRAUTMAN, AND PAUL GARTON, INC.

Copy editor
ANNE MCPEAK

Fact checker
PETER STEPEK

Proofreaders
TREVOR SCOTT BARTON, MARIE DUFFIN, KRYSTAL RENEÉ MILLER,
VALERIE SNOW, SALLY WEATHERS

Additional assistance
LAUREN HEINZ, NAOKI O'BRYAN, JILL PETTY, FERNANDO PUJALS,
TIANA PYER-PEREIRA, ADAM SOTO

Dedicated to the Chicagoans
who shared their stories for this book, and to the memory
of my mother, Naomi Elizabeth Jackson Petty

VOICE OF WITNESS

MᶜSWEENEY'S BOOKS
SAN FRANCISCO

For more information about McSweeney's, see www.mcsweeneys.net
For more information about Voice of Witness, see www.voiceofwitness.org

ISBN: 978-1-938073-37-3

VOICE OF WITNESS

Voice of Witness is a non-profit organization that uses oral history to illuminate contemporary human rights crises in the U.S. and around the world. Its book series depicts these injustices through the oral histories of the men and women who experience them. The Voice of Witness Education Program brings these stories, and the issues they reflect, into high schools and impacted communities through oral history-based curricula and holistic educator support. Visit www.voiceofwitness.org for more information.

CONTENTS

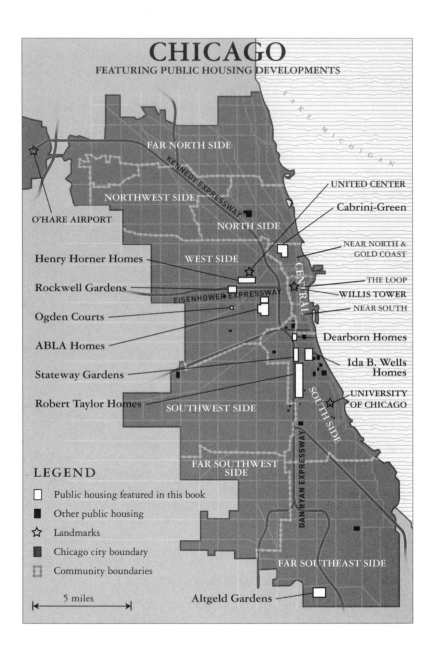

CHICAGO
FEATURING PUBLIC HOUSING DEVELOPMENTS

LAKE MICHIGAN

FAR NORTH SIDE

KENNEDY EXPRESSWAY

NORTHWEST SIDE

O'HARE AIRPORT

NORTH SIDE

UNITED CENTER

Cabrini-Green

NEAR NORTH &
GOLD COAST

Henry Horner Homes

WEST SIDE

THE LOOP

Rockwell Gardens

CENTRAL

WILLIS TOWER

EISENHOWER EXPRESSWAY

NEAR SOUTH

Ogden Courts

ABLA Homes

Dearborn Homes

Stateway Gardens

Ida B. Wells
Homes

Robert Taylor Homes

SOUTH SIDE

UNIVERSITY
OF CHICAGO

SOUTHWEST SIDE

FAR SOUTHWEST
SIDE

DAN RYAN EXPRESSWAY

LEGEND

☐ Public housing featured in this book

■ Other public housing

☆ Landmarks

▨ Chicago city boundary

▨ Community boundaries

|← 5 miles →|

FAR SOUTHEAST SIDE

Altgeld Gardens

VITAL
NEIGHBORHOODS

by Alex Kotlowitz

In 1987, when I first set foot in the Henry Horner Homes, a public housing complex on Chicago's West Side, I trembled—not out of fear, but out of shame. How could it be possible that people in the world's richest nation lived in such intolerable conditions? How could I not have known? These were places built on the cheap and then outright neglected by the powers-that-be.

Reading the accounts within this book of the physical decay and danger of now demolished high rises, I recall my own first glimpse of non-working elevators that became steel traps, open breezeways that cut through buildings, overheated apartments, caged-in walkways, and overflowing trash chutes. I remember one building at Horner where tenants complained of a stench emanating from the toilets, the odor of rotting meat. And so the Chicago Housing Authority sent workers into the basement where they found carcasses of dead cats and dogs, along with a trove of 2,000 rusting, never-used refrigerators, stoves, and kitchen cabinets that had long ago been forgotten. The high rises were structures simply too massive, too ignored, and too underfunded to become places where people could thrive. Indeed, at times their very existence seemed like a crime against humanity.

Yet here's the other thing about high rise public housing: these were rich, vital neighborhoods. It was, to be sure, an odd paradox. Here were places marked at times by utterly inhuman conditions, and yet residents considered these buildings home. Tenants in the high rises often felt they belonged to something—they were among family and friends, and they had neighbors to lean on. Any time of day or night at Horner, there were always people outside. Everywhere. Just hanging out. Playing basketball. Standing in the breezeways gossiping. Repairing cars. Shooting dice. Shooting marbles. Skipping rope. Playing chess. Barbecuing. There was so much activity, so much clamor, that when I would take some of the kids I got to know camping, the quietness of the woods unnerved them. Public housing, for all its physical ruin, was a lively, spirited place, whose residents—at least many of them—could imagine living nowhere else.

All that eventually changed, though. In describing Chicago's high rise projects in their final years I hesitate to use the word community, because by the end, violence had frayed the sense of commonweal for so many residents. Shootings came to define public housing in the media and perhaps contributed more to the razing of the high rises than their sub-standard maintenance. For the residents themselves, the violence left behind both physical and emotional wreckage so deep and so profound it altered lives. Virtually every voice in these pages speaks of having lost a neighbor, friend, or family member to the shootings. Yet even as these voices share stories from lives diminished by neighborhood violence, they still regard the demolition of their former neighborhoods—their former communities—as essentially tragic. It's what they knew. For some narrators, it's where they came of age. For others, it's where they formed lifelong relationships with friends who were fighting the same fights.

The scale of public housing's transformation has wrought immense change in the lives of those who resided there. At its peak, Chicago public housing made up a city the size of Des Moines, Iowa: 200,000 people. And then, just like that, in a matter of years, the high rises toppled one after another, so quickly it felt like someone had rolled a bowling ball through swaths of the city. It was as if once the decision was made to raze public housing, there was no time to spare. Indeed, public housing had become an embarrassment to a nation that likes to think of itself as generous and compassionate. And in some ways it's what I miss about the high rises: you couldn't drive through Chicago without taking note of them. They were reminders of who we are—and who we aren't.

And yet, of course, even though so many Chicago commuters were confronted daily with the high rises' facades along the Dan Ryan and Eisenhower Expressways, most of the city never had any idea what life was actually like inside the buildings. Even those who really needed to know. Once, Mayor Richard M. Daley held a press conference assailing water bill deadbeats, the largest being the Chicago Housing Authority. He flippantly suggested that the city start charging public housing residents for showers. The thing is, people in most public housing high rises didn't have showers, just baths.

As these pages so poignantly capture, the high rises were full of people simply aspiring to an American ideal, a place where education would afford opportunities for their children, a place where they could live in safety and security, a place where if they worked hard, success would follow. Now that the high rises are gone, former residents still struggle to attain that ideal, even as they and their neighbors have been scattered to the winds, many living in equally impoverished neighborhoods in the city. With public housing gone, in some quarters there's a notion that everyone's made it, that poverty has gone out of fashion. In sharing their stories, the voices in these pages remind the rest of their city—and their country—that they are still here, still striving for a place to call home.

Alex Kotlowitz
March 3, 2013

Alex Kotlowitz, the award-winning author of three books, is perhaps best known for the bestselling There Are No Children Here, *which the New York Public Library chose as one of the 150 most important books of the twentieth century. His stories have appeared in print, radio, and film, including his 2011 documentary,* The Interrupters, *which was selected as one of the top ten films of the year by numerous publications, and which was the recipient of an Independent Spirit Award.*

ON PLANS AND TRANSFORMATIONS

by Audrey Petry

Build up the cities.
Set up the walls again.
—Carl Sandburg, "And They Obey"

When the high rise buildings came down, footage of the demolition was posted on YouTube. There you can find—in montage, time-lapse, or real time—various stages of destruction of the Robert Taylor Homes, Stateway Gardens, Rockwell Gardens, Grace Abbott Homes, Cabrini-Green, Lakefront Properties. There are videos of each high rise of Lakefront Properties being felled by implosion. Collapse occurs not all at once, but gradually, horizontally, with thick, smoky vapors of dust rising in the wake. Other public housing structures were dismantled with cranes, excavators, backhoes. Aside from the jackhammers briskly knocking through windows and concrete, so much of the machinery seems weary. In one video, a wrecking ball appears to move in slow motion as it swings back and then lands, crushing a wall painted robin's egg blue.

When the high rises came down, there was official talk about progress. What was afoot was the Plan for Transformation: a $1.6 billion project and the largest public housing "redevelopment venture" in the United States. Announced in 1999, the ambitious plan reflected and reinforced national trends; many municipal governments in major cities (like New Orleans and Atlanta) demolished swaths of public housing structures and replaced them with voucher distribution programs and limited access to mixed-income developments. The Chicago Housing Authority (CHA) unveiled a major advertising campaign to promote its agenda, rebranding itself with a slogan "This is CHAnge"[1] and promising impacted CHA tenants, and the city at large, a fresh start. In Chicago, mirroring other neoliberal efforts across the country, planners have relied on the market to regulate the terms of what has been touted as full-scale reform. The vast majority of those directly impacted by wide-scale demolitions have been required to seek out housing in the private sector. For thousands, the outcomes have included displacement, multiple moves, and homelessness. In the current economy, the poverty rate is higher than ever in Chicago, as is the need for affordable housing.

When the high rises came down, TV cameras from all over the world were on-site. When the last towers of Cabrini and Robert Taylor Homes were toppled, coverage was the lead on the ten o'clock news. Scores of tourists and locals alike took snapshots as mementos, as proof. Now, thirteen years after the demolitions commenced, countless Chicagoans still know these lost places by heart. Eddie Leman clearly recalls Robert Taylor Homes where, for the first thirteen years of his life, he lived with his

---

[1] Media ads for the Plan for Transformation were designed pro-bono by the Chicago-based advertising agency Leo Burnett.

mother. "That's probably something you don't even see in a lot of cities anymore. Sixteen stories and what was it? About two hundred feet, you know? And about twelve, thirteen apartments on one floor. Each apartment got families."

I am a South Sider who came of age in the early 1980s, the child of native Southerners. My first neighborhood was all-black, middle-class Chatham Village. At age seven, I moved with my family to Hyde Park–Kenwood, a relatively well-to-do, racially integrated community, now best known as Barack Obama's adopted stomping grounds. When venturing out, I learned boundaries. Just across a field was busy East Forty-Seventh Street, lined with tenements, nightclubs, taverns, liquor stores, a meager grocery, a hardware store, and a funeral home. Postcard Chicago glimmered in the distance: the Sears Tower, the Standard Oil, the Prudential. Though my parents forbade me to traverse East Forty-Seventh alone, eventually I'd sneak across the much-trafficked thoroughfare to buy penny candies from the closest liquor store.

Ten blocks south of the townhouse where I grew up are the stately, Gothic halls of the University of Chicago. My forays onto the campus were more complicated. I wandered through quiet courtyards, intrigued by gargoyles crowning archways and alcoves, peeking through ivy. And I was regularly stopped short in my explorations, barred from entering public halls by uniformed guards who ordered me to leave. (Close to home, my brown skin often helped me blend into a crowd. But in the ever-emerging maze of the University of Chicago, it marked me as an outsider.)

To the west of my neighborhood, and closer to us than the city's downtown skyscrapers, stood Robert Taylor Homes. Twenty-eight high rise buildings. Together they formed an imposing facade. Though my memory often fits them into my daily vista, I couldn't actually see Robert Taylor Homes from my doorstep. Nonetheless, I saw them often—on the weekly bus ride to piano lessons, excursions to the ballpark, and fall and winter holiday drives to my aunt and uncle's place on the Far West Side. I saw them often and I also imagined them. As I imagined them, the buildings were always *over there*. Despite their physical proximity, the buildings seemed remote, vividly unto themselves. They were terminally run-down. Robert Taylor Homes were public housing, back then the largest public housing complex in the United States. And while the peak of the Sears Tower seemed entirely reachable to me as a kid, Robert Taylor Homes were ever unknowable, ever apart.

When those buildings came down, starting in 2003, I was grown up, a resident of Urbana (in downstate Illinois), and a frequent visitor to my hometown. Word of the demolition of places like Robert Taylor Homes didn't surprise me. City Hall's rationales were what I expected; I'd followed headline stories about high rise public housing nearly all of my life. Nonetheless, the eventual destruction of these landmarks stunned me. The absence of the twenty-eight buildings of Robert Taylor Homes compelled me to reckon with their enormity as a community. *What were those communities really like?* I wondered. *And where on earth did all those people go?*

Chicago's Black Belt took shape at the turn of the twentieth century. As a result of the Great Migration, the city's black population increased eightfold from 1910 through the 1940s, and this growing population was relegated to a space that didn't expand to accommodate the newcomers. Black Chicagoans were hemmed in principally to areas on the South Side (and secondarily on the West Side) of the city, forming what came to be called a "black metropolis"—a community of grand homes and boulevards alongside deplorable tenements. All too often, the tenement-style housing made infamous by Gwendolyn Brooks's *Maud Martha* and Richard Wright's *Native Son*—dilapidated and rat-infested—accurately captured the living conditions of thousands upon thousands of people in the Black Belt.

The Chicago Housing Authority was born in 1937 shortly after the New Deal Congress passed the Wagner-Steagall Act. The act provided funds for public housing construction and public housing subsidies to dozens of municipalities during the height of the Depression. Some of the first public housing developments in Chicago were designed as temporary housing for soldiers returning from war; others were open to applications from Chicago residents who could prove their family income was below an ever-changing threshold.

Early Chicago public housing was strictly segregated. It was in keeping with federal policy (the Neighborhood Composition Rule developed by FDR's Interior Secretary, Harold Ickes), that new developments were created in concert with the prevailing demographics of a given neighborhood—tenants of new housing developments were to be of the same race as their immediate neighbors. By the time the Ida B. Wells development was first opened in 1941, the Black Belt was dangerously overcrowded. So there was a great deal of optimism when the CHA opened a sixteen-hundred-unit complex consisting of two-, three-, and four-story brick apartment buildings in the Douglas neighborhood. Indeed, the Ida B. Wells Homes formed a highly coveted address for African-Americans. More than eighteen thousand families filed applications to live there.

One may not readily think of housing developments as large neighborhoods, but in the case of Chicago, politics and architecture converged to make this so. In opposition to early CHA policies that endorsed row houses and small multi-family buildings as more socially productive and family-friendly, Mayor Richard J. Daley (in office from 1955 until his death in 1976) and the CHA opted for the high rise as the new model of public housing. The Chicago public housing development became iconic: the high rise shouldered by matching high rises, expanses of grass framing the whole. In 1962, at the groundbreaking for Robert Taylor Homes, the mayor addressed the throng under a banner that read:

GOOD HOMES BUILDING GOOD CITIZENS

"This project represents the future of a great city," the mayor said. "It represents vision. It represents what all of us feel America should be, and that is: a decent home for every family . . ."

Robert Taylor Homes were named after the CHA's first black board member—notably, a man who resigned in 1950 out of frustration with the city's recalcitrance toward integration of public housing—and comprised twenty-eight sixteen-story buildings slated to house eleven thousand people. The Dan Ryan Expressway was erected in 1962, in tandem with the construction of Robert Taylor Homes, effectively keeping white ethnic neighborhoods (including Mayor Daley's own Bridgeport) on one side of the fourteen-lane expressway and the new public housing on the other. At its peak, in 1964, Robert Taylor Homes housed twenty-seven thousand people—twenty thousand of them children. Robert Taylor Homes became part of the State Street corridor, with four major public housing developments taking up four consecutive miles of city in all.

Defunded by city, state, and federal governments over the course of the 1970s forward, high rise public housing was chronically neglected and mismanaged. Common physical plant troubles encountered by residents have included backed-up incinerators, perpetually broken elevators, and infestations of roaches and vermin. These problems were compounded by ongoing crises that occasionally made the national nightly news: rampant gang drug dealing, turf wars, and gun violence.

Whereas Richard J. Daley ushered in the revolution in high rise public housing in Chicago, his son Richard M. Daley (1980–2010) was at the helm of its systematic dismantling. Summarizing his intentions, Mayor Richard M. Daley would profess his desire to "rebuild people's souls."

His CEO of the Chicago Housing Authority, Terry Peterson, would refer to the targeted high rises as "Godawful buildings." In 1998, nearly nineteen thousand CHA units failed viability inspection mandated by the Department of Housing and Urban Development, meaning that under federal law the Authority was required to demolish those units within five years. The following year the CHA initiated the Plan for Transformation. Approved by the U.S. Department of Housing and Urban Development in 2000, the stated goals of the plan are to renew the physical structure of CHA properties, promote self-sufficiency for public housing residents, de-concentrate poverty, and reform the administration of the CHA.

From the start, many CHA residents responded to the Plan for Transformation with skepticism and resistance. Tenant activists banded together to express concerns about their displacement, file lawsuits, and raise alarm about developers seizing coveted swaths of real estate for redevelopment and private profit. Current tenant activism has addressed the problem of wide-scale homelessness, voicing demands for the rehabilitation of empty buildings rather than their eradication. Organized protest has also resulted in the shelving of a 2011 plan for the mandatory drug testing of all renters in public housing.[2]

As of 2013, the city's ten-year project is now officially behind schedule, and the completion date has been extended to 2015. Rebuilding has not kept pace with demolition, and a great number of displaced families now find themselves in poor and underserved neighborhoods like Roseland and Englewood on the city's South Side, using housing vouchers to rent privately owned homes, some more distressed and dangerous than their former CHA-maintained properties. In so many critical ways, place matters in Chicago. As Dr. Doriane Miller, University of Chicago professor and director

---

[2] Although drug testing is not a requirement for all Chicago public housing recipients, testing still applies to residents of housing in mixed-income developments.

21

of the Center for Community Health and Vitality puts it, "In Chicago one's zip code is as determinative of one's health outcomes as one's DNA."

As a result of the Plan for Transformation, city government has demolished or rebuilt twenty-five thousand public housing units and simultaneously relocated tens of thousands of people.[3] And nothing is settled. For many outsiders, the disappeared buildings of Chicago public housing are too often considered in purely symbolic terms, with former residents easily categorized as troublemakers or victims. The truths of the matter belie such facile conclusions. The narrators of *High Rise Stories* describe the promise, the failure, and the success of the high rises. Their homes were once Cabrini-Green, Robert Taylor Homes, Stateway Gardens, ABLA Homes, Ogden Courts, and Rockwell Gardens. Some express their relief at having moved away. Others describe their fear of what comes next. Each and every one expresses the myriad ways they invested in their communities.

Most of the narrators in this book spent their early lives in public housing. Forty-seven-year-old Paula Hawkins describes the floor where she lived in Cabrini-Green as being filled with fellow playmates and a network of women who looked out for everyone. Summer days on the gated porch of that floor were spent together, sharing fun and games and homemade ice cream. "It was like a family reunion all the time," Paula muses. Decades later, in recovery from substance abuse and with children and grandchildren of her own, Paula would be turned away from public housing because of her background. Chandra Bell, forty-one years old, also grew up in Cabrini. Like Paula, she treasures close relationships with neighbors who were "like family" and fun-filled activities at the neighborhood public library, but Chandra also grapples with the ways

---

[3] For more on the impact of the Plan for Transformation on CHA residents' lives, see appendix V on page 246 and appendix VI on page 254.

neighborhood violence marred her childhood. When she was twelve years old, Chandra saw a school classmate shot by a sniper. She and her family were friendly with the families of Dantrell Davis[4] and Girl X,[5] two children brutalized—Davis was killed—on the grounds of Cabrini-Green. Whereas Paula moved away from Cabrini-Green in the late seventies, Chandra came of age there in the eighties, as deindustrialization bottomed out jobs for many residents. As the drug economy boomed, gun violence became rampant. Chandra remembers that the front porch of her building was one of the safest places little children could gather. She also recounts an incident where a child in her building fell down an elevator shaft. Chandra now lives in a new mixed-income development (blueprinted by the Plan for Transformation) not far from where she grew up. While she enjoys many of the physical accommodations of her new address, she is aggrieved by the fact that her son, imprisoned on a drug conviction, is barred from ever visiting her home.

Eighty-three-year-old Dolores Wilson spent nearly her entire adult life in Cabrini-Green, raising a family with her husband, working for Water Works on Chicago's Gold Coast, and becoming a community leader in the PTA and the Local Advisory Council for Cabrini. After fifty-three years in Cabrini, Dolores was hastily relocated to a public housing development south of the Loop.[6] She has lost count of the valuables that she left behind.

Dolores, Chandra, and Paula are among the twelve former CHA residents in this book who reveal how they made their homes, and how, in

---

[4] Dantrell Davis was killed at the age of seven. Davis was caught in crossfire between rival gangs during a morning walk to elementary school with his mother.

[5] Girl X was a nine-year-old girl who was raped, tortured, and left for dead in the stairwell of a Cabrini-Green building. The attack left her mute, blind, and wheelchair bound.

[6] Chicago's downtown district.

the face of (and in spite of) direct and structural violence, they resisted, connected, survived, and how, sometimes, they even thrived. These narrators also remind us that the story of high rise public housing in Chicago continues to unfold. *High Rise Stories* speaks from the inside of "over there," filling in the stories of unit after unit, floor after floor.

You are invited inside.

EXECUTIVE EDITOR'S NOTE

The narratives in this book are the result of extensive oral history interviews with twenty-six men and women from Chicago, conducted over the course of two and a half years. Audrey Petty and her team of interviewers spoke with former public housing residents of Cabrini-Green, Rockwell Gardens, ABLA Homes, and Robert Taylor Homes, among others. These recorded interviews—over a hundred hours of audio—were transcribed by a small corps of dedicated volunteers. Audrey and the editorial team at Voice of Witness then shaped those raw transcripts into first-person narratives.

With every narrative, we aim for a novelistic level of detail and a birth-to-now chronologized scope in order to portray narrators as individuals in all their complexity, rather than as case studies. To achieve this depth of detail, Audrey conducted numerous follow-up interviews with narrators, and with their guidance, we shepherded those stories through multiple rounds of drafts. The twelve narratives featured in this book are the end result: a collection of voices that offer diverse, eye-opening, and deeply moving accounts of lives shaped by public housing policy.

Some of the narratives were chosen because they demonstrate gross social injustices. Others are more subtle, reflecting the dehumanizing lack of dignity afforded to people from public housing, as well as the deeply rooted sense of joy and community that feature in the recollections of many of our narrators. It was rare for us to hear an account with a purely negative or positive perspective, and many of the stories are wrought with ambivalence and emotional complexity.

The stories themselves remain faithful to the speakers' words, and have been carefully fact-checked. Various appendices and a glossary are included in the back of the book to provide context for the narratives and some explanation of the complex machinery and history of Chicago public housing. Needless to say, *High Rise Stories* is not a comprehensive history of Chicago public housing; there are countless more stories to be heard. Collected in these pages are a vital few that we hope will bring more stories to light, not only from Chicago but from around the country. We thank all the men and women who generously and patiently shared their experiences with us, including those whom we were unable to include in this book. We make available additional interviews, audiovisual materials, and news articles on the Voice of Witness website: voiceofwitness.org.

—mimi lok
Executive Director
& Executive Editor
Voice of Witness

CABRINI-GREEN

DOLORES WILSON

AGE: *83*

OCCUPATION: *Retired city worker, community organizer*

FORMER RESIDENT OF: Cabrini-Green

We first meet on a sunny day in March 2011, at a coffeehouse situated about a mile north of Dolores's new apartment in the Dearborn Homes. Dearborn Homes is a public housing complex situated at the crossroads between Bronzeville (to the south), the McCormick Place convention center (to the east), Chinatown (to the west), and the Chicago Loop (to the north). Dearborn Homes was one of the Chicago Housing Authority's first public housing developments and remains one of the last standing—it now houses mostly senior residents. Dolores was relocated here last month after living in Cabrini-Green for the last fifty-three years, from 1958 until 2011. As we talk, Dolores is clearly distraught at the thought of her old building's scheduled demolition. "So many of my treasures are still there," she says. She goes on to catalog some of the valuables (family photos, trophies, clothing, books) that she had to leave behind during the hasty relocation process. Days after our conversation, 1230 N. Burling—Dolores's former home, and one of the last public housing high rises left standing in Chicago—was demolished.

THE STERILE WARD

I was born in Chicago in 1929. Cook County Hospital, Ward 32. I think that's the sterile ward. They had 31 and 32. If you're born outside the ward, your baby's un-sterile 'cause you could catch anything in the hallway.

After I got grown and got married and started having children, my mother told me the Cook County Hospital is the best hospital to go to. She said, "They have the best doctors." And I soon found out why, because it was like a charity hospital. You're not turned around. They can treat this, treat that, the doctors are learning all that they didn't get in school.

I had Chichi and Debbie at Cook County Hospital. Cheryl was born at Provident. Mike and Kenny were born at home. Those were the easiest births I had, Mike and Kenny. Chichi almost died because he was breech. Feet first. If the instrument that the doctors used to turn the baby had not been there, I would have died. But it was there when they needed it. I wrote my mother a postcard, and I said on it: "I almost died!" When I got home she said, "You don't never write nothing like that on a postcard where the mailman and everybody can read it!"

They had this nice sudsy water or some kind of solution and a swab, and they would just clean you afterwards. Couldn't nobody get an infection or anything in there. I loved the County. I don't know how it was after years went by. I hate that they're tearing it down. That whole hospital— they could have made it for the homeless. They had everything: toilets, kitchen, everything. All they had to do was just get security to make sure nobody was causing any problems. Now they gonna tear down Michael Reese Hospital too,[1] for some kind of high rise. Chicago is a capitalistic town, is all I gotta say. And that's why we're not in Cabrini anymore.

---

[1] Michael Reese Hospital was founded on the Near South Side of Chicago in 1880. Its founding mission was to serve all Chicagoans without regard to race, creed, or nationality.

ONE OF THE FIRST FAMILIES IN CABRINI

I lived in Cabrini-Green for fifty-three years. My husband Hubert and I raised five children there. When we moved there in '58 the oldest was eight, the youngest were two and one, and we loved Cabrini. Where we'd been living on South Side, on Sixtieth and Prairie, they were like fire traps. The buildings were just deteriorating. The placement at the private real estate office would charge us ten dollars to find an apartment, and at that time ten dollars was a lot of money. But we paid it, and everywhere they sent us were nothing but fire traps. They were no good, and some of them said they didn't want children 'cause they throw rocks and break windows—like every child will throw rocks and break windows.

So I kept looking, and after a while I thought, *Well, Altgeld Gardens and Cabrini was offered to us by the city.*[2] I wanted Altgeld Gardens, 'cause the complex was made up of family homes, with little front yards and backyards, but the city buses near there ran on a slow schedule, and I didn't want to be slowed down by anything. When I was ready to go out of the house and go somewhere, I wanted a bus that was coming in the next two minutes or something. So that's what made me ask directions all the way to Cabrini-Green. And I loved the apartment. The apartment had three bedrooms, and it was on the fourteenth floor. When I first stepped off the elevators and looked out over the railing I thought I was going to faint! I'd never been up that high. The cars below looked like little toys. I didn't even try to look at anything. I just looked down to see how high up I was. But after a while you get to liking everything. Just

[2] In the mid-1960s, the median CHA family was working class and two parent. Rents in CHA housing units were determined by building maintenance costs, not family income. Not until the 1970s, with the passage of the Brooke Amendment at the federal level, was rent indexed to 25 percent of family income, then later 30 percent.

like with people, I don't care what neighborhood you're in. I don't care if it's a diverse area or what, after a while you get to love and know your neighbors and everything and get along. That's the way it was with me and that fourteenth floor.

Me and Martha Williams, who is still my very good girlfriend, we were the first two families to move into 1117 Cleveland. She was on the second floor. After they started moving more people in on the floor, you get to have neighbors and all, and in the back of my mind I'm wondering, *How this heifer gonna be?* And I was thinking, *I don't want to be up here fighting nobody, telling me that they smell garlic.* I'm using that as an example, 'cause we did have Puerto Rican neighbors, like the Montanes, who cooked a lot of garlic. I can't stand the smell of a lot of garlic. Makes me sick. But they were wonderful people and even though they were young, my children always wanted to go to church with the Montanes. I was so happy to know that somebody on the same floor is taking time with my children. And they had about four or five of their own. Taking them to church. And they would cry, "Mom, I want to go to church with Miss Montanes! I wanna go to church with the Montanes!" My son Michael was the main one begging to go with them. And I'd be glad. The kids went with them all the time.

THIS IS A CASTLE

Ten years later, around 1968, we moved from 1117 because my husband's boss wanted him to be the assistant head custodian in one of the Green buildings, and that meant maintaining a whole building. My husband's boss was moving out, and he wanted my husband to take his place. I thought that was such an honor, but the assistant heads and the heads had to live in the building that they care for. That's why we had to move on to 1230 N. Burling. I was so mad that we had to leave our home. That's how attached you get to people. Ooohhh, I cried the whole time! My next door neighbor, Queenie, we were like sisters, and so she and her husband and her daughters and son helped my family move with some of the guys in the neighborhood. And when I got off from working at the Water Department that day, everything was in divine order cause I'd marked on the boxes, *This goes in this room, that goes in that room.* Curtains were hung and everything. I was on the sixth floor and we had four bedrooms and a bath and a half. I said, "Oooh, this is a castle." But I still was around strangers.

The move to Burling happened right after the '68 riots, after King[3] was killed. I remember my son Kenny, who was about twelve at the time, was heading out the door when the riots first started, and he said, "Mom, I'm going over to Pioneer." That was the grocery store nearest in the neighborhood. And I said, "Going for what?" They were rioting every where. And the police didn't care. They had the National Guard, but as long as you didn't go east across Wells, you would be safe. No harm would come to you. You could tear up everything else on that side, because the Chicago Police Department didn't care about the stores and businesses. And you know, most of the businesses didn't come back.

And I said, "What are you going out there for?"

He said, "I'm gonna get a shopping cart."

He wanted to join the looters.

I said, "No you're not."

And he said, "Everybody else is."

I said, "You don't do what everybody else does. You do what I tell you to do."

---

[3] Martin Luther King, Jr.

WHERE'S THAT MUSIC?

After a while, my husband became head janitor. So we lived rent-free. I'm telling you, I could see myself with a home in the sky. But the more money you get, the more money you spend. But it was wonderful, you know. And everybody, they just loved our family. They really loved my husband. All he was supposed to do as head janitor was just work with a pen and paper. But he didn't know nothing about doing no easy work. He wanted to help push and pull the garbage, and help with everything.

They called him "Old Man." They said, "Old Man, we got this, we got this." So they would help him push the dumpster. That building was spotless. People loved my husband, so they wouldn't even throw anything down on the floor.

I would come home and he'd tell me about his day and I'd tell him about mine. I worked for the Water Department. It was a secretarial job in payroll, and it was nice. Office was in the Pumping Station over on Chicago and Michigan, on the Magnificent Mile. Across from the Water Tower. Then they moved us to the purification plant near Navy Pier.

When we were at 1117 Cleveland, my husband started a drum and bugle corps. And there were kids from 1117 and 1119 Cleveland, and kids from certain buildings in our area and across the street from the Green section. And they were in three or four Saint Patrick's Day parades. And they weren't even in full uniform 'cause they didn't have the money for uniforms. They would practice outside on the black top or Father Sebastian would let them come to Saint Joseph Church and practice in their school's gym. But then it at all changed after the '68 riots.

More people moved in from other places that had been affected by the riots. We started seeing gang writings on the wall. Sniping at different buildings. Snipers were a problem for many years. These people would set up in a window of the towers and just shoot at anyone. Two police got killed.[4] I remember one day, a cop car was sent to my building and someone was sniping at them from the building facing my lot. And one young girl I remember seeing, she had on a trench coat. She was really running across the lot. When she got to the building, the back of her coat had caught a whole lot of buckshot. It was a miracle she wasn't hurt.

The Eighteenth Police District, they sent Commander Brash and Mr. Fred Rice, who passed recently, and they worked with us and they had officers patrolling in that area, so the kids in the drum and bugle corps were protected when they were coming to practice. They'd have patrols watching them coming and going. That's how they got safe passage from Saint Joseph's Church to our building.

My husband worked with kids for many years. He had a basketball team and a baseball team. Those teams won trophies. The drum and bugle corps got twenty-three trophies without even being in full dress. The kids played music by ear, and when they played that "Watermelon Man," boy, people would be looking. "Oh, where's that music coming from?" Especially in the Saint Patrick's Day parade. People be amazed. *Where's that music?*

They were called the Corsairs, my husband's group. My son Mike, he played that timbale, that's the three drums. Dolores, stop bragging! Okay. Can't help bragging. And all the gals liked him. There were the flag girls and the rifle girls. You know, the ones that twirl the rifles and the girls that twirl the flag. You know, all they say is: practice makes perfect. Beautiful! They were beautiful together. So when my husband passed away in 1981, one of the guys in the corps said, "Momma Wilson, what we gotta do is have a concert every May 11." That's the day my husband passed. He said we were gonna have a day to celebrate—a day for my husband. But it never came through because this one's living here, that one's living there.

---

[4] In 1970, Sergeant James Severin and Officer Tony Rizzato were crossing a field when they were shot and killed by a sniper positioned in an upper-story of a Cabrini-Green high rise.

GANGS THAT DIDN'T EVEN HAVE NAMES

I was the president of our Building Council for ten years after my husband passed away, from about '83 to '93. That's how I got into the Local Advisory Council and residents' management program. Every building had a Building Council, but in the late eighties, the residents in 1230 N. Burling started taking resident management courses. We pulled together and handled everything except the electricity and plumbing. The residents had jobs—work order clerk, janitors, maintenance men, secretary, treasurer, everything. We even collected the rent. Eventually our building was rehabbed after we went into resident management. All of the blinds, all of the kitchen, the refrigeration, double-pane windows, everything was brand new. I believe 1230 N. Burling was the first building in Cabrini-Green that went into resident management. The first President Bush, Daddy Bush, named us "a model for the nation." We met with Jack Kemp and then Henry Cisneros in Washington, D.C. And our building was incorporated in 1992.[5]

Back when I first got started, at my first meeting as president of the Building Council, there was a room of people—old, young, middle-aged—waiting to hear from me. I was so happy when I came in and saw all these people in there, but then I got so flustered I didn't even know what to say. "A dah-dah-dah-dah-dap. Uh-uh-uh dip-dip-dip-dip . . . we'll have a striptease next week!" I didn't know what to say, you know, all the

---

[5] Jack Kemp was Housing and Urban Development Secretary under President George H. W. Bush, from 1989–1993 and Henry Cisneros was Housing and Urban Development Secretary under President Bill Clinton, from 1993–1997. 1230 N. Burling was the first of Chicago's high rises to be granted resident management status, a designation applied nationally under the first Bush administration to provide Federal dollars directly to public housing residents to develop and manage their buildings. By 1997, seven Cabrini-Green buildings were under resident control, as well as parts of Dearborn Homes and LeClaire Courts.

different ages, waiting to hear from me. People with little babies and guys in there that belonged to gangs. Everyone was giving me suggestions. *We can do this with the building, we can do that with the building.*

But what really took off was working with the little kids. The grown folks, the older ones, they would make their appearances at meetings for maybe a few months, but the little kids, they're the ones that kept working with me, improving the building, picking up trash. "You better pick! Ooh, I'm going to tell Miss Wilson you threw that paper on the floor." They'd pick up that litter and throw it in the garbage. I'd put homemade paper badges on the kids saying they're elevator monitors, so that folks don't get on and leave trash. I'd have two on at a time and they worked those elevator buttons. They didn't even want to get off.

The older kids—the boys—they didn't join gangs because they wanted to, but in the eighties, with other gangs moving into the neighborhood, this made them form gangs in response, for self-protection. Gangs that didn't even have names. Even I wanted to carry a gun. There was so much slicing and shooting and carrying on. I said, "I'm gonna start shooting back," but I didn't have no gun. One lady was shot at who had a baby in the stroller. They were just sniping from that one building, I'm telling you. And 1150 and 1160 Sedgwick. One group just took over those two buildings, and guys that used to live in the building had to go along.

My very good girlfriend, she moved over there on Sedgwick, I guess 'cause she wanted a larger place, I don't know. But that made her son, you know, when in Rome do as the Romans do. So a lot of 'em had to be a part of that gang. Now, I'm so glad to know that this guy, he's into the Word. He sang at a funeral for a friend of ours and to hear him speak, you wouldn't ever think he had to pick up a gun. A lot of them, they have to join—either you shoot me or I shoot you.

The way our building was, if you come out one side you had to shoot, and if you came out the other side there was another gang waiting for you.

Oooh, it was terrible. August 5, 1991, my son Michael was standing in front of our church at the corner of Hobbie and Larrabee, which is Holy Family Lutheran, the same church I've been going to now for forty-three years. And he got shot right there, standing there. The shot came somewhere from way up high. The bullet came straight through him. He died. He must have been forty years old.

A lot of folks knew who did it, and when the detectives came, I'm trying to tell one of the detectives who did it. He'd say, "Well, it's just hearsay, we don't know, we don't know." But I know. I heard who did it. I told him, "I want you to go up there." They wouldn't even go, 'cause a lot of times they don't even care. That's what bothers me.

IN CABRINI, I'M JUST NOT AFRAID

Not too long after my son got killed, must have been in the fall of '91, I was at a benefit dinner, something to do with my community work, and this reporter came up to me and said, "Aren't you Ms. Wilson?" When I said that I was, he said, "Aren't you afraid of living in Cabrini with all this shooting and stuff?" I said, "No. I even leave out at night and go to the store," which I did. I said, "Only time I'm afraid is when I'm outside of the community. In Cabrini, I'm just not afraid." It's like I told my boss, "If I'm going to live somewhere all these years and be scared, I'm crazy."

In '93 I retired after nearly thirty years of service with the city. I got some congratulatory letters and tapes that people made for me. Janitors and clerks and everybody. Over the years on the job, so many people there wanted to ask me how I survived Cabrini. They had extreme ideas about what was happening there. I'd get to work in the morning and somebody would come up to me: "Ooh, Dolores. Did you get hurt? I read in the newspaper about this and that shooting." I'd say, "I don't know nothing about it." What got to me was the reporters didn't put down no address in their stories. Cabrini is a big neighborhood, from Halsted down to Sedgwick. But the news would just say, "It happened at Cabrini," and a lot of times, things would happen outside of Cabrini or nearby and they still pinned it on Cabrini. So folks wouldn't want to come up in there. Even my own brother. He would flat out refuse.

One day, I'm waiting on the bus in the dead of winter, to get to work. Waited so long I finally tried to flag a cab down. One guy stopped and said, "My boss told me not to pick up anybody in Cabrini, said if anything happen to me or this cab, my family don't get no compensation or anything." And then he said, "But I'm picking you up. You look like a nice lady." I said, "I *am* a nice lady." I could hardly lift my hands to shut the cab door, they were so frozen cold.

THEY MADE ME MOVE TOO FAST TO HOLD ON TO MY MEMENTOS

My building, 1230 N. Burling, is still standing. Supposed to knock it down in just a few days. When the last family was moving out, I felt so sorry for the lady who had just moved out of one building that they tore down. Everybody in that building had to move. You know, it's sad when you get a little age on you, you got your place the way you want it to be, and then they're talking about how you got to move.

When they told us that we had to leave, I'm thinking, *fifty-three years in Cabrini.* They gave us letters letting us know how many days. I think it was maybe 120 days, and I thought, *Oh, well I got time to move.* But I was still surprised. I thought that they were only going to tear down the buildings that were degraded and not working. It was such a rush to do this and do that. And it was hard for me. I was eighty-two years old when I moved. I didn't want to give up my apartment, and it was only two bedrooms. By then, I was on the eighth floor. Me and my youngest son, Kenny, we were the only ones still there, till he passed four years ago. But it was still my home and it held everything I owned since we were in 1117 Cleveland, including memories.

I had so many mementos and they made me move too fast to hold on to them. Now I cannot find my wedding pictures. I don't have one picture of me and my husband and my parents and his parents and our wedding cake that my aunt made. She had a bakery and I cannot find that one picture. I can't find a picture from one of our meetings with Bertha Gilkey. She was a public housing activist from St. Louis. Bush came. Daddy Bush. And he met with all the board, not all the residents. We met with Bush and he had his picture made with each one of us. I can't find that picture either. My husband and I went to Jamaica so many times. I don't have one picture from Jamaica. My sisters and I went to the Bahamas two or three times. I don't have a picture of that. It was in the house. I'd boxed it, and I'm trying to think 'cause things was happening so fast, and they were telling you you gotta get out by this that and other, you know. My husband's trophies are gone now. I didn't have the help to get those out of the closet, you know, and no boxes! I just had to leave them.

And I said, "Oh well." Now my stuff is probably off in some dump.

I got a brick from Cabrini, from our first building at 1117 Cleveland. And I got a brick from when I traveled over to St. Louis with Bertha and a group of public housing resident leaders; got a brick from where Pruitt–Igoe[6] once was. I saw the remains. Said it was gonna be a huge parking lot.

The last day I was allowed to be in 1230 N. Burling, I was so happy that the manager let me go back in there. Mostly I went in looking for my wedding picture. And three times she let me in. I thought that was

---

[6] Built in 1954, the Pruitt–Igoe housing development of St. Louis was one of the first high rise housing developments in the U.S., and also one of the first to be demolished. See appendix IV, page 237.

so nice of her, 'cause I didn't think she had to. But I was still rushing and I just couldn't find that wedding picture. You see, I didn't have a pickup truck or anything to help me put stuff in storage—I couldn't afford it, and they didn't provide. They didn't give me nearly enough boxes! And I didn't find out there was storage for people who were forced out. Didn't learn that until the day the movers showed up. But, oh well.

A lot of people had to move. Everybody, you know, you look out the window, you see long trucks. This one moving, that one moving. Different ones were using different vehicles, pickup trucks or whatever. I just didn't have it together. They gave me and my daughter one long truck. We were each supposed to have one truck because she was moving to a new place, too, so I was rushing and I didn't pack what I needed. And if I didn't get out on time, I'd have to pay rent for both places.

Everybody was moving in all directions. The housing office kind of steered you to where they wanted you to go. I'd been interested in Hilliard Homes[7] and Parkside,[8] but they said those places weren't taking applications. Quite a few of us headed to the Dearborn Homes, where I live now. My daughter's right nearby. But we're not all in the same building. The people I've known from Cabrini are all in different buildings. And when we see each other, it's "Ohhh ahh!" Like we haven't seen each other for a thousand years. And a lot of them, their sons come to visit, "How you doing, Ms. Wilson?" 'Cause I'm there by myself. "Are you all right? You being taken care of okay?" And they come back and keep checking. "You want anything from the store?" All times of day and night they stopping in, I can hardly rest, but I get up anyway and say, "Thank you for coming."

---

[7] A forty-nine-year-old public housing structure on the Near South Side, consists of two sixteen-story buildings reserved for elder housing and two eighteen-story buildings reserved for low-income family housing.

[8] A mixed-use development of townhouses on the Near North Side, blocks away from where the Cabrini-Green high rises once stood.

Young guys, their mommas probably send 'em to ask me. That's the way it's supposed to be. That's family. That's what it is.

I'm still getting used to things at Dearborn Homes. It's like that song says, "a house is not a house, a home is not a home" until you live there. My new place is okay, but I'd really like to be in a larger space. I always joke that I can sit on my sectional couch and cook on my stove! It's okay. It's not Cabrini. It's funny—now I like to be up high! I like to see the sun set, but from where I am now, I can't see anything set. From my window, I see the building in front of me and the parking lot and a little bit of the street, and I can also see the playground. God is good all the time. You know, for a while I was so stuck on seeing the sun set, one night I saw the moon, and I got all excited and said, "Ooh, thank you, Father. Thank you, Father." He said, "Where have you been staring all these years?" I was stuck on the sun setting, and he said, "Look at the moon."

ROBERT TAYLOR HOMES

DAWN KNIGHT

AGE: *48*

OCCUPATION: *College student, ordained minister*

FORMER RESIDENT OF: *Robert Taylor Homes*

As Dawn Knight recounts, growing up in Robert Taylor Homes in the 1980s was not easy. Dawn describes a time of crowding, rampant drug selling, and violence against women that she still doesn't understand. She recounts a number of abuses at the hands of corrupt police officers and men "looking to take over women's households." She reminisces about her love for the neighborhood library, her place of refuge. And with intense immediacy, she remembers the mysterious death of a younger brother that occurred in an elevator in the Robert Taylor Homes complex. Dawn moved out of Robert Taylor Homes in 1991 but would return nearly ten years later to do ministry outreach. Today, Dawn is a mother, an ordained minister, and a DJ for WCSU Radio at Chicago State University, where she is in her final semester of studies as a communications major. We first meet her in the library at Chicago State. Names in this narrative have been changed at the request of the narrator.

YOU GROW UP WITH THAT FEAR

When I was a small child, we used to live in an apartment on Sixty-Eighth and Wood in Englewood, and over there, white people would march through the blocks picketing for us to move. The march I most clearly remember was in 1976. They didn't want black people in their neighborhood. They didn't want us to move past Cermak or Western Avenue—I guess that's where Marquette Park started. We couldn't cross Marquette Park.[1] We couldn't cross Western. We knew that. How far black folks lived over there, I don't know, but we knew *do not cross Western. Do not even go near Western. You'll get hurt over there.* That was something our parents told me and my siblings. The white people marched down past where we lived, and we four kids would just run in the house. I had a mental image that they were going to lynch us. They would have bullhorns and signs, and the only thing I knew about white people is that they hated us, you know, we were slaves and they lynched us. So you grow up with that fear.

Years later, when I was youth pastor at a church in 2004, a youth group from South Dakota came to Chicago. They invited me and my youth group to a gathering in Marquette Park, and I instantly got offended. I thought the lead minister from South Dakota was trying to insult me. I thought, *I can't take these black teens to Marquette Park! Why would she even ask that?* I hadn't been over to that area since I was a small child. So I said, "No, we can't go." But the woman that invited us, she didn't know. She was from South Dakota.

---

[1] A neighborhood on the Southwest Side of Chicago; the park itself was the site of a Chicago Freedom Movement march (a demonstration devised to bring attention to housing discrimination in and around the city), headed by Martin Luther King, Jr., in 1966.

WHERE CAN I GO?

My parents had split up when we lived in Englewood. We moved to Robert Taylor Homes around 1979, when I was thirteen. My brothers, my sister, and I, we lived with our mom in one building, a Gangster Disciple[2] building. Moving into the projects was really crazy because there were certain buildings and areas within the community you couldn't go because you were from a different building. So it was like, *Where can I go?* When we moved to the projects, I didn't understand young children being left by themselves. I didn't understand the elevator and the hallways smelling like urine, the writing on the walls, men just standing under the building. It was scary. I didn't know they were selling drugs. I just didn't get it. So the first year I moved there, I would come home from school, go to my room, and read magazines.

I found out there was a library in 4429, so I would go there. That was my escape and it was definitely my alibi for not hanging with the so-called cool kids. I could say, "Nah, I'm going to the library." Once you got that rep they didn't bother you. They'd say, "Aw, she's a book head." But then one day, I went to the library and some people in front of it said, "The library's closed down." I was crushed. After the library closed, I ended up hanging with the kids in my building. They got high on weed and before long, I was getting high, too.

The kids I knew, a lot of their parents did hard drugs. Not reefer, but cocaine, heroin—they shot dope. My mom drank, which was terrifying, but I didn't understand everybody else's parents doing the other drugs because I was never exposed to that. Even with my mom drinking, she had drinking buddies, but I was like, *What is this? Everybody's parents do*

---

[2] A gang in Chicago. For more information, see glossary, page 217.

drugs? Not everybody, but a lot. It was heavy.

I was filled with a lot of hopelessness. My dad would always say, "Just go to school. Go to school, stay away from people who don't want anything out of life." There was just so much craziness to deal with. Going from one place to the next, you might encounter guys coming from another building and you didn't know what they were up to or how they were going to treat you. Even though I wasn't with a gang, I understood that they could use that as a reason to hurt me. These are guys I walked past every day. It didn't matter. You just never knew what they were going to do. Once I started using drugs, I understood. It was all about the money.

A GOOD TIME WAS LIKE A TEARDROP IN A BUCKET

In 1984, my little brother Will was shot dead in an elevator by a guy we knew. We used to hang at the guy's house. They said the guy was just playing with the gun. I didn't care. I lost my little brother. You know, I was eighteen and I'd just had a baby, and me and my little brother was tight. People who didn't know us thought we were going together because we were together so much of the time. We'd gone through a lot. When we lived over on Wood, after my parents broke up, there were people in our house that never would have been there if my dad was living with us. People drinking and fighting. And so we took that to the projects. There you had men who wanted to take over your house. This guy whose whole family is scared of him is trying to take over your house because he sees a woman with kids who drinks. That's a vulnerable situation. Me and my little brother often had to argue with this guy, to tell him, "No, you're not going to punk us. You're not taking over our house." It was just me and him, with no one else to defend us.

My extended family, my mom's people, didn't live there, and no one ever came to visit us. As a child, that's something I was upset about. No one came to check on us. Altogether my mother had eight siblings. A couple of uncles would come when they needed somewhere to stay. Other than that, no one came to say, "Hey, how are you?" It's not like they brought their kids to visit and play with us. When we lived in the projects that was the excuse they used. I'd call my auntie, "Can my cousins come over?" And she'd say, "Naw, we can't come to the projects."

But when my little brother was killed, you saw everybody. *It took my little brother getting killed for you to come by.* I didn't want to talk to them by then. *So you coming to be supportive? I don't even know you.* I just didn't understand why now you would be coming. I just didn't get it.

Back then I was drinking beer and smoking weed to deal with my personal issues, but the night my little brother was killed, afterwards, a so-called friend gave me some heroin. And I snorted it, and the pain was gone. I didn't know I was high. I just thought to myself, *The pain just went away.* It was downhill from there.

I went to crack because there was a drug raid and there was no more China white dope in the neighborhood. That was it, there. Once I smoked crack, that's all I thought about. I started turning tricks, doing whatever I needed to do to get a hit. I didn't care. I smoked up the food stamps I got. Smoked up my baby daddy's check. He didn't even know about it. He comes in the building and he's got to pay the drug dealer. So now we're fighting. And the thing about smoking: I could justify marrying Satan. You know what I'm saying? I could justify anything. Yeah, we had good times. But there were so many bad times. A good time was like a teardrop in a bucket. Because you knew death was coming. It didn't matter *when*; it was more like *who*. Who's going to get shot next?

THEY CAME IN: FOUR BIG DETECTIVES

Around 1991, someone shot and killed a policeman in the neighborhood. The shooting happened in the evening and the gunfire came from one of the buildings. A few hours later, early morning after the shooting, there were dozens of policemen lined up on the fire lane right outside. It was four or five in the morning and it was hot—even if you have a fan, the apartment gets so hot you just can't sleep—so lots of people were out on their balconies, trying to cool off. We saw the police in formation. It took a while to figure out that they were about to go door to door to search each apartment. Now, it's sixteen floors and there are ten apartments on each floor. And it's probably eight to ten buildings. They went to each building, each apartment with CHA management, and they searched our apartments. And if you were visiting me that night, they would've escorted you off the premises, walked you to State Street, and ordered you to not come back on the property. This is what they did.

They did all of this without a warrant. At the time we didn't know they needed one. I found out later they should have that. But to degrade someone like that, invading people's homes—we were already the lowest of the low. It's sad that the cop got shot, but where were these raids when children were getting shot? They never went door to door when a little kid got shot. They never went door to door when a woman was abused, or shot or whatever. What was so different? Why was his life valued more than our lives? I never understood that. I remember this reporter, a pretty black girl, walked up to me a few hours after the police sweeps happened. She asked me which building I lived in. When I told her 4410, she said, "Well, which building is the worst?" That blew me away. What did she mean? It's the projects. Did we have rankings? This let me know how the outside world really saw us. Did we have a worst building or the worst drug dealer or the best crack head? Stuff like that makes you realize, *Wow, this is hopeless.*

Sometime later that year, detectives knocked on my friend's door while I was visiting her and asked about this guy she used to date. She said, "Yeah, but I haven't seen him in two years." They said, "Well, we need to search your place." And as they were saying it, they came in: four big detectives. Plainclothes policemen. These guys were big. It was her and me and our children. I'm glad she didn't tell them they needed a warrant, because that can get you hurt. They came in and searched the place, the kids are crying, and I'm trying to tell them just be quiet, it'll be okay. Eventually the police left, but that was common.

One thing I want to make clear though is that there were good policemen. A lot of times, if you saw them getting somebody, that person had pretty much done something questionable. It's not like they just came and picked on the people in the projects. They did their job. If it wasn't for the good police, I could have been beaten really, really bad by my ex. It was just a few thug cops, and you knew their names. I grew up seeing them do things that weren't right. It was crazy, but it's like the police were the government. So you were taught and you learned: this police is cool and this police will hurt you. If they said you did something, don't try nothing, don't disagree; if they try to take you, you just go on down to the police station and sleep it off. If you challenged the abusive police, you'd be seriously hurt. When I see police today, I feel like, *Oh God. Oh my goodness.* I'm just not sure what's going to happen. It's been a long time. I'm an adult now and I'm terrified of them. It's crazy.

"YOU CAN COME AS YOU ARE"

I lost my apartment around 1991. I was getting high. I wasn't paying any rent, so I had to leave. I stayed with my sister for a month or two, but I ended up moving in with my kids' father, on the Far South Side of Chicago, over on Michigan. I got high. He drank. It was just a dark situation, and I knew my kids were going to end up like me but at an earlier age.

I was messed up, and this guy was messed up. But we lived together for several years. Then one day in the spring of 1995, he jumped on me, and I knew it was time. I called the police. Had to sneak to a neighbor's house to do it. When I came back through with these officers, he was still there, drunk and passed out asleep on the couch. I didn't want nobody waking him. I just wanted to leave. I grabbed my two kids, put on their coats, and the police drove us to the L stop at 95th. They told the driver to give us some transfers. I went to a battered women's shelter. Eventually I came back to the neighborhood and stayed with my friend.

Living in the projects, we had churches right nearby, but none of the members ever came and invited us to their church. Not long after I got to my friend's place, these white people invited us to come downstairs for their church outreach. They were all the way from Minnesota. They did a skit about Jesus right there out on State Street, right on the sidewalk. They had fake blood and everything, and the little kids loved it. These church people acted out the Passion of the Christ, with Jesus being whipped on the way to the Cross. When they whipped him, the blood would show up on his white robe. My friend told me that this church would come out every summer and have programs and services right out in the open field on Forty-Seventh Street. I'd never been to any of it. Seeing them just blew me away. *Wow, white people coming to tell me about Jesus, but how come churches across the street don't come over here?*

I remember a lady from that church prayed for me, and a year later, I left Chicago. Me and the kids. I took the check and put the food stamps in the bottom of my shoe, in my sock. I bought an Amtrak ticket for Minneapolis, and my kids and I left with just a change of clothes and some underwear. At the homeless shelter where we ended up in Minneapolis, there was a lady pastor who invited us to church. I said, "I'm broke." She said, "That's okay." She'd drive us there or we could get there on the bus. When I told her, "We don't have anything to wear," she said, "You can come as you are." I was thinking, *This is some Jim Jones type of stuff*, because in Chicago you had to dress up to go to church. Women couldn't wear pants, especially no cutoff shorts. Minneapolis was totally different. The church I went to was that same church that had members performing the Passion Play on State Street.

In Minneapolis, everybody lived together. Once I saw a black guy hugged up with a white girl, and I grabbed my kids and I crossed the street, because I thought the police was going to roll up any minute and beat this guy. I didn't want my kids to see that. But in Minneapolis, it's not segregated. Everybody lives together; it doesn't matter. A biracial couple? I had never seen that.

I saw a lot of young people come to the church in Minneapolis— people who were hurting, who were damaged like I used to be. Once I was saved and delivered from drugs, I was able to see things clear. It was on my heart to help young people. When I looked at them, I saw myself, when I was young, when I lost hope. I volunteered as a youth worker at the church in Minneapolis and I went on to ministry school.

I CAME BACK TO THE PROJECTS AND I COULD FEEL THE DARKNESS

The person who asked me to come back to Chicago was my pastor in Minnesota. By this point, around 2000, I was a youth minister with my church in Minneapolis, and they wanted me to serve in Chicago with a church they'd planted on La Salle Street. I couldn't believe the man asked me to go back to my old neighborhood. I asked him, "Are you crazy?" I didn't understand it, but I agreed to do it.

I was terrified when I went back to visit Robert Taylor Homes. I was able to see the oppression when I came back. The people standing around the building when I left in '91 were still doing the same thing in 2000. Almost ten years later. And now with a new generation of drug dealers. I saw people who didn't used to get high and I looked in their faces and could tell they were doing bad. It was sad to see that. And it was terrifying because, I'm like, *Okay, am I next?* Little kids who were now grown were standing out in the open selling dope. So I was just feeling scared and guilty. I used to get high with these kids' moms, and a couple of them said, "Hey, Ms. Knight." And what could I tell them? *I'm here to tell you about Jesus?* Eventually, I did get around to that, but I wasn't expecting to see what I saw. All I could think was, *God brought me from this. I used to live like this.* I knew something was wrong with it back then, but God opened my eyes. I came back to the projects and I could feel the darkness. To me, people looked demonic. Some of the people, these same people getting high, were the same people who'd encouraged me to stay away from drugs.

When I went inside the apartments, they seemed like little boxes. They were really small. I went to my old apartment and thought, God, this was my room? The bathroom looked like a closet. It was unreal and very sad. And so many of the people hadn't left. Ten years later. And now with a new generation of drug dealers. I thought, *Maybe I'm not ready for this.* But He kept me. We would do a ministry in this park right off of 37th Street. My coworkers wanted to call it Needle Park. And I said, "No, we're not going to give it that name. We'll call it Wall Street, because they already know they're on the low. We don't need to insult them. We're Christians. We'll call it Wall Street because they're so organized." This is something you had to see: all these different types of cars pulling up, getting in the dope line. They had a guy to direct you, and somebody would call a signal, and then you give one guy the money, and you go further down to get your stuff. It was so organized to where the police could not even catch them. They'd have a guy two blocks away calling back to let you know when the police was coming.

I would preach in that park and there would be people there selling and getting high. But I would preach, and a few people would get saved. I knew they would, because I know how the Word pierces your heart. I worked there for months. I would talk to the teens and pray with them and try to explain to them why our communities are the way they are, and I'd do it from a Biblical perspective. I saw kids change spiritually. I didn't focus on whether they were saved. To see the kids smile, to see them open up, it was what really mattered.

I WANT TO MOVE THE HECK UP
OUT OF CHICAGO

These days I'm studying communications at Chicago State University. I love the sound board, I love audio, video. I like to make movies. I've always loved sound. My favorite time in the projects was when one of my best friends and I would search the incinerators for parts of stereos or component sets. People would throw stuff out. When we first found something, we had to go door to door, asking, "You got some roach spray we can use?" 'Cause we had to spray the stuff down before we brought it in my momma's house. After we sprayed the equipment, we would rewire the receivers and speakers, and hook it up. We'd make our own stereo system. It would be raggedy, but it would sound better than anybody else's. That was fun. Because you know, we were entrepreneurs. We just didn't know it. We would build the set and people would buy the system. And it sounded great. We would play the *Control* album by Janet Jackson for-*ever*.

Now my kids and I live in Englewood. I lived on LaSalle at the church staff house, but I wanted to go back to school, so I moved out. I'm just getting to know people in the neighborhood. It's no project, but a lot of people come from the projects there. I thank God that my kids have better chances than me, but they have friends that can't cross Fifty-Ninth because their brother is in a gang. Same old stuff.

I encourage my kids to not listen to that type of stuff, gang-banging. I tell them, "Don't be pulled in by it. Don't be tricked by it. You're not going to be dressing like anybody." It's so many different rules that I tell them, because it's like the gangs have upgraded their slickness. It's different. I know I have to be careful, because a lot of people know how to influence young people and pull them into doing darkness because they themselves were pulled into doing darkness. And I often have to explain to my kids about how to handle rejection and where rejection led me. I went to school. I was an honors student, but I wouldn't even get into the honors society program because of the way my mother drank, I felt I wasn't good enough. So I tell my kids, "As long as you have food on the table, clothes on your back, a roof over your head, and no one's in here abusing you or anything, you have to appreciate that. You have to thank the Lord for that, because everybody doesn't have it."

Sometimes my daughter's friends will come over because their family be fighting. I let all their friends come. I let them know they can always stay if their family is tripping. I let them know I have to call their moms, but I want them to know they have a place; that they don't have to go smoke or lay with a guy just to have a roof over their head.

Once I get my degree, I want to move the heck up out of Chicago. I don't care for Chicago for raising children. Just too many people here. It's a big city and it's too cold. I want to go to Atlanta. I've been there. It's beautiful. I want my children to be able to go outside and for me not to worry, *Will they get shot?* I worry about that every day.

56

ROCKWELL GARDENS

DONNELL FURLOW

AGE: *31*

OCCUPATION: *Carpet cleaner*

FORMER RESIDENT OF: *Rockwell Gardens*

We talk with Donnell at a dining room table in the quiet basement of St. Leonard's House, on the city's West Side. Anchored by two late nineteenth-century row houses, St. Leonard's provides interim housing and supportive services for formerly incarcerated men. We are only blocks away from Rockwell Gardens, the high rise public housing community where Donnell lived throughout his childhood and adolescence (from 1981 through the late 1990s). Donnell has been in residence at St. Leonard's for nearly three months, readjusting to life on the outside. In 2005, he was sentenced to eight years for aggravated battery with a firearm after shooting his mother's landlord in a stand-off altercation with guns drawn on both sides. As Donnell recounts, the violent confrontation occurred after a series of arguments about the landlord's impromptu inspections of Donnell's mother's apartment. As we speak, Donnell describes his early induction into gang life, the sense of belonging and purpose he felt as a member, the routine hazards of gang combat, and the police abuse he experienced. Just as eagerly, he describes the new chapter of his life since his parole in 2011. He prefaces his story by gently expressing surprise at being asked to share it. "I didn't think nobody really cared about what we went through in the projects."

I'M LITTLE, BUT I'M NOT TOO LITTLE

I first started learning about the streets at three years old, maybe four. My brothers would come in the house and tell me, "Here, come put this gun up." And so I'd hide their gun for them.

By the time I was ten, the biggest gun I ever handled was probably an AK-47. I can't lie to you. I didn't feel fear, because that's what I knew. I felt more safe holding something *this* big than holding something *that* big. If it was real big, I felt it was going to protect me from *anybody*. When I did get the chance to help out—"Here, go hold this" or "Here, go clean this big old AK-47"—it happened at an early age. I knew how to break the gun down and clean it. I knew how to put it back together like it's never been took apart. I realized what it meant to hit somebody, to kick somebody down the stairs. I realized what it meant to play with a real gun. I learned the rules and regulations to the streets—to know that if someone got jumped and I seen it, I knew to say nothing about what I seen.

I'm the youngest in my family. It was me, my sister, my two brothers. My momma worked for the free lunch program. All the kids knew her from that. In the summertime, people from the housing office come around, and they put a lot of food out for the kids in the building. Everybody calls it "choke" or "free lunch." She also used to take care of people in an old folks' home. My father used to fix cars up there on Madison Street for $25. It didn't matter what was wrong with your car—your windows could be busted out, your tires could be flat—he could fix it for $25. Whatever was wrong, he'd make it right. He was good.

My brothers' friends—the guys I grew up with—those guys would come up to our apartment every day, and my one brother would always have the music on. And I'm little, but I'm not too little. I was always curious, you know what I'm saying? So when they come up there, they come up there with gun cases *this* long. When they come in and shut the door, I see them put the buggy chain on the door—I *know* we can't leave, and ain't nobody coming in, so I sit back and watch them fire up a joint.

I had to be about eleven. They smoking a joint. I'll come over there and peek around the couch at them and they'll be like, "Hey, come here, lil nigga," and grab me up around the collar and pull me up there to them, like, *here*. They give me the joint. I look at the joint. They looking at me. And I think, *I'm going to do what you just did. I'm going to hit the joint. I'm gonna inhale it. I'm gonna exhale it.* The first time I did it, I felt out of my body. I felt high.

After maybe three or four days, I liked that feeling, you know what I'm saying? I liked that feeling. I liked that smell. I liked to be around my brothers' friends because it was like they knew what I needed. So when they come around, I was there. I caught on. They wearing hats. *I got to get me a hat.* I didn't have no money to get me a hat, so I went outside and caught somebody my size that ain't from the projects, beat him up, and took his hat. Now I'm back around them turning my hat the same way they wear their hat. They would give me a gun and give me the bullet, tell me to load it back up. At age ten or eleven, I knew what it was. "That's a 6-shot. That's nothing." I load it back up. It just escalated, because they seen what I did and was like, "Okay, he down."

I spent daytime with the guys. The only time school existed for me was when the principal or other people called wondering why I wasn't at school. By the time I was in grammar school, I was learning how to clean guns, how to shoot a gun, how to hide a gun, how to bag up cocaine and how to shake dope. I could sell something small as my thumbnail and get $10 for it. And I had my first of three daughters when I was thirteen, fourteen years old. I had other things on my mind besides school.

There were rules. The guys I was growing up around, they put me in a circle and told me that this way was the way it goes. They said that they were going to violate this one guy because it was supposed to be that way. I seen guys get their head hit on the stairway and two or three people stepping on their head. After the violation, I would just see the guy lay there and shake as blood's coming out of his mouth. I've seen that happen. As I got older, about thirteen and fourteen years old, I had to carry out the same violations to guys that were doing wrong or being disrespectful.

MY NEIGHBORHOOD WAS THE
WORLD TO ME

I didn't see much happening inside the building. Outside the building, we did it all. We shot at police. We robbed the trains, trucks. Robbed each other. We did it all. We were at war with opposite gangs. It got to the point where no parents could leave the building and take the kids to school. There wasn't no coming out that building. It didn't change over time. That's the way it was. The beefs may have been over something small. It might be because someone literally bumped into your girlfriend. It could be over something real small as that.

We always had this saying about Rockwell: "If you're not from here, don't come here." And we always said, "What goes on in the projects stays in the projects." We just didn't like outsiders. It was a neighborhood thing. I've seen people in their cars get burnt up: other guys that we fighting against, getting caught in the wrong area, trying to slide through without being seen. If you're driving, you still got a chance to get away. So we flipped the car to make sure you don't get away. We turned on the fire hydrant so you'd have a hard time pulling away.

We always called Rockwell "a devil's home." What we really meant was: if you made it out, you made it out. If you didn't, then you didn't. It was just like, *Oh well*. But my neighborhood was the world to me. My neighborhood was better than downtown. To me, back then, I looked at it like, I don't care how many buildings are downtown, as long as we got those buildings right there, that was all that we needed because there was money to be made. When I say money, I'm talking $2,300 a night. That was off cocaine alone. Off dope—stuff people put up their nose—you were making a good $15,000. When weed came along, that was another profit right there.

It was mostly people outside the neighborhood coming in to buy. We had people from everywhere. Humboldt Park, the Latinos. People from the South Side and further back out west. Off Central and Western. Off Pine.

Had a lot to learn about how to read people when I was on the street, selling. I learned who to trust and who not to. We had this one white lady. She tall. Her name was Suzy. I couldn't never forget her name. I could honestly say she was the only white lady that came in our building and had some heart.

She wasn't scared when she first came in the building. Everybody did the quiet thing. Everybody just looked at her. She was like, "Where the shit at?" And everybody was like, "We don't sell drugs down here." We played with her like that for a minute. She was like, "I spend money with y'all all the time. I know you all sell that shit down here." The guys said, "Shit, what you looking for?" She said she was looking for the rocks. She pulled out a roll of twenties, and she said, "I'm fixing to spend all this with y'all. You want me to take these $500 and give it to the boys over there?" We were like, "Hell naw. Wait a minute!"

She was a regular. She came to 117 South Rockwell one day and we sitting there under the building smoking weed. Suzy warned us that there was three police cars close by, stationed on the corner of Madison and Rockwell. She'd come by that day to get two jibs, but she didn't have the money on her. Two whole jibs! The guy I sell drugs for, he was looking at me and I could see he was like, "You fixing to give her two jibs and there are twenty-four rocks in one jib?" Two jibs is forty-eight. And we selling dimes. Ten dollar rocks. I walked to the back of the building, go in the trunk, put the speaker to the side, reach up under, grabbed two jibs, and I said, "Here, Suzy," and handed them over. She said, "Thank you." I told her, "I stay upstairs on the sixth floor, room number 602. My name is Donnell. Don't make me come look for you, lady. I got a little trust with you because you always shop with us. So don't make me come look for you." She was like, "All right."

She stayed gone for about a week. I walk through the building, wondering, *Damn, is this lady really going to bring back the money or what? 'Cause if she come and get $200 worth of shit from me, she know she got to give me $500 back.* That Monday morning, a pickup truck pull up to our building. She jump out the truck, she walk in the building. I was standing inside the building like this—I got a TEC[1] on a shoestring hanging down from my coat. I'm mad because I think she ran off with this stuff I gave her. And now I'm gonna have to work it off or maybe get my ass whipped. So I got this big old TEC and I got it for two reasons: one, I ain't gonna let nobody jump on me; and two, if she didn't come, the next time I see her I'm going to use the gun on her. But she jump out of the pickup truck and walk over there to me. She's like, "Hey, Donnell." I'm standing there shaking a little bit, tears wanna run down my eyes. And it was like a big relief. She walk up, she say, "Here are the $500 I owe you. And here are another $500 for your pocket." And she say, "that go another $500 for trusting me." And I got that money in a rubber band. And I'm like, "I have $500 that you owed me, $500 for me waiting, and $500 for me trusting you?" She said, "Yeah."

When I told her to take all her money back because she was a good customer, she said she wanted me to keep it. She said, "I might need you to do that again for me." I said, "If I do that again for you, you know you

---

[1] A TEC-9 semi-automatic handgun that supports high capacity magazines.

still gonna have to pay me for that?" She was like, "Yeah, I know." So I took the money. I told myself I could go spend it.

When I called the man I was working for, he said he was on his way. He come from the suburbs. He pull up and I lean over in the car and talk to him because the police are on the corner. As I'm talking to him, I just drop my money on the car seat. And he says, "We gonna go to The Circle. There are going to be some strippers down there. We gonna be in some black and gold. We gonna be doing our thing. Are you down?"

I said, "Solid, Joe," and we made our plan for the night. He pulled out and I went back to the building and thought, *Dang, I got $1,000 for myself. That's whassup.* I went to the crib. My sister was there. She's older than me. It was rough for us. My momma was barely making it paying the rent and keeping food in the kitchen. We had a stove but the gas wasn't on, so we had to make it through a hot plate, you know what I'm saying? At times our lights be on. Sometimes our lights be off. If Dad made enough money to pay the bill, he'd pay the bill. It was about time for them to pop the lights back on.

PACMAN TRADED FOR ALL TYPES OF THINGS

Back then there was this police officer. His name was Pacman. He was a Traveling Vice Lord.[2] Let's say you're one of the home girls and you're walking down Western or something, and Pacman and his partner catches you with a gun. He might ask you, "Is you plugged?" He might ask you what your affiliation is. And you might say, "I'm a Four Corner Hustler Queen."[3]

---

[2] A faction of the Vice Lords, a prominent gang in Chicago and rivals of the Gangster Disciples. For more on prominent gangs in Chicago, see glossary, page 217.

[3] A gang closely allied with the Vice Lords.

Pacman and his partner will come to our building with you in the backseat, handcuffed and everything. The guys always send me out to the police car to talk. I was cool with them then, and I'd ask, "Whassup, Joe?" And he be like, "Man, nothin'." Then I'd look in the backseat and then I'd look at you, right? And I'd ask, "What did she do?" He'd say, "Aw man. She walking down Western and something was poking out of her side." That's him telling me right there that you got caught with a pistol. But I'm gonna ask that question anyway. And I'd be like, "So what you saying, that she got caught with a knife or something?" And then he'd go in the little glove compartment and pull up the gun that you got caught with. Then it'd be my turn to ask, "Man, what you want for these two peoples?" I'm talking about the gun and you. And he'd say, "Man, give me a TEC." And I'd say, "Hmmm . . . you might have to take her to jail, man. Straight up." That's bullshit talk, to try to get him to trade you for a gun that's littler, 'cause a TEC probably holds about 150 shots in it.

But at the same time, that all depends on the mob, too. If you not valuable to the mob, the guys would let you go to jail and we'd bond you out. If you're valuable, we'd make an exchange then and there. I'd go on back to the building and tell the guys, "They want a motherfuckin' TEC!" Then they'd send one of the other guys to go get the TEC and put it on the side of the Beacon House, where the kids go and play ball at. I'd come back to the car and give Pacman and his partner directions. "There's a TEC on the side of the garbage can, over there by the Beacon House. Pull up right there. Brown paper bag." They'd ride down Rockwell, turn up in the Beacon House. His partner would jump out. Brown paper bag. He'd pull the TEC out the bag, look it over for a minute. Then Pacman would let you out the car. He'd uncuff you and tell you to go get the fuck on about your business. Once you're freed and they've gone about their business, that TEC that we just lost? You have to work that off. You have to replace that TEC. We paid $2,000 for a TEC. Now you got to go sell all them drugs again to get that $2,000 so we could get the gun back.

Pacman traded for all types of things. Could be money. Could be information. Could be for anything he might be looking for. Especially if what he wants is coming from that area. They'd want to try to get information about guys we ran with, but we'd play it cool. "Y'all know Boomer?" Why wouldn't we know him? "Y'all know Angelo?" Why wouldn't we know the man?

It was another police over there too, a black dude. Tall. Kind of big. They called him Batman. He was cool, but he was sneaky. When there was other polices around, he did his job. But when he's just cruising the neighborhood by himself, that's when his sneak side come out. He'd pull up and I could be serving someone and I'd be like, "Here. How many? Five?" And I'd give the customer five. And I'll be like, "Whuuuup, Joa." He'd be like, "What up, little homey." But if he had another officer in the car with him, then he'd jump out and chase you, rough you up, beat you up, break your nose and stuff like that. He talked about you, disrespected you, talked about your parents, the way you living.

THEY WAS KICKING ME, PUNCHING ME, CALLING ME A NIGGER

You know how many times I been jumped on by the police? I'm gonna give you an example. I was seventeen. I was on Western and Madison one night, going to the gas station. And these dudes ride up on me and they say, "Man, little homey. Where they got some weed at?" And I looked in the car and I was about to say, "Shit. I got some," but they looked too healthy and too clean to be customers. So I said, "I don't know. Y'all gotta go check down that way or something." They pulled off. I went to the gas station. I bought a pack of Newport 100s, an RC pop, and two blunts. I'm walking back down Western, fixing to go back to my building, and the blue and whites, the Chicago polices—one black, one white—they pull up on me. And they say, "Hey, you. Come here." I look in the car. I say, "My momma told me not to come to strangers." And I walk. The black police say, "Hey you. Bring your fucking ass here right now." I look at him and I keep walking. He jumps out the car. When he get over to me, he grabs me. He doesn't grab me and throw me up against the car. He doesn't put me down on the ground. He runs up on me. Bam! By his being the police, I just go ahead and hit the ground. I ball up, right there on Western and Jackson. The white police jumps out. They're kicking me, punching me, calling me a nigger. Telling me I ain't ever gonna be shit, that I'm gonna die on the street. And then after that, they handcuff me. They lean me up against the car. They search me. I said, "I ain't got nothing." My nose was bleeding, my mouth was bleeding. My head was busted. They bent my arms way back. I said, "Man, I ain't got nothing on me. Nothing." They said, "Well, you do now." They went back to the car and go into the trunk and brought a whole bag of cocaine and they say, "This yours."

They take me to the station. Another police officer seen the drugs, he look at me and say, "Where you get those drugs from?" I say, "From them other police officers." He's like, "What?!" Then four or five officers took me in this other room and jump on me for like twenty minutes. I was in there screaming like a little girl. I actually had a police holding my arms and the other ones just hit me from my chin down to my body. My whole face was just swollen. And did I go to the hospital for it? Naw. They gave me an ice pack, two Tylenols, and told me to go to sleep, that I would be all right. I was glad to go to the county jail. I was glad to get around the other guys because they helped me out. They gave me a warm towel. They kept me in a room until my swelling went down. They actually helped me out.

Another time: I was at a house party. A project party. The police come in there, they looking for somebody. They flash that light in my face. They say, "Hey man, what's your name?" I'm being polite. I say, "My name is

Donnell Furlow." They say, "Well you look like this boy right here." They showed me a picture. I knew exactly who he was. Went to school with the man. I said, "Naw, that ain't me." The police said, "Your name Seneca Sanders?" I said, "No, I just told you my name." He asked for my name again. I said, "My name is Donnell Furlow." They said, "Come with me." They grabbed me by my arm and put me in the car, no handcuffs on or nothing. I could've done anything to them. They didn't pat me down or nothing. They took me to the station. They run a fingerprint and put me behind bars for about two hours. Now I know those fingerprints came back 'cause this ain't the first time I be in jail. I know them fingerprints told them my real name, where I live at and everything. They *still* didn't let me go. The next day they let me go, but they didn't just say, "You free to go." They took me to a neighborhood where I am not known at. They dropped me off there. Trying to get me hurt.

Now I'm walking down the street and some guys get up behind me. Now they're not speaking directly to me. They talking to they selves, but you can tell that they're talking about me. They're walking close behind me and they saying, "We don't like them punk ass Vice Lords." And I'm saying to myself, "Pssh, here we go . . ." They say, "We be killing Vice Lords." I try my best not to say anything. They say, "If we catch any of those hooks[4] around here, we going to kill them." That was enough for me right there. So I turned around and I tell them, "I'm a hook, now what?" And I'm ready to just deal with the dudes, but then I look up and here come an Astrovan. Now, I'll fight a few dudes and get whooped, but I ain't about to fight an army of them. I had to take off. They chased me. After a few blocks, these Latinos rolled up on me, they asked what was up. I was thinking, *Man, I'm fixing to get killed.* My heart was getting this sensation.

---

[4] "Hook" refers to Vice Lords, who use canes and crescents as symbols.

I just couldn't run anymore. I thought it was my time to die. These dudes knew I was getting chased. They said, "Were you just getting chased by them niggers back there?" I said yeah. They said, "Come on, bro. Jump in." They said they were Latin Kings and I asked them to prove it. They showed me the tattoo with the crown and the five-point star.

When I got in the car, they asked where I was from. I knew I was taking a chance, but they was being pretty friendly to me. They said, "You are cool as hell, bro." One of the younger guys, he handed me a pistol. It was like a .357 Magnum, but it was like a shorter version. And I took it. I thought, *Well if they try anything, I have a piece.* I was like, "Okay, cool." I asked them what they wanted, and it turns out they were at war with them dudes that were about to jump me. We shoot back down to where they were. We saw two of them boys coming out of Popeye's. The Latinos asked what I wanted to do. I wanted to beat their ass. I didn't want to shoot anyone. We caught one dude and stomped his head, kicked his rib, stomach, mouth. A Popeye's worker came outside then, saying she was going to call the police. So we jumped back in the car and they shot me back home. When we got there, I got out and asked my man to give me a Ziploc bag full of weed. I told him, "The Latinos in the van, Joe, they just saved my life." I gave them that bag. I said, "Y'all have fun." From that day on, I never went down that way again by myself. From that day on, I always had a gun with me, everywhere I went.

"SOME OF Y'ALL GONNA BE THE GANG-BANGERS"

Police are always going to look at us as gang members or terrorists. They're always going to see us like that. I ain't gonna sit up here and say that being up in a gang is the right thing to do. I'd be lying. But I didn't have a choice like that. That's all I knew. My parents were there, but they weren't there. I learned more structure from the gang than I did from my parents. I wish I had stand-up parents, I wish I had someone to stand on me to go to school and stuff like that, but I didn't, so the streets had to raise me. I practically had to raise myself. Times started getting real hard for us once my oldest brother got hooked on drugs and he started stealing from the house. My brothers started to fight a lot, and both my parents were just trying to keep up with things the best they could.

With the gang I was in, there was structure and there was rules. We had to respect the people in our building. We made sure there were lights in the building. Wasn't none of those guys I grow up with be disrespectful to you. We did things our way and when we wanted to do it, but we didn't rape or anything like that. Wouldn't none of those guys take anything from a lady. Like me, if I helped you with your groceries and you offered me two or three dollars, I had to tell you no. 'Cause we had to look at it like you were helping keep up this building because you lived there. I couldn't take any money from you. I couldn't be disrespectful around you. But what I would do if I see your son ditching school, I might kick his little butt. He'd come to you and say, "That boy downstairs jump on me," and point me out. And you'd talk to me and say, "Why did you put your hands on my son?" I'd say, "I know you were trying to send him to school, but I seen him down there at eight o'clock this morning. He was down there ditching school. I kicked his little butt because he was missing school."

We respected the people that came to buy drugs from us. We even respected the different gangs that came to buy weed from us. But the thing is: if you had a nephew who was coming in from out South to see you, it was fine but he could not be carrying a gun in there because he was going to get searched. He might say, "The boys down there pulled a gun and searched me." Yeah, I searched you 'cause you wasn't from round here!

The way I grew up—the older guys used to tell you, "Some of y'all gonna be gang-bangers. Some of y'all gonna shoot the guns and pop the pistols. But some of y'all ain't got that. Some of y'all gonna grow up to be lawyers, doctors, police officers. Just don't forget about where you come from. Don't forget about who raised you." I didn't want to be no gang-banger. But the household I grew up around, instead of me being turned off from gangs and sex and drugs, I was turned on to it. I can honestly kind of say it was maybe meant for me to do all the things I did.

In 2005, when he was twenty-four years old, Donnell was arrested and sentenced to eight years in prison for aggravated armed assault after a gunfight with his mother's landlord. At the time of his trial he had three daughters, ages three, six, and ten. He spent six years in Dixon Correctional Center, a medium-security facility one hundred miles west of Chicago. In May, 2011, he was released to the custody of St. Leonard's halfway house to serve the remainder of his sentence.

"DON'T GO GET YOURSELF IN NO TROUBLE"

A couple weeks back, I wanted to go back to my old ways, because it got to the point where I was feeling frustrated, like, *There just ain't no respect out here.* I was just ready to go off. I still know some of these guys around the neighborhood, but there's a whole new generation out here, too, and some of them just don't know me. Nobody told some of these new guys who I am, that I been around here for a minute.

I was with my girl, we were going to the store, and one of the guys that hang out in front the store called out, "Look at that nigga with that white girl," and I turned around and I walked up in his face, and I was like, "Who are you calling a white girl?" He said, "I'm talking about that little honky that you with." I said, "First of all, she ain't white. She Puerto Rican. Second of all, skin color shouldn't matter, man. As long as you happy with that person, that's what count." He said, "Hey, man, you at that place over there called St. Leonard's. I advise you to go on back over there because this ain't what you looking for." And I looked at him and said, "You know what? You right. I'll be back."

We walked back from the store and my girl asked me, "What you thinking about?" I said, "C'mon. Let's go on and get what else you need. I'm fixing to walk you home, 'cause I'm gonna go back and spin on him and see what he made of." She said, "Don't go get yourself in no trouble. You just came home from jail." I told her, "This is what he looking for." After I walked her home, I made two phone calls and had some guys I known a long time pull up out here and we drove back in front of that store.

When I got out of the car with them, that guy walked over, shook their hands, then he got to looking at me and he was like, "Y'all know this dude?" And they told him, "Dude is the reason why we came down this way." I took off my shirt and got up in his face and I said, "What was all this bullshit you was talking, homey?" My guys told him, "Do you know that dude used to come through here and shoot people and now you gonna be getting up in his face?" After they told him who I was, he looked at me with his eyes all big, then he stuck out his hand to shake hands with me—we call it "showing love." When I shook his hand, he said, "Whassup, I can't get no love?" He was waiting to be showing gang signs with me. I said, "I ain't on that. But just listen: when I come through here with my girl, I'm not here to start nothing. I done been there, done that. Just because you see somebody that you ain't seen before, it doesn't mean that they don't have family or pull. I been in this thing since I was ten years old, and I done learned the hard way."

Dude was probably about twenty-one, twenty-two. If I met him when I was about seventeen, I wouldn't have gone to get those guys. I would have gone and got a pistol and come back and shot and maybe killed him.

"Just say whassup, man. That's all you got to do." That's what I finally told him. Then I had to ask him: "Do you know the basis of what you claim? Can you tell me the basis?" He said, "I really can't say." I told him, "You out here gang-banging, turning your hat, but you don't really know what it means. If you go to a max,[5] someplace like Stateville, you can't come up there and claim, 'Yeah, I'm a Vice Lord,' when you don't even know the basis of what you claim." Dude was out here claiming something, but he don't know the law.

Now he'll come up to me when I see him at the store, "Aw, whassup, Joe." He knows I smoke cigarettes and he comes around sometime trying to give me a square, but I'm like, "Naw, that's all right." But he asked me one day if I had a minute to talk, he wanted to know, *What's this mob thing I really should know about.* I told him that the main thing he should know is when the Vice Lords and other organizations got started. "If you can't tell someone that's older than me that it started in 1958, you in trouble. You got to know who the king of this mob is." I'm thirty-one years old and I've been in this since I was ten. When I was twelve, my brothers made me learn what was what. I couldn't go outside until I did. *Who's the crooked ones? Who's the straight? Who we got beefs with? Who died for us? What year we start?* I told him our foundation was really about protecting the neighborhood, we were trying to build something in the community. We had health clinics, after school programs and everything. But over time, it became more about the gang-banging stuff. Then he said, "If you don't mind me asking, how did you get your stars?" He saw my tattoos that day we had clashed. I told him, "From the streets." From the wrong things I did in the streets and when I got in the penitentiary. I had to prove myself there. There's a big difference. Out in the streets, you can get

---

[5] Maximum security prison.

a gun, but in the penitentiary, you can't get a gun. So that's where your heart come in at. Are you gonna go in a room with someone twice as big as you—a room ain't no bigger than that laundry room—is you gonna go in that room, shut the door, and fight with him? Go on in there and fight and you know that ain't but one of you gonna come out standing?

After we talked for a while, I knew he wanted to keep talking. He said, "Maybe I can come around here and you can give me some insight." I said, "Talk? Naw." He asked me why not, I told him, "Been plenty of nights I seen you coming around here, being loud with a stick in your hand, hollering and cursing. You don't know who know the person you out here selling drugs for. I wouldn't want to be out here on the grounds, talking to you and be taking my chances that way." And then I finally had to ask him, "Why you judge me that day in front of the store? Why me?" He said, "There'll be other guys who'll come by here and kick it with us, but I always see you look over here by us, but I never see you mingling. I don't know what made me fuck with you. Guess I thought you weren't from around here."

I REALLY APPRECIATE YOU TAKING
A CHANCE ON ME

I got three women out here. One that's sixteen, one that's twelve, one that's nine. I want to be out here for my daughters. That's what's on my mind now. My oldest, she tease me. One day I told her she better pull up her pants, she was trying to wear them all sagging, like she didn't know no better. She said, "Dag, Daddy, you getting all old. You act like you fifty instead of thirty-one!" And I told her, "I ain't getting old. I'm just getting wise. I'd rather act like I'm fifty and be around for a long time, so pull your pants up when you with me."

I'm still getting myself together. I've got a little job. It's better than what I used to do. One of my friends recommended me. Been cleaning carpets. I'm guessing that the owner likes my work because he calls me a lot now. He tells me to keep my phone on, in case he needs help.

We be in Chicago Heights, Aurora, different suburbs. The owner wanted to take me to New York with him to do eight houses, but I knew it couldn't work right now with my parole. Even though it's travel for a job, my movement is still limited. I got to wait until I'm off parole in 2014. I stick with this job, leave St. Leonard's, get my own apartment, save some money. Then I can go to those out-of-town places. Billy, the owner, he says business picking up, the company doing really good. "I really like the way you work," he tells me. "You get in and do your job and y'all ain't sticking around, taking up people's time."

The way he show it to us, it's real easy work. Shampoo it real good, vacuum up, and you out. I work with the same guy most of the time. His name's Ray. There's other guys working for the company, too. If we done doing our job, if some of the other guys call and need our help, Ray will drive over there and he'll be like, "Joe, y'all go on in there and check this out." Some people don't know how to get stains out. I'll run back out there and get the brush from the truck. *Let it set for five minutes, go over everything else, then come back to this same spot.*

Billy be telling us, "I really appreciate you working for me." And I be thinking to myself, *I really appreciate you taking a chance on me.* It's a lot to look forward to. When I first started, honestly, I was nervous and scared. I knew what was expected, but where I come from, with the way I carry myself and how I dress, I look at the houses these people are letting me into, and I'm wondering, *How are these people looking at me?* The first time I got on a job, I still got my same mentality and I'm unsure of myself, but I know that if I can say on the phone, "Hello, this is St. Leonard's House, my name is Donnell Furlow. Can I ask who's speaking?"—I know if I can do that, then I can introduce myself on my job. The people introduce themselves, they take us right to the spot and we get the work done right away.

What makes me happy is when customers come out their room and say, "That smells good. What's the name of that? Y'all got that for cars, too? That smells too good!" People been friendlier than I expected. You don't have people wanting to watch you. They say, "You hungry? You want something to drink? Y'all can sit down on the couch, watch TV for a minute." Sometimes, my working partner will say, "The *Maury* show on. Let's sit down for a minute and watch the *Maury* show." But I tell him no, I ain't interested. And he say, "Why you taking this so serious?" Later, when we out the house and get in the van, I tell him, "It's not the point of this being serious. For one: it's a job. For two: if it wasn't for this job, I wouldn't be here in this people's only, as I'm not trying to get comfortable able or become friends. We here for a reason. Let's do this reason and be gone because next thing you know they gonna give us their number, asking us over on the weekend for a drink." I try to keep it professional.

We go to rich people houses, that have parties, beer stains everywhere and you know you have certain guys who have hired us, their wives, their girlfriends, anyone they be messing with, walking around in they bra and panties. And Billy told us, "If you can't deal with this, don't take this job, if you can't handle those enticements." Billy warned us about it. "This is what you gonna have. Peoples like that, they really not used to being around people like y'all, the way y'all talk to each other, they're gonna want to mingle and be friends with y'all because y'all bringing something different to the table." And he said, "What I want is for y'all to go in and do the job. When I get paid, y'all get paid." That's the way I keep it.

Billy, he make you feel comfortable. He give his customers good deals on getting carpets and couches clean and stuff, and he give us the things we need to do our job. He told me, "By you being in St. Leonard's, don't get into no trouble. On weekends, I advise you not to go out there and drink or get high, because if you mess up at St. Leonard's, you basically messing up with this job." I don't do that no way. I don't get high or drink alcohol.

Now I'm in the process to be moving out of here to go next door to Andrew's Court.[6] Gonna get my own little studio apartment. Other than that, I'm just taking it day by day. You got to crawl before you can walk. Nowadays, if the police come and stop me, at least I can go in my pocket and pull out a check stub and say, "No sir, I wasn't there last night. I got a check stub in my pocket. I got a job."

Now that I'm home from prison, I want to live right here on the West Side right where I grew up at because it mean a lot to me. I'm real with my neighborhood. Even though it's totally different peoples here now. It's a whole new atmosphere, but I'd still love to be right here because I have shed blood here just like I have caused blood to be shed over here. When I get old and die I want to die right here because this is where I'm from. My whole family is here and this is where I'm from. My history is right here.

---

[6] St. Andrew's Court is a residence that is owned and operated by St. Leonard's halfway house. St. Andrew's offers residents more space and less institutional control than St. Leonard's housing.

CABRINI-GREEN

YUSUFU MOSLEY

AGE: *61*

OCCUPATION: *Prison reform activist, restorative justice worker*

FORMER RESIDENT OF: Cabrini-Green

Yusufu Mosley was born Lonell Mosley in Columbia, Mississippi. Yusufu was a
name first given to him by a Tanzanian minister who visited his family's church
in 1967. The word itself is Kiswahili for "one who encourages." When he was
eight years old, Yusufu's mother and stepfather moved the family north in order
to provide more opportunities for their children. He lived in Cabrini-Green in the
early through late 1960s. His experience of racism in Chicago politicized him
and spurred him to travel back south to volunteer in the Freedom Schools.[1] As a
young man, Yusufu became involved in organized armed resistance and violent
activity. He says, "We thought the revolution needed to be fought with knives and
guns rather than minds and hearts." In 1974, Yusufu was convicted of murder
and attempted murder and was incarcerated in southern Illinois. He remained
a dedicated student of history during his incarceration, enrolling in a college

---

[1] Freedom Schools were seminars designed to teach civic engagement. They were a feature
of the Freedom Rides—campaigns to register Southern African-Americans to vote in the
early to mid-1960s.

program through Roosevelt University and earning a bachelor's degree. During his imprisonment at Menard Correctional Facility, Yusufu co-organized a Black Cultural Coalition to bring African-American scholars and community leaders from Chicago into dialogue with prisoners there. Since Yusufu's release in 1996, he has done extensive training and work in restorative justice, with a particular emphasis in mentoring young people. He is also an organizer for the prison-abolition organization, Critical Resistance. When we make his acquaintance, Yusufu lives in a group home in Englewood. We meet for several conversations over breakfast at a pancake house in Hyde Park, where a teenaged Yusufu once worked as a busboy.

CHOPPING COTTON

We left Mississippi because my mother and stepfather didn't want me and my siblings to grow up to be sharecroppers like them. I had three brothers and three sisters at the time. I remember picking cucumbers, peanuts, and other vegetables as a child, and I remember being in the cotton field back in Mississippi. They don't call it picking cotton down there. They have another name for it, *chopping* cotton. I don't remember doing that kind of harvesting myself, but I remember seeing people I knew with the long bags walking row-by-row. And taking full sacks of cotton to the place where they'd pull the seeds out.

I remember the confusion a lot of the whites had toward my father and grandfather. Both of them refused to be called "boy." They wouldn't respond. Which is where I probably got my sense of resistance. I remember white men's pursuit of black women. They hated everything that wasn't white, except black women, black horses, black cars. Black men—they hated them especially. That's what got me making a lot of inquiries about why they hated us so much. As a child, I asked my father first. He said, "Ask your mother." I asked my mother, she said, "Ask your father." When I kept asking, my parents finally said, "Ask your grandparents." My great-grandmother was still alive at the time and she's the one who would talk to me about racism. She said, "We came here as slaves from our home country in Africa. We worked to build the country for over two hundred-something years and then they freed us, but they never really liked us." And my ma's mixed blood—she claimed that she's Seminole Indian, and my great-grandmother told me how most whites really hated the Indians. "So this is your history," my great-grandmother said. "Let me show you what your great-grandfather used to do. He was a Pullman Porter." And she had pictures of them together, with him wearing his uniform and everything. He traveled all over the country. He died before I got to know him. My great-grandmother told me that she and my great-grandfather had both been in bondage in Florida. When she laid it all out, I was curious. It didn't feel good once she told me about my great-grandfather, about how he'd been nearly blinded as punishment after trying to escape once. But he and my great-grandmother had come far since then.

THEY DID THE BEST THEY COULD
WITH WHAT THEY HAD

We traveled to Detroit from Mississippi with my parents and grandparents around 1960, when I was eight, and then we moved to Chicago about a year later. I lived on the West Side when we first got here. My grandparents took care of the four oldest kids when we first arrived. They did the best they could with what they had. I got my first pair of dress shoes from my grandfather. What we used to call "roach killers"—Spanish boots with the elastic in the middle. They had about an inch heel. I got them one size too small and I didn't know it at first. But I was cool. And that's what I wanted to be: cool.

After my stepfather and my mother split, my mother moved us to Cabrini-Green reluctantly. This was in the mid-sixties. I was in ninth grade then. My mother wanted to be a nurse, but there were a lot of us kids to tend to. Nine of us in all by then. And I was the middle one. The one who caught all of the flak from both sides. When the little ones messed up, I got blamed. When the old ones messed up, I got talked to like I was one of the old ones.

An early memory I have from Cabrini was seeing the first Daley, Richard M. Daley, visit for the opening of an outside swimming pool. Mayor Daley and some other city officials came over for the dedication and we met some of them directly. I never really questioned things politically or economically then. We watched the mayor give a speech that afternoon. He treated my siblings and me like good little kids.

At the time, I didn't know it, but I know it now: my mother, she had sold her vote to the Democratic Party. And they gave her, all of the people, little bitty envelopes and inside were two dollars. I do remember seeing my mother's name on her envelope. Two brand-new dollars. The local committeeman would distribute the envelopes. He'd have a meeting and call over to each person who had an envelope. *Here's yours, here's yours.*

WE CALLED RACISM "PREJUDICE" THEN

I had all kinds of jobs as a boy. For a while, I was up at four A.M. delivering papers—Chicago's finest, *Sun-Times.* We boys would go down to the branch with our wagons and get our paper load. I started off making $20 or $25 every two weeks. I also delivered bottles of milk from a little milk truck. Later, when I got to be a teenager, I'd work as a bag boy at the A&P.

The stepfather who came into our family's life when I lived at Cabrini was named William. I don't remember exactly when that was. He met my mother when she was working as a waitress at a lounge called the Outer Limits, right up on Sedgwick and Larrabee. She met my stepfather there and she brought him home and he had that look on his face, like,

"All of these kids—oh my God, what did I just step into?" He didn't say anything, but you could tell. He had that stunned look and I thought that he was going to be gone. My mother had had other boyfriends, but not ones we saw—they would come and go. William was the first one that actually came in and at an appropriate time, like seven o'clock. We were watching a show on our color TV and he came in and all of us looked at him and, like I said, he had that look. And he stayed, he stayed, he stayed. He was a stand-up man.

I kept up with school very well back then. I'd had black teachers in Mississippi, so seeing all these white teachers in my schools in Chicago was still a novelty to me. I think it wasn't until fifth grade when Jesse White was my first black teacher at school here. My teachers took an interest in me; as much as I read, I read slow. But this one Asian teacher taught me how to read real fast, with some kind of machine that had a light across the page. You could increase the speed of the reader and at the end of each reading would be questions about comprehension. That helped me turn a lot of corners, 'cause now I can read three or four books at a time. One of my most supportive teachers was Mr. Koob. Mr. Koob was a white guy. Of course, Koob is *book* spelled backwards. And that's what he would always mention. "Anytime you see me you should grab a book." And my brother and sister were like, *Yeah, right. You know what you can grab.* But I would grab a book. Since Mississippi, I was reading as much as I could.

Jesse White—now the Illinois Secretary of State—he was our gym teacher. Jesse White was a very strong disciplinarian but he was also a community man, and that used to shock everybody 'cause you don't see your teachers after school. The man went door-to-door to every building, asking parents, "What you want your kids ending up doing?" He inspired me to do community work. He got the kids together, playing sports.

I was also a Boy Scout, in Troop #146, and we went on camping trips to scout jamborees, where all of the scouts from across the country get together. There were other black troops coming from other places, and of course we gravitated toward them. And there were these little Girl Scouts there, and the brothers were, "I'm taking that one over there. And you talk to that one over there." And when we'd go to the campfire, we'd sit next to them. Some of the white girls were kind of liberal with the colored brothers, but the majority were apprehensive. Lots of white Boy Scouts were outwardly aggressive towards us. They said the N-word. They called us black SOBs. And said, "We're not gonna work with them." I don't know how they got any merit badges. My troop talked about it at our meetings. We called racism "prejudice" then, and my thing was to ask why. *Why is it they just don't like us?* People would make excuses. "You don't know what you're talking about. So-and-so said something to him and that's why he called him a nigger." But I'd noticed how things went down and there wasn't any real provocation. And we tried to sort it out, but Jesse tried to smooth over that people just disliked us.

LEAVING CABRINI AND GETTING
INTO REAL TROUBLE

Leaving Cabrini one day was when I got into real trouble. It happened when I was fourteen or fifteen. I was going over to my grandma's, like I did sometimes. She lived on the West Side and I'd have to cross over the Ogden Bridge to get to her. The walk there was problematic because it wasn't straight to the West Side. You had to go over a very long bridge and then pass through several different communities. You had to walk a little over a mile. If I remember correctly, one Polish, one Italian, and one Irish community. This one day as I was walking, I heard the fabulous words that some people used to like to speak in those days: "Nigger, what you doing over here?" And I turned around and I saw the man shouting at me and I gave him the finger. The man was a tall burly kind of white guy, looked like he'd been playing football. Muscular. He was blond-haired, blue-eyed and a little bit older than me, in his twenties. He was a big guy and I wasn't about to try to fight him, and when I gave him the finger he charged at me and pulled out one of those little itty bitty baseball bats they called Louisville Sluggers, and started swinging it at me. I was fortu nate enough I ducked out of the way, and in ducking I started moving into the street, and in moving into the street of course I stopped traffic, and when I got into the street he was still out there literally swinging at me like he was trying to hit a baseball or something. And when I got out of the way one time it hit one of the cars that was stopped and beeping and telling us to get out of the streets and all that kind of stuff. And when it hit the car the guy jumped out the car and said, "What you doing, nigger, what the, you trying to destroy my car?" And I say, "It ain't me with the baseball bat, sir," and it just kept on kept on.

Finally some people, I guess they got tired of it, and they came over and tried to break it up. Someone had called the police. They came and instead of grabbing the guy that had been attacking me, they grabbed me. I asked, "Why are you grabbing me? He's the one who was trying to hurt me." "You in the wrong neighborhood, boy." That's what I was told. I snatched away from them and one officer pulled out his pistol and said, "You're coming with us."

They took me to the police station and they charged me with assault and battery. I think they later dropped it when they found out that I was a youngster, but they kept me detained there. They asked me questions. "What are you doing over there? Why were you going through that neighborhood? Where do you live?" The questions would come almost all at once. And they had me handcuffed to a ring in the wall. The handcuffs was probably as tight as they could be 'cause my hand started swelling up. The two who were questioning me were doing the good cop/ bad cop kind of stuff and I guess that counts for something because the good cop would come and loosen them up a little bit.

What I remember most clearly from that day were the spectators. Me and that guy were almost in the middle of the street and these people were stopping their cars, getting out of their cars, and surrounding us, so that I wouldn't have too many places to go when I stepped back. And they were just standing there. Nobody trying to do anything, nobody saying nothing. Not, "That's wrong," or "What are you doing?" They just stood there like what was happening was an everyday thing. Spectators. I can say it now, I didn't do it then, but it was straight-out Mississippi racism, here in Chicago. I had walked that way many times before, had gotten called nigger, but nobody ever confronted me. This was the actual first confrontation. It's one of the experiences that got me involved in the Civil Rights Movement more earnestly.

MY POLITICS WERE GROWING
LITTLE BY LITTLE

My politics were growing little by little. There was a deacon in the local Catholic church. His name was Smith. I don't remember his first name, but he and his wife took a liking to me and they took me to one of my first operas. I was like, *What are they singing about? I don't know none of that stuff.* Something happened in the story and I said "Boooo," and Reverend Smith said, "You don't boo. You either clap your hands or snap your fingers; you don't boo." *Oh, okay.* And it was so horrible. Four acts and I had to sit there. I don't understand a word they're saying and they're singing at the top of their lungs. And the people are clapping and giving a standing ovation. And none of them look like me; I don't think they had anybody black up on stage.

Back in '65, Reverend Smith convinced my parents to let me go back to the South on the Freedom Rides. Reverend Smith was always talking to us kids about rights and duties and all those things, and he asked if we were interested in the Civil Rights Movement. He convinced me to sit down and he talked to me about Dr. King. I was a hyperactive kid, but I guess I must've showed some sign of interest 'cause he kept talking to us about Freedom Rides. I didn't know what he meant at first: I just knew "riders" as passengers on the Greyhound bus. But Reverend Smith convinced me, and I went to talk to my mom and my stepfather and my mom said, "No. Hell no, I don't want you going down there. I ain't gonna open your coffin if they send it back." But I was my feisty self and my stepfather supported me. He said, "Why not let him go? He needs the experience, he needs to know this world, let him go." And they argued for two or three days before she finally agreed. She was scared half to death about my going back through We were quite conscious of Emmett Till.[2] Reverend Smith had to convince my mother it was in my best interest. He told my mother that I was mature enough to make the trip and he told her I'd be traveling with a group and staying with good families. My mother kept reminding me of Emmett Till. She showed me the *Jet* magazine.[3] We saw the pictures. Wasn't no WVON[4] or Channel 9 covering it. We had the *Jet* and the *Defender*.[5]

---

[2] Emmett Till was a fourteen-year-old African-American from Chicago who was murdered in 1955 while visiting relatives in Mississippi. He was reportedly murdered for flirting with a white woman at a local grocery store. Days after his visit to the store, Till was kidnapped from his relatives' house and driven to a barn, where he was severely beaten and tortured, then shot and dumped into a nearby river. After his body was returned home, his mother insisted on an open-casket funeral. Photographs of his body were first published in *Jet* magazine and helped galvanize a national Civil Rights Movement.

[3] An American weekly magazine marketed toward African-American readers; founded in Chicago by John H. Johnson of Johnson Publishing Company in 1951.

[4] A Chicago radio station that was founded by Leonard and Phil Chess (of Chess Records) in 1963 and which geared its programming toward an African-American audience.

[5] A Chicago-based newspaper founded in 1905 for primarily African-American readers.

I went back down South for a little more than two months. I lived with families and I worked to sign people up to vote. I also got to volunteer in the Freedom Schools, working with the elementary and high school students, helping to make the young folks more politically and socially conscious. It seemed like nothing had changed there since I moved away, but I had changed and I felt like I was doing what I had to do.

One of the highlights being back down South was meeting Ella Baker.[6] She wouldn't have remembered me, but I was part of the audience when she spoke. Ella Baker was one of my heroes. I always use her model for organizing, as opposed to the Saul Alinsky model.[7] See, the difference between him and the kind of organizing I am talking about is that the Alinsky model relies on a leader to mobilize people and to challenge particular issues. Ella was talking about a whole structural kind of assault, and a paradigm shift, so we can look at things in a collective way. It's not about individuals. And that's why they obscure Ella Baker in history.

DIDN'T MANY PEOPLE KNOW ABOUT BLACK HISTORY

When I was around sixteen, in 1968, we moved within Cabrini. From 1340 to 1160 Sedgwick. My oldest sister got married and my two brothers eventually moved in with their own girlfriends, so we had reduced living

---

[6] Ella Baker (1903–1986) was a leader of the Civil Rights Movement.

[7] Saul Alinsky (1909–1972) was a leading community organizer who worked for decades to address concentrated poverty in Chicago and across the U.S. His influential book *Rules for Radicals* (1971) proposed organizing social movements around charismatic leaders, among other strategies. Alinsky's approach contrasted with that of Ella Baker, who avoided media attention. Unlike Alinsky, Baker believed that the most effective social movements are carried through broad public participation without figureheads or visible leaders.

space. If you ever saw *Good Times*,[8] the building that JJ and them lived in was the building we moved to. They'd show that building in opening credits. And so we lived there. We didn't have any Thelmas, but we had a lot of Willonas, and by that I mean we didn't have any special-looking ladies like Thelma. And I've seen the actress who played Thelma in more recent years at different events tied to Chicago public housing, and I told her just that, and she asked me, "What do you mean you didn't have nobody that looked like me?" And I had to tell her, "We didn't have no beautiful black women like you in the projects. We had your mom and your next-door neighbor; those were the people we looked at." If there'd been a Thelma walking around the neighborhood, there would have been a fight daily! When I told her that, she said she didn't believe it. And I don't believe it either, but it's kind of true. I saw that show with my mom a couple of times while we were living in 1160 Sedgwick. We didn't have JJs in the neighborhood neither. Let me tell you: JJ couldn't have survived in Cabrini; he was too foolish. That "dy-no-mite" stuff? JJ wouldn't have lasted there. He woulda been dynamite. Remember the character Booker, the building custodian? We had custodians like him, but their behavior wasn't comedic. They were trying to get sexual favors or whatever kind of favors, because 90 percent of the women were single.

Eric Monte, the guy who helped make *Good Times*, grew up in Cabrini. A lot of other famous people grew up in Cabrini-Green as well. Curtis Mayfield—he grew up there. And Ramsey Lewis was from the neighborhood. You could tell he was going to be something 'cause he was always playing the piano. His talent was remarkable.

But most of us didn't grow up understanding who we were or where

---

[8] A CBS sitcom that aired from 1974–1979. Focusing on the life of an African-American family, *Good Times* was set in a public housing development in Chicago. The series was produced by Norman Lear and co-created by Michael Evans and Eric Monte.

we'd come from. Didn't many people know about black history. We didn't know about Langston Hughes or other great thinkers. There was Negro History Week: an upgrade from Negro History Day. We learned a little about Booker T. Washington and George Washington Carver. But we didn't learn much. We just thought of Carver as the peanut man. He was a genius. Little did I know this man had a skill for nature. I'm glad to have that fuller picture of him now, but it was good to have some exposure like that because we could imagine that our history was more than just slavery.

Once in school I wrote a poem about what the Fourth of July meant to me. I can't remember what I wrote, but I know it wasn't nice. They asked me to rewrite it. Something more appropriate that could be published in the community newspaper. I was a radical. And I was ugly. People looked at me and thought, *Either he's going to be dead or he's going to be way out so far they gonna never catch him.* I didn't even think about Cinderella or things turning around like that. But I was one of the smartest kids.

In 1974, Yusufu was convicted of murder and attempted murder, and he was incarcerated in southern Illinois. After his release in 1996, Yusufu became involved in restorative justice, an approach to mitigating the damage that violent crime causes to the larger community. Part of his work includes counseling young men who have recently been released from prison.

YOU DID THAT FOR ME?

For the past few years, I've been living on the South Side, doing training and working with young men in restorative justice. Troy Davis,[9] the

---

[9] Troy Davis was sentenced to death in Georgia for the 1989 murder of a police officer in Savannah, Georgia. He maintained his innocence up until his execution in 2011 and won the support of numerous public figures and human rights groups.

brother they executed in Georgia, I was anguished about that. Troy himself showed a lot of dignity. He said, "Don't let this end with me." And I started wondering: how does one deal with a case like this through restorative justice? I talked about this last week at an event called *Englewood If.* How could things be different in Englewood? What if there were more resources in that community? What resources are most needed? People are looking for answers, but they're stuck in the same paradigm. People think they're getting something new, but it's the same thing repackaged.

I give credit to CeaseFire.[10] They're doing a great, heroic job, but you can't just stop violence, you have to stop the roots of violence. It's not the violent gang chief I'm worried about, but the mentality that produced it, where you have to use violence to get what you want. We're in a culture where violence is equated with manhood.

I've seen the distress in our communities. I've seen it when I was working in juvenile courts and the Community Justice for Youth Institute. Too much instability. I worked with a lot of kids whose moms were doing time in prison and whose dads were wherever. When those kids thought I was a probation officer, they'd tighten up, talk hard. I'd have to tell them, "You don't have to talk like that to me. I don't work for probation." It's something that tugs at your heart. *What can I do? I'm just an old guy working with the court.* I try to find the links that they need with welfare programs, but it's not enough.

Back when my mother was on welfare, I swore it would never happen to me. It created a dependence in her that was just heartbreaking to me. She never got off of it. And she passed away when I was in prison. Now I'm underemployed and I need assistance. When I first went to get my Link

---

[10] An anti-violence program and initiative, first launched in the West Garfield neighborhood of Chicago in 2000.

card,[11] I was in line like everybody else and the scene there is depressing, full of impatient people and people who are so down and out. When I got up to the table, the lady said, "Will you step over here?" And when I stepped over to the side with her, she said, "What are you here for?" I said, "I really don't know, but I'm supposed to get the Link card." She said, "Okay, you stay right here." She went to the back and took my application out the back and she said, "Come out of the line." She asked me to come back the next day.

When I got there the next day, I was the third person in line. She pulled me out of line and gave me the paperwork. She said, "You go back to that room right there and you'll get your Link card." When she came back to speak to me, she said, "You don't remember me. You helped me with my son a couple of years ago over at the juvenile center. I literally moved your name up on the list." I said, "You did that for me?" She said, "You talked to him and he's in college right now. And if it wasn't for your talking to him, he wouldn't be there." I said, "I thank you for that."

---

[11] In Illinois, benefits for the Supplemental Nutrition Assistance Program (formerly Food Stamps) are provided on the Illinois Link Card, an electronic card accepted at most grocery stores.

BALCONY, ROBERT TAYLOR HOMES

EDDIE LEMAN

AGE: *43*

OCCUPATION: *Hospital employee, entrepreneur*

FORMER RESIDENT OF: *Robert Taylor Homes*

We meet for the first time at the library at Chicago State University, where Eddie is enrolled in graduate courses in business administration. Eddie maintains a busy schedule, studying, coparenting, working at the Hines Veteran's Hospital, and developing his own brand of granola mix. Over the course of many conversations, Eddie shares personal photographs, newspaper clippings, and inspirational quotations, from Ann Landers to Buckminster Fuller. One of his favorites is from Gandhi: "You may never know what results come from your action. But if you do nothing, there will be no result." A self-described chameleon, Eddie attributes his flexibility and fortitude to lessons learned during his childhood in Robert Taylor Homes. He speaks of the fourteen years he lived there (1968–1982) with a mixture of affection, wonder, and regret—Robert Taylor Homes was where he enjoyed connection with an extended network of family. By the time we meet for our final conversation, Eddie is living in a suburb west of the city with his fiancée and her daughter. Names in this narrative have been changed at the request of the narrator.

WE CALLED IT OUR PENTHOUSE

I had a cart. And back then you'd get a refund on bottles. A nickel or a dime, you know. As a little kid—six, seven years old—I used to go through the buildings with my cart and collect bottles and take them to the supermarket to redeem them for money. I was a bottle hustler. I supported myself and my mother. I remember going to the stores, paying for things. My mother was on stamps. I can still remember I had to count the stamps out, because my mother really couldn't count.

My paternal grandmother, her name is Zola Washington. She lived in 4525 South Federal—the building that was right next door. This is my father's mother. She had seventeen kids. So to start off with I had about sixteen uncles and aunts. Throughout the years, a lot of them passed and everything. But we had several people in 4425 in our family. We got several people in 4429 that was in our family. Several people in 4444. So our family of Jacksons, Lemans, Eberharts, and Perrys was scattered throughout that one block of buildings.[1]

The apartment me and my mother lived in was 4429 South Federal. A one-bedroom apartment on the fifteenth floor. It had a kitchen. It had a pantry. It had a let-out couch that I slept on in the living room. It had a floor heated from the tiles. If we go on the porch, we'll see the front. The State Street side. If we look from the back, we'll see the Federal side. The Federal side is all the parking lots. And right after Federal, the Dan Ryan Expressway. And we could see across the expressway to some of the other homes and houses. You know, we called it our penthouse.

---

[1] Robert Taylor Homes was made up of twenty-eight identical sixteen-story towers. The buildings were arranged two-blocks deep between the Dan Ryan Expressway and State Street, and ran from Thirty-Ninth Street to Fifty-Fourth Street. Originally planned for 11,000 inhabitants, Robert Taylor Homes housed as many as 27,000 residents in the seventies and eighties.

GROWING UP, I NEVER SAW AMBULANCES

I heard stories when I was a child, from my uncles and people that lived there, that the Robert Taylors were built as a housing project very strategically. If there ever was an uprising or something: easy access for tanks to come down the Dan Ryan and target the buildings. Or motorized military vehicles. And I thought about that even as an adult. Mostly all the projects are next to expressways in Chicago. Easy access for military vehicles.

They built the police station over on Forty-Third Street, but this was years after the Robert Taylors were built. They built the station in the late '90s or something.[2] Before that, I think the closest station was so far away—Fifty-First Street, over on Halsted, Well, there were so many buildings at Robert Taylors and sometimes the numbers were torn off the building, so if you called the police and told them, "I'm in 4429," they probably wouldn't even know which building that was, and so that might have contributed to the police not coming when residents called in emergencies. And another thing: if you tell them what floor you're on, it's sixteen floors in the building, you know? If the elevators ain't working, then nothing's moving, including the police. They're not about to walk up all those stairs.

Even when the elevators were working, the lights were out half the time. They used to call them death traps. People got their arms or their body caught up in there. The elevator closed tight, like a clamp. You'd have to hold it with both hands and try to open the door if it was shutting. There was no safety sensor. People were routinely stuck, hurt, trapped in there. They had one red button bell in there to ring, but that didn't do anything.

---

[2] The Chicago Housing Authority Police Department was a police force established in the late eighties that was dedicated to patrolling public housing. See glossary, page 217.

The only way to open the elevator safely was to use this long six-inch key. It was like a stick and you'd open the elevator with that, but those keys weren't never around, so you'd have to pry yourself out. And when you climb out, you've got to jump down or climb up. You'd be stuck between floors. You get on the elevator, you risk getting stuck, you risk getting hurt, you risk getting robbed. That was every day, all the time. And I lived on the fifteenth floor, so you know I had my exercise on.

When I was growing up, I never saw ambulances. There was so much crime around there, maybe they didn't come because of their safety. In Robert Taylor, they had little chain-link fences along the parking lot held by metal beams. And these metal beams had sharp edges. When I was a little child, eight or nine, I was sitting on one of the metal beams and I got up to play. The metal beam ripped my leg open. We waited for the ambulance, but it never came. So my mother got a ride and we rode to Provident Hospital.

Provident was just a tragedy. I remember seeing roaches, bloody tissues, everything. Ten stitches I needed for this cut. It was about two inches deep, two inches wide. Because it was unsanitary in the hospital, the cut got infected and it didn't heal right. And when they stitched it, they didn't stitch it closed. They had it wide open. Ten stitches. The scar is about three inches long. Big as a finger. The stitches are about half-an-inch apart. Looks like a centipede. It's disfigurement. And I got to carry this all my life.

YOU GOT TO REALLY NAVIGATE WHERE YOU GO

I was always a young man who was into the streets, you know. Not gang-banging, but hustling. My mother was on drugs, she was out there bad, so I kept our house in order. I'd cook, clean, everything. Zenos Colman was my first school. We ate breakfast there, lunch there. The teachers at Colman had several different types of punishments for us, you know, without laying hands, but we had to do duck walks and hold books up straight in front of us and hold our arms up until our shoulders were about to fall off. It was a learning experience. And we had to navigate our way to school real carefully. Going down the fire lane—it was about a two-block walk from our building to school—we had to really listen to what was going around us. In case there were any cars zooming around through the fire lane, or shooting, or things getting thrown, because back when I was there, they didn't have fencing on the balconies. When I was there, there was half a fence, so people would tend to throw things over the sides. So we had to constantly look up. I didn't see anybody get really hurt. I never seen anyone get their head busted because people pretty much respected the fire lane. I seen plenty of water. Plenty of furniture and trash.

Sixth grade was when I really started concentrating on schoolwork. I started excelling in school. It was '81 or '82 when they pulled different children who were gifted out of the projects, from Fifty-Fifth all the way to Forty-Third, and put them in Beasley Academic Center. And I was in the first graduating class of Beasley. I had to go further from my block when I started going to Beasley. The only thing we was fearing back then was getting jumped. With the Robert Taylors, there were two separate kinds of buildings: the white buildings and the red buildings. And each section has different gangs, so you have to know who's governing your hood. In my case it was the GDs and Gangsters.[3] You get transported to someplace that's another hood where there's Vice Lords and Disciples, like Fifty-First, then you got to really navigate where you go. If you on school ground, you'd better stay on school ground. So that was the only part that concerned a lot of the male students.

---

[3] Branches of the Gangster Disciples, a prominent gang in Chicago. See glossary, page 217.

THEY GAVE ME A CHOICE

In eighth grade, I had a teacher named Mr. Adamak. A white guy with a blond Afro. He enrolled me in this program called "Unto Perfect Manhood." And I won an award while I was in the program: a scholarship to Hales Franciscan High School.[4] At that time I was going through a lot of changes. My mother, she was pretty strung out. I was getting older and my cousins wanted me to run with them. They were all in gangs. My maternal grandmother who lived out in Chicago Heights was always concerned with me and my living situation with my mother. My mother and my grandmother gave me a choice. It was a hard choice because I'm in eighth grade, you know? I'm thinking, *If I stay here and go to Hales Franciscan, I'm still gonna be living in 4429 with my momma and I'll still be susceptible to gang violence and then there won't be no girls.* I'm thinking about girls, too. Hales Franciscan is all boys. So I'm thinking, *If I go to the suburbs with my grandmomma, I'll be living a lot better and I won't have to worry about my safety, and there'll be girls.* My momma, she wasn't one to make decisions for me back then, so it was left up to me and I decided to go with my grandmother.

I had some ideas about what it would be like. I used to go out to Chicago Heights and my aunt's family had motorcycles and toys everywhere, a big backyard and a refrigerator full of food. So that's what I'm thinking. *I go there, I'll be living part of the good life.* When I'd been out that way, I never socialized with people in the same ways I did in the hood, but I fit in because I knew how to talk to anyone. When I actually moved out there, I was pretty much on my own, 'cause all I known is gangs. I was a freshman in school doing prayers, you know. I was regulating things, hosting prayers[5] in the bathroom on the GD side. The kids are like, "He's

---

[4] A Catholic high school on the Near South Side.

[5] Gang prayers occur when meetings are called to order.

from the city. Straight G, man. What's happening?" I brought it there. It was some people who knew about GDs already, but I brought it there. When you're a freshman and you first go to a high school, you kind of want to get a group of people around who you can feel safe with. And the only thing I knew about was gang-banging, so the people around me, they were into gang-banging too. Or they wanted to get into it. And we weren't into robbing-type stuff. It was more of a little brotherhood thing going on. I wasn't no Board member[6] or nothing, but I've got a lot of family who taught me a lot of loves and prayers, you know.

It was like I was in-between when I first went out there. I was coming back to Chicago nearly every weekend. But the thing was, when I came around the old neighborhood, I felt like a visitor. I still knew a lot of people — a lot of my family, they still lived in Robert Taylor, but it's like, I cut it off. My uncles and aunties, some of them was pretty much out there on drugs or they were alcoholics. Once I left the projects, my extended family still treated me with love. I know in their hearts, they didn't feel no jealousy. They wanted an opportunity like mine, but they didn't have it. Still they were gonna try to support me as much as they could.

Before too long, I got a few friends in Chicago Heights and we developed a little network. Some were selling weed and all that stuff. But I had to make another decision when I was a sophomore. Cause my grandmother was like, "Naw-uh. Hold up." I think what broke the camel's back was that she came in my room and she saw some baggies with some joints in it. I didn't have anything hard, just some joints and stuff, and she was like, "No, you got to go." She put me out right there. She sent me out to live with one of my cousins, and I stayed out there for a minute. Then my grandmother and my cousins, they moved to Park Forest just south of the

---

[6] "Board member" refers to a leader of certain gangs such as the Gangster Disciples.

city, and she pulled me back, and I got back to books and studying more. All this happened in a one or two-year period.

My senior year, I made a big change. I was in a motorcycle accident. I wasn't hurt bad or anything, but I thought, *Damn, I almost got killed messing around in the streets. What am I gonna do?* And then they had a recruiter come to the school from the Marine Corps and he told us about this program called Delayed Entry where you sign the papers before you graduate, so they lock you in. I signed the papers for the Marines.

I GOT A CALL FROM THE CHAPLAIN

Couldn't nobody pay for college for me, so I saw the Marines as a means to an end. I also saw it as another adventure. I'm thinking to myself, *I did it all. I been a gang-banger. I took care of myself. I done been through the projects. I did all this. So, if I'm gonna join the service, I want to join the best one it is.* This was in '85. I was eighteen when I went to Camp Pendleton, over near San Diego. When I first got there, it was kind of a shock. Back then, they were still able to put hands on you. It wasn't like they just beat you down or nothing, but they'd grab you and yank you or do whatever to you. And it clicked in. Sometimes when you're in a lot of violent situations, and then you go to a subtle situation, any kind of violence will trigger a—*hey, hold up!* The Marines triggered me. And my survival instincts kicked in. But you know, I took it. I embraced it. 'Cause I was confident that wherever they put me, whether it was in a field or a foxhole or whatever, I knew I could adapt. I know how to wash my hands with ice or rain. I know how to start a fire without a lighter or match. Get an MRE,[7] I'm gonna make a gourmet meal out of it because back when I was living in the projects,

---

[7] A military ration. MRE is an acronym for "meal, ready to eat."

I got used to making do with what I had. So I embraced the military. I didn't make too much money out there, but I became a platoon leader, a squad leader. I had two tours while I was in the Marines overseas.

During my second tour, one of these tours, in '87, I got a call from the chaplain. They told me my mother had passed. My mother was an addict. When she died, my aunt had to bust down the bathroom door and call for the ambulance and the police to come because my mother was dead with a needle in her arm. It took them over an hour to come—the EMT workers. My aunt said when they did finally come, the body was so . . . not decomposed, but something was wrong with it. Bio-hazard, they said. They wouldn't touch it. They took the stretcher back downstairs and they brought a wheelbarrow. They took my mother's body out of 4429 Federal in a wheelbarrow.

Once I got to the closed-casket funeral, I couldn't cry. I don't know if it's conditioning from living in the projects. I don't know if it's conditioning from the Marine Corps. But you know, I felt a hole in my heart. I felt empty. It wasn't like I didn't want to cry, you know. It's just that I'm looking at all these people, and I know we lived in the projects. And the way my mother died was off an overdose—a speedball with cigarette ash contaminate—in the same apartment I lived in all my life. So I'm like, *Okay, I left to go to high school and the Marine Corps and y'all didn't take care of my momma. Here she is. I won't give you the privilege to see me cry. I won't give you the satisfaction.*

I always knew that my mother used to be in the gambling house[8] a lot, and I remember being there with her, looking over a table and seeing her playing cards and getting drinks for everybody. So I know the kind of people she was dealing with. So when I came home to her death, my mind was so confused that I fantasized about taking out *every* liquor store, *every*

---

[8] A bar or residence where gambling takes place off the books.

gambling house. I was in bad shape when I came home. If I hadn't been shipped out again after her funeral, I might have continued to get worse. Of course, I never intended to harm anyone. And now that I've grown and gotten back to society, I know that everybody has a choice to go to a drug dealer or a liquor store. But back then, I was thinking it was something the liquor stores were doing to people. Once I left Chicago and went back on tour, I had to turn off my anger again. I had to turn the streets off again. Everything I brought here that trip home, I left here.

I loved the military. I loved fighting. I loved serving my country. I went to Asia. I went to Hong Kong. I went to the Philippines. I went to Korea. All over. All my life, I've been accepted in so many places, but I couldn't stick around. In 1989, the end of my four-year tour of duty was coming up and I was in San Bernardino, living with a lady and her child. And every time we got a leave, I'd go out there. I was still living on base. But that was closest I got to my own home. Over in San Bernardino, this lady's father worked for a homogenizing plant. He had a job for me, fifteen dollars an hour. That was beautiful. I had a car, the woman's beautiful and everything. But around that time, my grandmother got sick and I had to go back to Chicago. So I didn't sign the re-up papers. I got my four years, got out. Honorable discharge.

My grandmother got me a job as a mental health technician on the North Side, in Uptown. All my life, when I was smaller, my grandmother used to take me there. I remember realizing back then a lot of people there were different. I remember the clients there all respecting my grandmother. I remember the offices being so clean. And people were so nice and professional. So it was a positive experience going there. I had another friend of the family who I grew up with, my grandmother's co-worker's son, he was a shorty too. We used to go in the basement, play house music, down at the center. And we had good times there. Then when I got out the service, everybody there already knew me from when I was a little kid.

I WAS INCOMPLETE IF I DIDN'T HAVE
A LOT OF RESPONSIBILITY

I had to go through plenty of training for the work I did in mental health, but that couldn't really prepare me. It was hands-on learning that made it real. My grandmother told me, "You know why you so good at this? You got a little mental illness in you and, you know, it takes one to influence one!" I said, "All right, grandma, all right." She was halfway teasing, but she was also telling the truth. I worked it out instinctively. Living in Robert Taylor, you're under a lot of stress and you learn to adapt, but there are people you get to know who have their own difficulties and sometimes the pressure is too much. Being in the military, I learned different personality types through observation. Both the military and public housing put you in extreme situations. By the time I started therapeutic work, I had pretty much run across mental illness already.

During the time I was first working at community counseling center, I started my college studies at Chicago State. I also met up with the woman who later became my wife. My wife grew up in Robert Taylors, too, and I was friends with her aunt back in the day. Her aunt lived in my building. We'd play cards and be kicking it. I knew who my future wife was before I joined the service, but she's two years younger than me, and back then I thought of her as a little girl. I didn't really meet her until I got back from the service. She rode in my car after a group of us went to her grandmother's funeral in Memphis. That night, after we got back to Chicago, she and I went to a party across from where I used to live, in 4429. We kissed at that party. She fell in love. I fell in love. She already had two baby boys. So young they weren't walking yet. I'd raise them with her.

All my life, I was incomplete if I didn't have a lot of responsibility. I was like, *Bring it, bring it!* I did the work at the Edgewater–Uptown

Mental Health Center from 1989 to 1996 and also joined the sheriff's office in '95. My wife gave birth to our three girls in those years. Our youngest was born in '93. Two days later, we finally got married. For the first eight years of our relationship, my wife didn't have to work. I told her, "Baby, you don't have to work, all you got to do is satisfy Daddy and you gonna be all right!" For almost two years, I was working two full-time jobs: at the community center and also with the county sheriff. That was when my wife and kids was living right next door to the Mental Health Center, and I worked the midnight shift there and managed to get a little sleep. And when I woke up, I had to go down to Twenty-Sixth and California, work at the criminal courts.

I was the best sheriff I could be. I got commendations. I got noticed by my superiors. At first, I was working in receiving at Twenty-Sixth and California, helping process people brought before a judge. I worked receiving from '95 to '98. I didn't like it, but I did what I had to do. Then I got transferred to the front door. Because I'm thinking to myself, *violence every day*. I had to put hands on my young brothers. I asked for a transfer to the front door and I worked the metal detectors for the next few years. That was a lot better. That was more like social work. You get to help people. And I was real good at that job. Anybody who ever went to Twenty-Sixth and California from '98 to 2003, they'll tell you: "Black guy with the glasses? Oh man, he's real cool, but hard as paint."

And then, like on holidays, I was a hustler, too. Selling things on the corner. I sold scarves, hats, gloves in the wintertime. In the summertime, I sold little balloons. I had a van back then. I took my sons out, showed them how to do it. We did mostly events like the Bud Billiken Parade.[9] I always had a cart at the Bud Billiken Parade. My father-in-law, he always

[9] The Bud Billiken Parade is the oldest and largest African-American parade in the United States.

sold fish and on the side, you know, I sold other cooked things. He had a fryer and everything, and me by his side. We were business partners for a long time.

I GOT THE SAME TIME AS A BIG
DRUG DEALER

In 2003, there was an FBI sting. The FBI had an informant at the court at Twenty-Sixth and California, and his job was getting other people to participate in a theft of money from a drug dealer. I had a friend at the court who was recruited by the informant. They asked me too, and at first I refused. They got me on tape three times saying no. But then that one time, I needed money. I'd been in a car accident. A drunk driver hit me when I was in the squad car and I was in bad shape. I couldn't work no overtime. I couldn't take on extra work, you know. And he asked me to do it and I said yes. So we drove and met him and this other dude. I never saw this other guy before. We met at the movie theater over on Eighty-Seventh. They told me, "You don't have to do nothing. All you got to do is do lookout and we'll take care of everything." They broke into a parked car. I played lookout.

I ain't gonna say I didn't do nothing. I did participate in a theft. But anyway, as far as hands on, they were the ones who broke into the car. Now the guy who my friend was with, he was the one who was working for the FBI. And he was the one who was supposed to break into the car and take the money. But, along with the money, the Feds had put some fake drugs in there, too. So the informant took the money and the fake drugs, but he didn't show anybody the fake drugs. Now, the informant was wired, and on the drive back he said one thing that made a big difference in the case. He was like, "The coke goes to my man." That one sentence, that put me away for seven years because they argued that when he said that, I knew

109

drugs were involved and I still accepted money from them for the theft. The drugs led to additional charges.

They ran this sting seven different times to seven different people from seven different agencies. Seven different black men. From probation officers to sheriffs to CHA police. The same set up. The informant breaks into a parked car, and they get the outside dude to play lookout. The lookout guy faces the same charges for the whole crime of theft and possession. There's this law called the Pinkerton Law that's all about conspiracy. If you participate in any kind of crime, whatever the other people do, you're liable for it, too.

I was bitter at first, but I did participate in a theft, so I wasn't innocent. But the main thing I was bitter about was everything I done before wasn't a factor in how I was treated at all. I served my country, I worked with mentally ill, I was in law enforcement—I did all this, and they gonna forsake me? They gonna do this to me? Man, I was heartbroke over that. Then I started thinking, after sentencing, I'm like, *They sentenced me to all this time and I never even saw no drugs or touched no drugs.* It would be different if I was a drug dealer and I had all the cars. Traveled to different places. Got the memories of exotic things, then, *Okay, y'all caught me. I'll lay it down. I done did my dirt.* But I wasn't that guy. I've been working since I was sixteen getting a paycheck, and I got the same time as a big drug dealer.

My whole life has been sevens. I got seven years working with mental patients. Seven years as a Cook County sheriff. Seven years in jail. Three sets of sevens. I went in in 2003 and got out in 2010. First, they shipped me to Ashland, Kentucky. The first three years of my bit. I did three years with no incident. And then they shipped me to a camp. That was in Duluth, Minnesota. In a medium security, you get ten-minute moves. You're locked down pretty much all the time. It's more restricted. In a camp, you get free movement, you know, you get more leniency. Because the camp is like the next thing before society. You're still locked up, but you don't have no bars.

When I was incarcerated in Duluth, I didn't have nobody to send me money. My wife and I had separated. I told her that she was released from our marriage contract if she was ready to move on. We stayed friends, but I didn't want to ask her to wait for me. But I still wanted to do what I could to support our kids. And so I had to try to make money the best way I can. Now in prison, there's very few ways to make money. One way is you can steal. Steal from the chow hall, re-sell it. Steal from other people, risk getting messed up, whatever. That's one way to make your living. Another way is to gamble with cards, dominoes, anything else available. And the third way is to get a legit product from the store, make it or bake it or cook it, and then sell it. I did the third. That's how I got going making my granola.

IT'S LIKE IT WAS A DREAM

Once I was released, I was in a halfway house for six months. In a halfway house, you're pretty much on lockdown, unless you get passes to go certain places. The only way to get out is to have appointments, go to school, have a job interview, whatever, so that's what I'm gonna do. I was going to school every day. I was in a halfway house when I got my bachelor's. I finished in six months.

When I came out, I think they were just starting to tear down the Robert Taylors. Or they were almost finished. They were doing a lot of construction, too, when I first got out. A lot of construction on the Dan Ryan. And I was thinking to myself that I was kind of glad they were doing those demolitions. I got some good memories as a child up in there. But it's a lot of tragic memories as an adult from there. And to have people living like that, on top of each other, in this day and age, it's a shame. This is 2011, you know. That's probably something you don't even see in a lot of cities anymore. Sixteen stories, and what was it? About two hundred feet, you know? And about twelve, thirteen apartments on one floor. Each apartment got families.

Sometimes when I be driving on the expressway and I look in that direction and I see those little storefronts, it's like those buildings, well, it's like it was a dream. A lot of memories come from them. The mother of my children, she was from there. She lived over on Fifty-First. My extended family, they lived there. My children were used to going there, visiting. So it's a lot of history with them. But as far as breaking it down . . . My mother died there. I can do the research to find the article on my mother. I can do it, but I don't want to. I don't even have her death certificate. I couldn't even cry at her funeral.

Where I want to live now is anywhere I don't have to watch my back. It's been so long since I relaxed. I want to live in a neighborhood where I can go out, walk around, and not worry about getting shot or jacked or whatever. Some young people out here are so brainwashed, they think that just because you look presentable or nice that you're an easy victim. They don't know about your history, where you been, what you did. I'm not going to get out here and put on pants to my ass or wear a starter jacket like I'm gang-banging. I'm wearing my pea coat and I have my shit together. I'm thinking I may need to move from Chicago.

LIBRARY IN CABRINI-GREEN, PRE-DEMOLITION

SABRINA NIXON

AGE: *43*

OCCUPATION: *Freelance writer, college student*

FORMER RESIDENT OF: *Cabrini-Green*

We meet at a diner a few blocks away from the Wicker Park apartment Sabrina Nixon shares with her two sons, aged seventeen and twelve. Currently pursuing a degree in medical transcription, Sabrina has written several novels, a memoir, and a play. She recently penned an essay about the demolition of the Cabrini-Green high rises for the Chicago Tribune Red Eye *daily supplement. Sabrina lived in Cabrini for twenty years from 1974 through 1993. She regularly ventured outside of her neighborhood in her youth, attending grammar school in the mixed-income Old Town (where her grandparents lived) and high school in the more affluent Lincoln Park. In her narrative, she describes how this shuttling required her to learn how to safely navigate gang territories. She also recounts her experience of witnessing her older sister being shot in their apartment, and the neglect of ambulance workers during this harrowing event.*

FROM REAL LIFE

Langston Hughes is one of my favorite authors. Back in grammar school, I had to recite his poem "Mother to Son" for a school play. "Life for me ain't been no crystal stair . . ." I went to George Manierre School back then, up on Hudson, in Old Town, not far at all from Cabrini. We actually lived in Old Town until I was five, and then we moved to Cabrini. One thing I loved about Manierre was that our teachers made such a big deal out of Black History Month. You had to be a part of the Black History Month play. I don't care if you were a tree, a plant, or something; you were going to be involved in the play. And I remember having to recite that Hughes poem, and I didn't like it, because I didn't really know the meaning of it.

At Manierre, they focused a lot on reading. The teachers made sure we had good penmanship. They made sure we pronounced words properly and they really encouraged a love for books. Do you know the nonprofit called RIF? Reading Is Fundamental. They used to come around once every six months, and I looked forward to following the *Encyclopedia Brown* series through their book club. All the fast girls, they were into the Judy Blume books. *Are You There, God? It's Me, Margaret*; *Deenie*; and *Blubber*. I didn't have to rush to go get *Encyclopedia Brown*, because I knew he was going to be there. All the other girls was beating each other up trying to get the next Judy Blume! I just strolled on over there, glanced on the table, "Oh, *Encyclopedia Brown Goes to the Farm*." I hated it when I missed school the day RIF came, because that meant that someone else would pick out a book for me, and then I would get something like *Spot Goes to the Farm*, and I'd be so angry.

That's really when my love for reading started. As an adult, soon after I had my sons, I started writing. I kept a journal about everyday stuff. Later, I just fictionalized it. I've written a play, three novels, and my fourth book is like Christian nonfiction. It's called *Grace and Hope*, and it's about how God blesses me on a day-to-day basis, with me dealing with my lupus and my boys' autism. I became interested in Langston Hughes again as an adult, once I started writing. I read his biography, and more about how he used the urban experience for the backdrop of his works. The "Mother to Son" poem, I understand it now. I tell my son, "Life ain't that easy," which is what that poem meant. One of my favorite Hughes poems is "The Ballad of the Landlord." The speaker is basically threatening the landlord, like "come and see about what I want." Langston Hughes wrote so many good, funny poems, and they come from real life.

IT'S EQUAL, BUT SEPARATE

Some of the most vivid memories I have of Cabrini Green are from when I was a teenager in the 80s. That was when the neighborhood became more crime-ridden. There was a lot of gang activity. A lot of shootings. Wasn't too much drug activity back then. Crime was related to territory, turf, like the movie *The Warriors*. You couldn't wear certain colors. Stupid things like that.

Remember the phrase "separate but equal"? In Cabrini-Green, it's kind of reversed. Equal, but separate. Cabrini-Green is one big community, but it's sectioned off into different neighborhoods. Everyone there is equal as far as having low incomes. But the separate part is the location of where each building is. We had the Reds and the Whites. Within those communities, you had buildings going against each other.

I vividly remember heading to school every day, walking into my old neighborhood. There's different gangs over there. The Vice Lords were over in the Old Town area versus the Gangster Disciples inside of Cabrini-Green. We pretty much took a chance with our lives just going to school. We had a boundary. Larrabee Street. Once you crossed that street, you were in a whole new ground of gang activity. I remember getting phone calls from my mom, if we were at school, or at my grandmother's saying, "Okay, don't come home right now, because they're shooting." Sometimes it could be days before the shooting subsided. We'd stay over at my grandmother's, at 1426 Mohawk, about a mile away. That was the most frustrating and critical time, just trying to go out, just doing every day things, and my mom, you know, she was so worried.

A PERSON SHOT THROUGH OUR DOOR

It happened when I was thirteen years old. It happened at nighttime. It must have been summer, because in Cabrini, most of us would leave our front doors open when it was warm out. My oldest sister was eighteen and she was dating someone who was at the house that night. Me, my parents, my older sister, my middle sisters, and one of my brothers—we all were there. My mother was pregnant with my youngest sister at the time.

The guy my older sister was dating, he wasn't a gang member. He was just on the wrong turf. My sister's boyfriend was "from the other end," as they called it, from over near Old Town. That night I was braiding my older sister's hair, with my back turned toward the door. We had the front door open, and I got up to close it. A minute after I closed it and was heading back through the apartment, a loud bang went off. I probably thought somebody threw a firecracker at our house. We heard firecrackers all the time. But a person had shot through our door, and my older sister was wounded. We think that someone used a sawed-off shotgun.

Cabrini was brick inside and out. The door wasn't steel, but it was really thick, good quality wood. The thickness of the door must have slowed the force of the bullet. My sister was shot in the back of the head. So much of what happened afterwards is just a blur.

We lived on the thirteenth floor and I think my father had to walk down the stairs with my older sister. The elevator wasn't working and no ambulance came. My father wouldn't have been able to catch a taxicab. You rarely saw cabs in the neighborhood because of the gang activity, so my father must have drove. My mother went with them. They went to the local hospital, Henrotin, over on Oak. My sister was treated there for maybe a couple of weeks. I remember when she came home, her face was really, really swollen. She didn't suffer brain damage. The shooting didn't paralyze her. She survived, but to this day, she still has buckshot in her. When it rains, she feels sore and stiff. She still has pain.

The thing about ambulance and police at Cabrini is that when there were reports of shooting, they'd come eventually, but they didn't come right away. It wasn't a hurry. Police knew that shootings happened in the neighborhood on a constant basis. Nine times out of ten, they weren't going to risk their lives when they knew it was plain-out gang activity going on. It was the norm, so to speak. I'm sure that's how a lot of them looked at it. *They'll just kill each other off.* They didn't care.

For months after the shooting happened, me and my younger siblings were afraid to walk past the door. The way our house was set up, the bedrooms were in the back and to get to the living room or the kitchen, you had to walk past the door. I was fearful to go the kitchen or the front room. I didn't want to pass the entrance because I was scared someone was going to shoot through the door again. I didn't have nightmares or anything like that, but I had a fear of walking past that door. My younger sister would just run past it when she was going to the kitchen. It was pretty much the same thing with me. When the door was open, it was fine, but once it was closed, that's when the fear came.

WICKER PARK

When I was coming out of high school, what was clear in my mind was to get out of my surroundings because I got tired of the shootings. I got tired of just living at home. I wanted to build my own life. I lived in Dallas for a while, just to get away, and I moved from the 1230 N. Burling building of Cabrini for good when I was twenty-five and I had my oldest son. He was five months old when we moved out to Wicker Park. And that's where we live now. It will be eighteen years in September.

I'm an online student now, completing a degree in medical transcription. You have to have a love of vocabulary and language in general to be good at medical transcription, and you have to know punctuation. It's not just something that you can learn overnight. My love of reading and writing was linked in to my choice of study. My overall goal is to work from home because of my children and because I have lupus.[1] I wouldn't exactly call it a trade, but it's like being a mechanic or a hairdresser, people are always going to be in need of people with those types of skills. Eventually, I'd like to work in a private medical practice.

I wasn't studying transcription when I was first diagnosed with lupus, or while I was very ill—I became ill in 1999 and I'm in remission now—but taking transcription courses, learning medical terminology and pharmacology has given me greater understanding of what to expect when I go to the doctor's office. It makes me more confident when a doctor prescribes something for me or for my youngest with autism. He's on a couple of medications. Now I can decipher some things.

Of course, I keep writing. Writing is something I love. The hard work is in trying to network, but I wrote these books for a reason, so I've made up a mantra for myself: every day just try to do something productive towards your goals. I try to do as much as I can while the children are at school. My whole life is pretty much centered around Kameron, my youngest. Whenever he's out of the door, there are a million and one

---

[1] After years of illness and misdiagnosis, Sabrina was diagnosed with the autoimmune disease lupus in 2004.

things I want to do, but I have to prioritize, because once he comes back home, that's it. He wants all my undivided attention. And him being non-verbal is kind of tough.

My angle is to eventually get a bigger place for my children to live, 'cause right now they're sharing their room and they need their own space, you know. I love the neighborhood, because it's residential, as well as business-oriented. And I've actually got the ideal place in mind. It's down the street from me. Three bedrooms and two bathrooms. I don't want to leave Wicker Park. It's easily accessible to everything.

SEEING ANYTHING TORN DOWN
IS HEARTBREAKING

I wrote an article last spring about the demolitions for the *Chicago Tribune* on a whim. I'd emailed the editor and asked about the criteria to become a contributor. She wanted just two five-hundred-word essays, to see my writing style. I submitted them and after that, she signed me up for that one assignment. That was a blessing because I haven't worked for many years because of my children's needs due to their autism.

When I wrote my article, people were still living at Cabrini-Green, but I knew it was going through a transformation. Some buildings were already closed down. I don't like to watch the TV news because it's too depressing, so I first heard that they were moving forward with the demolitions on my building from people on Facebook. My cousin posted something like, *Oh man, it's coming down.* And then my sister, she would come over to my place, she'd ask me, "Man, did you all see what they did to the Burling side? They spray-painted a picture of a big rat on the public side of the building." And I'm like, *Oh, whatever,* you know. Then I kept just hearing little tidbits here and there. Our building was the last. My father would call, "Yeah, Burling, coming down. They're chopping it in half, it's getting chopped down." *Whatever, I still ain't seen it.* I wasn't really motivated to go over there. People were saying, "Oh, let me get over there and go get a brick, go get the last piece of brick from there." Honestly, I really, truly, did not want to go by there. I thought, *Let bygones be bygones.* I know the history of Cabrini. I know what could have been. Whatever, que sera, sera.

Lo and behold, I had to drive by Cabrini on my way somewhere. It was meant for me to see it. Part of me felt it was heartbreaking, because it was like the end of an era—for some people a good era, for some people a bad era. Just seeing anything torn down is heartbreaking. Not so much that I cared it was 1230 N. Burling, but to see years and years being put into something, and then to see it come down . . . well, I look at that metaphorically. You could just build your life on something for so many years, and at a moment's notice it's all taken away from you. Then after thinking about the people that had spent so many years there, I started looking at the demolition technically, thinking about the construction of the buildings. I'm like, *Hmm, why am I thinking about the construction?* I should be thinking, *Wow, you know, this place is gone, where I lived.* Instead I'm wondering, *Wow, who built this place?* What is wrong, you know? I almost started to cry.

Then as I passed through my old neighborhood, I was suddenly not sure where I was exactly, since I didn't recognize my surroundings anymore. The whole landscape had changed. *Oh my God, where am I?* Finally I saw 1230 N. Burling in the distance. But that was a scary feeling, getting lost in your own neighborhood.

In Sabrina's Red Eye *article, published in April 2010, she writes, "I started to cry about two months ago as I was driving down Chicago Avenue going west and encountered a detour on Larrabee Street. I made a wrong turn down Kingsbury Street and thought I was in another world. In the midst of driving down this street with its strange and beautiful homes, I saw the landmark of 1230 N. Burling in the distance. I was lost, in a neighborhood that was once my own. If that building hadn't been there, I wouldn't have known where I was or where to go." Demolition on 1230 N. Burling, the last of the Cabrini-Green high rises, took place in March of 2011.*

GATE, CABRINI-GREEN

PAULA HAWKINS

AGE: *45*

OCCUPATION: *Cab dispatcher, student*

FORMER RESIDENT OF *Cabrini-Green*

We meet Paula at her apartment in the Englewood community. Her living room is decorated in royal purple, her favorite color, and is often filled with the birdsong of her parakeet. On more than one occasion, Paula quotes the filmmaker Tyler Perry: "He said something and I'll never forget it. 'Two places you should have peace: in your home and in your grave.'" Paula lived in Cabrini-Green from infancy until she was eleven years old—between the late 60s and the late 70s. Her treasured memories of childhood in Cabrini-Green include going to church services in the neighborhood with her grandparents, witnessing her twin brother's Evil Knievel–inspired, daredevil capers, and riding her ten-speed bike through her neighborhood and into the neighboring Gold Coast. Paula identifies her youth in Cabrini-Green as a very happy era in her life. The challenges of adolescence and adulthood included her early motherhood, her struggles with addiction, and subsequent incarceration. Now ten years sober and staunchly grounded in her religious faith, Paula struggles to make ends meet and is locked out of many opportunities for support because of her prior conviction and imprisonment for prostitution.

AND I REMEMBER THEY SINGING

Union Baptist Church. Reverend Alexander. That's the reverend that played in the movie *Cooley High*.[1] I remember they singing, and they praising, they clapping they hands and they be shouting. And I remember this one particular time, my grandmother Rose was shouting, and my grandfather cut her girdle with some little scissors he carried in his pocket. And she said, "Lee, what you cut my girdle for?" And he said, "That's the reason why you shouting. It was too tight!" That stayed with me for a long time, so when I used to see people shouting in church, I used to say, "Ooh, they got on something tight. It's just too tight around here."

I don't remember my mother at church, but I recall my grandmothers, sitting there teaching us the Bible, showing us pictures from a special Bible book. I was there every Sunday, as far back as I can remember, listening to that choir singing, and I'd be joining in. Like the old men say, I was singing to the heavenly choir. I couldn't carry a note, but I didn't care. I loved it. I really got bonded to the church when they sung: "I love the Lord. He heard my cry." That grabbed me more than any song in my life. It's still one of the things I grab hold of. That song will bring you out of some things. He said, "Hasten to His throne." That means come quickly to Him. I tell you, that song kept me from really losing my mind.

FAMILY REUNION ALL THE TIME

My mother and father had two children. I'm a twin. Me and my brother Paul were tight. I remember my father from when I was a small child. I know he was there, but I remember my stepfather more. I adored my

---

[1] A 1975 feature film based upon Cooley High, a real Chicago high school, and the neighborhood school for Cabrini-Green families.

stepfather and it didn't make a difference if I was his or not, he loved me. He came into my life when I was about four. He gave me the kind of security I realize I've been looking for ever since. He was the one who laid down the rule that we couldn't ever use the word "hate" in the house. He was strict about that. I remember him getting ready to go to work. And he had a GTO, a blue convertible. My brother used to go downstairs and wait for him in the car. One time, we pulled the gears in the car, the gears shifted, the car rolled backward and ended up with a dent! We got in trouble for that.

When my mother and my stepfather divorced, I was ten. It was hard, but I was still a child. I still had fun. We moved to the fourth floor of our building in Cabrini. My grandmother stayed down the hall. I knew mostly everyone in the building. All the ladies helped each other out. Our neighbor Carmen, on the first floor, used to make this delicious homemade ice cream. Living there was like a family reunion all the time, and all the kids would play on the balcony. We used to sneak eggs out the house when the sun was out—the sun was beaming on the balcony and we would try to cook eggs on the metal surfaces. It didn't ever work. I learned how to skate on that balcony, I learned how to play hopscotch on the balcony, I learned how to jump rope on the balcony. We even did *The Gong Show*.

People talk about the projects being terrible, and I say, "I lived there too, but I don't remember all that crap." I thank God for placing us in the building where we was. God knew what he was doing. A lot of mothers in them buildings did work. My auntie worked, my grandmother worked, my mother was going back and forth to school before she started working. My mother went to Malcolm X College, right off the expressway. I was there when she walked across the stage to graduate. I was proud. I thought, *That's my momma.* And my mother was one of the prettiest ladies I ever did see. Her Afro with her reddish hair styled to a tee. She became a phlebotomist, and my auntie was a respiratory therapist. Anything you want to know in the medical field, them two sisters, oh my God, they was the two smartest women I ever knew in my life. And I can't exactly say my mother was an addict, because she was still able to maintain everything. She was functional even as she was using. You wouldn't never know unless she told you.

My mother's mother helped raise me. She worked in a factory where they made paper products. We had a lot of paper at home. I never bought school supplies because we always had it: notebooks, binders, book bags. To this day, my grandmother's sharp in the mind. She likes to say that nosy people stay alive much longer, and I believe her because she's eighty-something years old. She stayed in our life, she was in our business, and I just thank her. When my mother was using drugs, and a mess was going on in the house, my grandmother would come down and get us. "Yeah, come on out of here. Don't you know that I want to save you?"

A TOMBOY TO THE FULLEST

Coming up, my twin brother and I used to be together all the time. We shared a room in our place at Cabrini. As a little boy, Paul wasn't as keyed in to what was going on as me. I was always grown-like, but he was Batman and Superman in his mind. Still, we stuck together because we was the twins of the family and he kept me in trouble for the things he did. Trying to jump his bike over rows of boxes and nearly breaking his neck, accidentally setting stuff on fire. My mother would say, "Paula, you the oldest," and I would say, "Yeah, twenty-nine minutes." Then she would say, "Then you got twenty-nine minutes more good sense than he do."

I was a tomboy to the fullest, but I just didn't do some of the dumb things the boys did. I liked to run, jump the fence, pop a wheelie. When they wouldn't let me play, guess what Paula did? I fought. My stepfather would always say, "You are more important than anybody else. You can do this and if you wanna play, go play." And I did. I was intrigued with how boys lived. They played hard and I played hard with them. It was a daily amusement park. I'd go out to the top of this one tree, and my momma told me, "Paula, stay out of that tree!" But the tree called my name.

"If the boys can climb the tree, why I can't climb the tree, Momma?"

"You a girl, you gotta play with the girls."

And that would be my biggest punishment. The girls just played on the swings, and they was dressed all pretty. My hair was all over my head. I had a torn T-shirt. The boys were over there sweating and having fun. And the girls would say to me, "What you gonna cook?" *Cook?!* I didn't want all that prissy stuff, and I didn't want no babies. When I started getting older and developing, boys was starting to pay attention. But I wasn't really paying attention because I didn't wear no bra. I didn't. My mother always saying, "Put it on!" A dress? I didn't want that. Some patent leather shoes? I didn't want that.

I spent time indoors when I was a girl, too. My mother had me taking classes over at the Lower North Center, a community center right near Cabrini. I took up ballet, I took up tap dancing, piano, because she wanted to occupy my time and she wanted me to be a girl and I didn't want to be a girl. I wanted to be a tomboy! But she exposed me to all these subjects at the center, and I thank her for it. I love ballet. It was my passion. The grace, the softness, just like you're floating on air. I learned all kinds of arts at the Lower North Center. I learned how to use a sewing machine. I did tie-dye. It was a great place to be.

I TOOK THEM ON ONE BY ONE

I'll never forget this boy from the neighborhood named Shaun Brown. My first crush. He was two or three years older than me, and he stayed in the next building. We'd be outdoors playing all the time. I guess the virgin state had left his mind, he was sexually active, and he was going with a girl in 1157 N. Cleveland named Norma. But he loved me, it was puppy love, and Norma would fight me. She hung out with her gang-banging friends, and they'd jump on me. My mother would send me to school with this silk blouse, hair all laid and clean and looking put together and they would tear my coat off and mess up my hair, and my momma would say, "I'm tired of you coming home like this." I was scared of 'em. There was too many of 'em. My momma got a .45, cocked the handle back, and she said, "You go out there and handle your business." She came out there with me, and she told 'em, "Any of y'all wanna fight her, fight her one by one." I fought 'em. Oh I did. The sun was up when I started, but the sun was down when I got through. I took them on one by one. Right after that, those girls wanted to recruit me to the Disciples. That's when my momma said, "It's about time to go." Before long, we left the neighborhood.

I was going on twelve when we moved, and I was raped around that time. That's really what finally prompted us leaving. I don't remember packing no clothes. My brother and I went to school, came back, we was in another place, moved to an apartment further north, not far from Wrigley Field, over on West Addison.

I was thirteen when I got together with Ron. After I was raped, he protected me. Didn't nobody touch me. That's why I fell in love with him. I first met him through my cousin. They were supposed to be kicking it. He invited me to smoke some weed and he had a beautiful car. It was shining. It was shining! I was a still a tomboy then and that's how we first started hanging out. He was an entrepreneur, a mechanic, and he had his own garage. That man knew his stuff.

Ron wouldn't let me use the word "dumb." He didn't like the word at all because he couldn't read. He told me, "Ain't nobody dumb." He kind of kept me on the path, you know. He didn't need to be with me, as old as he was, but I thank him. He molded me to be who I am. He was a father figure and I never wanted for anything. He taught me how to cook, taught me how to maintain a house. I watched him drive and that's how I learned how to drive. Surprised him with that. I drove his cars, and I even stole his motorcycle!

I started being a "wife" at a young age. Ron was already married and he had a whole lot of kids. He'd leave his wife and then he'd go back to her. I have to say, he loved each and every one of his kids. He also had a lot of girlfriends and I was jealous. I busted out all kind of car windows. I won't even tell you all that I did. I went through some trouble with that man. I dealt with him for twenty years. I got my son and my daughter by him and that's all the kids I got. I thought that was the man I was gonna marry.

But you know, I tell people that story and they say, "He shouldn't have been messing with you as a baby." But he was there. He protected me. I see *that*. My mother? She knew about him. She couldn't tell me nothing. Still, I wish she would've fought him. Hard. Sometimes I wish she would have took him to jail. You know. Same with my father leaving. She gave up so damn easy. What the fuck? I'd fight tooth and nail about my kids, but she was more *don't ask, don't tell*. But my mother had her own problems that I didn't know about when I was younger. When my mother finally got honest with me about her addiction, I was seventeen. That was about the same time I found out I was pregnant with my son.

RELEASED TO THE GENESIS HOUSE

In my twenties my life started to take a turn because of my emotions. I lost my mother, and I felt such grief. I had turmoil in my relationship, a lot of conflict with Ron. And I had got caught up in addiction myself. Then addiction took over my life when I was in my thirties. I was over on the West Side then and I was tired of my life. I thought I'd done everything for other people, but I was the people that needed to be done for.

About ten years ago, I was walking down the street, screaming up the heavens, and saying, "What is my purpose? It can't be using drugs. It can't be for prostitution. It just can't be for this." And then a miracle happened. I went to jail. I was arrested for prostitution. I went to jail and started seeing things in a different way through recovery.

I was high when the police took me in, claiming it was for prostitution. When I went to jail, they kept me in there with other women who were in on charges of murder, of assault. And I thought, *They got me here for selling some kitty cat![2] I'm on the wrong tier. I ain't supposed to be here!* I went in my room and laid down and I prayed to God.

When I went before the judge for sentencing, he said, "Give me a reason I shouldn't send you back to prison." I told him I was ready to change, that I wanted to be released to Genesis House.[3] They'd come out to the prison to run group sessions for women with addictions. One lady with Genesis—her name is Vicky—she told her story of turning her life around. Vicky was so honest about everything she'd been through. Her success made me think I could turn things around myself. She instilled that feeling in me. There was a way she'd look you in the eye. When this judge was sentencing me, he gave me a chance to go through rehab when I was released. He said, "You could go and change your life, but if you come back here, you're going to do your time and some more." That man gave me a chance. Genesis House turned out to be at West Addison in the same building where I lived when my momma first moved us out of Cabrini.

At Genesis House, they give you group therapy, STD testing. They help you get clothing. One of the programs they recommended was

---

[2] Prostitution.

[3] A Chicago organization that provides housing and outreach services for women involved in prostitution.

Prostitutes Anonymous. It helps you learn not to prostitute. I had to learn that when I heard a car horn to stop automatically looking inside the car. I developed a habit and it became my character. When I was first released, I wasn't out in the street, but sometimes I would still prostitute. Their support helped me to stop. My recovery took off so quickly. I had a strong support system. You see somebody and they tell you something and it catches and it holds. I remember my sponsor Tyrone once said, "The reason why we're sick is that we won't tell the truth about ourselves." He said, "Stop keeping those dark secrets." And I haven't shut up since. I will tell on me.

ONCE THE BELL BEEN RUNG

When I came into my addiction, my grandmother had my house keys, and she stayed in a three-apartment building with my mother. The whole family took care of my kids, so I didn't drag them with me into my messes. I dragged me and me with me, though I understand their feelings of abandonment. I understand that part, but it's over. I'm here now. When I came home and took recovery, I sat my kids down and said, "Anything you wanna ask me, I'm gonna be honest." I didn't have to go into graphics. But I'd tell them, "This is what your mom did, I'm sorry, and you know, I'll do better. All that other stuff is gone. I can't change it." As they say, *Once the bell been rung, you can't unring it.* So what do we do from here? When I first started recovery, I made a promise not just to myself but to God that once my life got on track, wherever I'd live, there'd be room for them to live there too.

But I've had my conflicts with my daughter. She had her own daughter when she was fourteen, fifteen. I was mad about it, but I was already in my own madness. A couple years later, when I was in recovery, she was messing around with this older guy, same age I am now. I tried to tell her it wasn't no good, but she was like my brother used to be with his stunts. "I know what I'm doing." I remember going to that man's place and I told him face-to-face, "I'll have you locked up, I will kill you. You are not gonna ruin my daughter's life. Let her live her life." He wanted to say something crazy, but I think he could see it in my eyes. I was gonna kill him. And my daughter was upset. I told her, "Girl, ain't nothing he can do for you that you can't do for yourself." It's hard to get that girl to listen sometimes, it's like she trying to live *my* life through her own life. I tell her, "You have a part to play in your own life."

A few years ago, my daughter had to do some time in jail. That's when I decided to take custody of my granddaughter. My daughter was released by the time I moved here. We lived together for a while, and I dealt with her as long as I could. She wouldn't follow my house rules. We'd be clashing all the time. She wasn't working, wasn't cleaning up after herself. One day, I had words with her, she cussed me out and called the police 'cause I'd put my hands on her. Police came and told me that if I put my hands on her again I was going to jail. I ended up putting her out—the first time I ever put her out and not let her come back in again. It devastated me, it really did, but she had to find her own way. Everywhere she ever been she got put out. She moved around with her friends for ten months before she finally got her own apartment. I gave her a hundred dollars and I rented a truck to move some of her stuff she still had here.

I'm proud of her now. And the thing is, I'm trying to talk to her now. She's starting to listen. That's the best part. I said, "Well, maybe because you thought you was going to run my house that you didn't have to listen, but now that you on your own you can listen." I try to motivate her and tell her to stop depending on a man to do anything for you. It's okay to have fun, but it ain't enough, 'cause God bless the child that got his own. Go get your GED. Then your values and your morals and your standards are high. Yes, you can have high expectations. If the dream is reachable, then go. Go!

WILL I EVER BE WHAT I REALLY WANTED TO BE?

I've been at my current job for over five years. I talk on the phone. I make orders. I deal with cab drivers. They don't have a maternity or sick leave, and I pay it forward on insurance, I can't understand why we don't have benefits. I like my job, but I don't want to have to struggle. It says in the Bible, whatever you want you have to work for by the sweat of the brow. But, damn, don't they see the sweat of my brow? I'm forty-five. What will I have for my retirement? A credit union, and decent benefits—I want that. That's why I want to get my GED. I need to secure some things.

Not long ago, I had to take off work for almost a month and a half. Doctor's orders, because I was recovering from surgery. I'm paid hourly, but I couldn't get unemployment because I was still working. I needed a medical card 'cause I can't pay these hospital bills. The total hospital bill was a thousand and something dollars—hell, that's my rent! Then I got light, gas, food. I don't get food stamps. I have full custody of my granddaughter, and she's a growing girl. She needs clothes, she needs to eat. Now I got to buy her a coat. She needs things for school. The state gives me $100 for my granddaughter and I'm grateful that she has a medical card. I still need some help. Low-income housing. My own medical card.

When you go look for an apartment, they check your criminal background. That's what happened when I got my place here. The landlord said, "You got to pay more money to move in." I'm like, *What? I don't make money like that.* "Two months security plus the rent." That's ridiculous. I try to fill out for a Section 8. They did a background check and they denied me. They denied me. And I said, *Oh, well. Somebody else needed it more than I do.* I justified that in my mind, but here I am just trying to pull it all together all the time. The system sucks! I made a mistake in my life. How long you gonna keep holding it against me?[4] I applied for Section 8 three and four years ago. Every time they were taking applications, I tried. Some people get it, some people don't. But don't they see I'm trying? I'm out of the "menace-to-society" part. I'm paying taxes, I'm doing this, I'm doing that. I'm being productive.

When it comes to my background, I'm not ashamed of what I did, but I'm not proud of it. Problem is: it's hard to move forward because this past is stuck with me for the rest of my life. And people look down on it, but I'm a changed person. Everybody talks about how they want the crime to stop, but when the person stops doing the crime, and they got some baggage back there, you ain't willing to help. So now they left me struggling and fighting and even getting pissed off up in my mind. It tears at my self-esteem, and I know I'm not the only one that feels that way. My background is holding me from a lot of things. If I hadn't made these mistakes in my life, where would I be? Will I ever be what I really wanted to be?

I love music. I ain't too fond of rap. Some rap I can get with, but I love old dusty stuff, jazz, love songs, some classical, and even a little Handel opera. And I love dancing, always loved it. That's been one of my dreams ever since I was a little girl. My mother danced. African dance and jazz dance and modern dance, and she made sure I took those dance classes at the community center. When I hear a certain song and I'm driving, I envision me dancing. I have this dream: I want a place, a center for some teenagers to do they little dance, they figure out their little footwork moves and all that. I want a place for them because they need it. I want

---

[4] Rules for obtaining Section 8 (Housing Choice Vouchers) vary from housing authority to housing authority. The CHA has strict criminal background checks for all voucher applicants.

to make a difference where teenagers live. Girls that's been abandoned—that's who I really want to help. I want to do things different for my granddaughter. I try to teach her certain things, tell her to watch her back, to be aware of things. They say I'm overprotective of her, but I have my reasons. I have my reasons. To pay attention is to be alive. At home, we're sewing together, she do all her chores, she's good in school. Now she's on a girl's volleyball team. I've been going to see her play.

Been ten years sober now, and I see my purpose. God had to save me for me to take care of my family. I've got custody of my granddaughter. Now here goes my grandmother. I'm getting ready to take her in now and she's going to live here. Sometimes I have to wonder, *Is this a boarding house?* But I believe in the family.

My road is a narrow road, but I'm like a tightrope walker. I'm gonna keep walking that road and I'm gonna move forward. My grandmother's in her eighties. We don't know exactly when she was born, so we gave her a birthday. She's about eighty-four years old now. They diagnosed her with dementia. She was lonely where she was living. I told her, "When you come stay here, you won't be lonely." I got a bird up in here that makes all kinds of noise. I got a granddaughter running in and out. There's always something going on over here.

LANDMARKS

About two years ago, I went back to Cabrini and took my keepsake pictures. I knew they were getting ready to tear everything down.

I wanted to capture the building I was in, and the tree I used to love to climb up in, and the curb where my stepfather always parked his car. And then I went back again not too long ago after the demolitions happened. I was in a relationship at the time, and I was very upset with the person I was seeing, and some kind of way, when I drove my car, I wound up over there in my old neighborhood, and I rolled through, looking out the window all the while. Some of the things that was not so pretty, things I'd been through—I was just thankful I wasn't there no more. And I went on, I went to where I got raped that night. After that, I started remembering being mistreated by my kids' father, and I wasn't there no more either. And I came back home, and I was like, *Okay. All right. I ain't there no more. I'm here right now.* So those past things, all them things happened. I'll never forget it, but I know I'm not there no more. Got to move forth in life.

The thing is: we the landmarks. Forget a building! People are the landmarks. I take it back to what I read in the Bible. In the beginning, God created all the things—the flowers, the birds, the bees, you know, everything—He seen that was good. He created Adam, and then he seen that was good. But Adam was down here sad, so he created Eve. So he said, "Go forth and multiply. Be fruitful." This is how I believe. To know your history is to know yourself. And we human beings, we are the landmarks of the world. God gave the world to us. Just like he gave it to Adam and Eve; he gave them everything, until Satan did what he did. We go around and we do drive-by shootings, we raping, we doing these things that's tearing down the spirit. This earth is the house that God built, and we dwell here. I believe all foundations can be re-mended. All foundations can be restored.

ABLA HOMES

SONOVIA MARIE PETTY

AGE: 38

OCCUPATION Author, public speaker, and organizer for
incarcerated mothers
FORMER RESIDENT OF: *ABLA Homes*

*During her early childhood—from 1974 until 1982—Sonovia Marie Petty
(no relation to editor) lived in the ABLA Homes, on the city's West Side, with her
older brother and her grandparents. We first meet Sonovia in downtown Chicago,
at the headquarters of the Chicago Coalition for the Homeless, where she works
in data entry and serves on the Speakers' Bureau. In her partnership with the
Coalition, Sonovia has found her calling. Her goal is to make affordable housing
available to the underprivileged, particularly the formerly incarcerated. As she
puts it, "I've always been told, 'You got a gift for gab.' After working a while for
the Speakers' Bureau, I figured out what I had to start doing was telling different
stories, sharing all of me to make a difference." In addition to living in ABLA
Homes, Sonovia has lived in subsidized housing for the elderly (as a caregiver for
her grandmother), and in homeless shelters and group homes with her children. She
has also been incarcerated. In her narrative, she reflects upon how all of these forms
of institutional housing (and lack of housing) have shaped her life.*

WHERE I FIRST EXPERIENCED VIOLENCE

At about four or five years old, I knew my address: 1440 West Thirteenth Street, apartment 101. It was an ABLA building, one of the Abbott high rises, when you make that right onto Laflin. It's like a turnaround. We called it the circle.

That's where I first learned how to skate. It wasn't the roller blade kind of skates, it was the kind with the iron wheels. I used to go back and forth from one end of the hall to the other. We didn't have a backyard 'cause this was a high rise building—but in back of the building, we had a pool and a playground. That's where I learned how to swim. Well, someone actually pushed me in the pool, and that's how I learned.

ABLA is also where I first experienced violence. I remember this one man. His name was Alvin. He was with his wife and daughter in their car, and he was murdered in front of the building. He laid on top of his wife and daughter so they wouldn't get shot. My window was right above the street where it happened. I remember the scene. At the age of five or six, I was used to the sound of gunshots. I knew what my grandma had taught us—get up under the bed, don't be looking out no windows. I finally peeked out after it got quiet, and that's how I knew what had happened, 'cause I knew Alvin's car. I told my grandma. Never heard why it happened.

Me and my older brother were two years apart. On my mom's side, there's four of us. On my dad's side, there's nine. But our grandma had legal guardianship of me and my brother until we was twenty-one. Our grandmother was a well-put-together woman. We went to church every Sunday. We did Bible study on Wednesdays and choir rehearsal on Saturdays.

I still see my grandma's apartment in my head. As I'm entering, I walk into a living room. My grandma had velvet blue furniture and she had two end tables where the top was wood but with white trimming and the sides was also blue velvet. That was to my left side. The chair was right up against the wall as you walk in the door, and then you got the long couch—the love seat. And to my right was a grand piano. My grandmother loved to play the piano. She also played in church.

I lived at ABLA Homes for eight years back in the late seventies, early eighties. When I look back on our little apartment in ABLA, I realize it was like a cell. How those walls were made. How things were laid out. It wasn't spacious. I see it clearly now, since I've been incarcerated. Prison reminded me of when I stayed in the projects because the walls was cinderblock. You bump your head, trust and believe: you gonna get brain damage. Even down to the toilets, the same materials. We was on the first floor at ABLA, so we had bars on our windows. I think about it now and wonder: what if there were a fire or some thing? We only had one entrance to get in and out. It was horrible.

I used to go to Jefferson School, the only one in the community. We walked there every day. We crossed into a big, open field. It was like a desert. Back then, it just felt like poverty. My surroundings, my environment was poor. My walk to school took me over manhole covers, the smoke coming out of there was so hot, it could burn you. Now it's different over there. It looks nice with those row houses. All those stores they've built. We didn't have none of that when I was there.

My cousins stayed in the Horners.[1] And we stayed over there some-times. There was a lot that ABLA and the Horners had in common. Stuff being dropped from windows. Elevators not working. Lights always out. A couple of women had got raped in our building 'cause the elevators weren't working or the lights in the hallways and stairwells was out. The stairway was a public bathroom as well. That was just routine. Horners

---

[1] Henry Horner Homes. A high rise public housing development on the West Side of Chicago, not far from ABLA Homes.

also had the cinderblocks. The apartments was smaller, but they had a similar layout to ABLA. Exact replicas of prison.

Eventually, my grandparents found a better place near our church. When we all moved out of the apartments at ABLA, it was a relief to me. I was glad I didn't have to be raised up my whole life in the projects. We moved to K-Town,[2] on Gladys. A few years later, my grandma got a bigger apartment and then a house, still on the West Side. My grandfather had left in '87, when I was thirteen. Eventually, my grandma had to move to a senior citizen building. By then I was sixteen and I had two babies, and we couldn't stay in the senior citizen building with her. So I went and stayed with my dad's people in Englewood for a little bit, and then my grandmother called me and said that she needed me. She was a diabetic and she needed help. So I went over there with her—me and my two kids. She'd completely stopped walking. I was over there trying to take care of her and people in the building started complaining when the kids were crying at night. So I had to go.

I WAS ALREADY INCARCERATED BEFORE I WAS INCARCERATED

Someone told me about Human Services. When I went to seek housing and shelter for me and my children on my own, instead of accommodating me with housing, they made me a ward of the state. They placed me and my kids in a group home. I went back and forth to group homes. I kept leaving. I kept running away back to family. I couldn't go back to my grandmother's because they'd come and get me. But I'd be here, there, all over.

When they first put in me in a group home, I thought it was proper

---

[2] A neighborhood on Chicago's Far West Side.

protocol. I thought, *Oh, I'll be here for a couple of weeks and then I'll get an apartment.* I was sent to a place out on Sixty-First and Drexel. I forgot the name of the place, but come to find out it was an old mental health hospital. I figured it out because of the way the rooms were arranged. They just kind of renovated it. I thought, *This is an old hospital bed.* I asked around and that's how I came to found out for certain that's what it was.

Me and my two kids shared a room with this other girl who had three kids. We was in this one room together. Imagine: it's a hospital room. There were baby beds all around. It was too crowded. We had to all share a shower and we were monitored when we did. I couldn't come and go as I pleased. I had to get escorted everywhere by the staff. Everybody did. During the day we didn't do anything but take care of our kids. When we had doctor's appointments, the doctor came inside. When we had dental appointments for our kids, they used to pile us all up in the bus and take us out. I was already incarcerated before I was incarcerated. I had no freedom in that place and I didn't want to stay there. I wanted to go with my dad and that side of my family. Even though I wasn't supposed to be with them, I was still attached to them. Some of the girls that lived in the group home told me I'd have to run away. They wasn't just going to let us leave. Everything was locked. When they took us down to eat, they'd put us in an elevator. I couldn't just turn a knob and go out.

After three months of being there, I earned a four-hour pass. But by the time I got out to the West Side to visit family, it would be time to turn around. I knew that wasn't going to work, so I decided to run away with my kids. I had to throw some clothes out the window in secret so I could take them with me.

At that time I had a case worker and she called my grandmother. My grandmother knew what happened, but really, my family couldn't do anything because they had put me back in custody as a ward of the state. They'd ask my grandmother, "Do you know where she's at?" and my grandmother would call me. I was over at my uncle's. She told me that I needed to call these people. My uncle and them were so money hungry and greedy, they called over to Human Services and said I could stay with them so they could get the money. They took the money that the state was giving me, they were supposed to give me an allowance out of that, but that never happened. They were already getting a check from the government and then when I got money from public aid for my kids, they took that, too. I didn't stay there long at all because my uncle was a creep. I would tell my boyfriend what was going on and he got so angry that he wanted to go do something to my uncle. Eventually, he told me, "Come on." I stayed with him for a year and a half, nearly two years. I stayed with his parents. His mother would get my check. She would give me my money and everything was okay.

When I was about to turn eighteen, my boyfriend's family was moving to Mississippi. His momma asked me to let her take my kids, and I should have. She said, "Just until you get situated. You can always send for them when you ready. You can come down there as well." She wanted me to come down with them, but I said I couldn't leave my grandmother, since she couldn't take care of herself. Send my kids away? No. My boyfriend's parents moved out on the day I turned eighteen. So I had to start back all over again. My boyfriend didn't move down South, but he was out of Chicago a lot, doing his thing. Me and him had parted ways by then and I was pregnant. He looked out for me, but I wasn't going with him anymore.

After they left, I had to go back there with my uncle and them again. But I couldn't do it. I guess they got tired of me turning them down and leaving these places. They called me into court and took custody of my kids for inadequate placement. I wasn't able to take my kids home with me. I had a nervous breakdown. It made me have that baby, and they wouldn't let me take my child home with me from the hospital. Now I'm eighteen. I got an apartment, but they wouldn't give me my kids back. They said now I had to go through DCFS[3] to get them back. By this time, I'm damaged goods. I'm messed up. *I need to get my kids.* They said they were going to give them back to me and they weren't doing it.

OUT INTO HOMELESSNESS

I met my youngest kids' father when I was twenty-one. Howard lived near ABLA, but we didn't meet until we were out of high school. We met over on the West Side. He was in the car with his two friends and they didn't know the neighborhood. One of them, a real ugly guy, was driving. His friend pulled up to me and asked me for directions. I looked in the car and saw Howard. He was slim with a nice face. A real GQ type of guy. He was gorgeous. I got in the car and I showed them where to go and Howard struck up a conversation with me.

I was still taking care of my grandmother at the time. She'd left the senior citizen building and moved to an apartment. Howard and I went and got food that afternoon. He dropped me off, we exchanged numbers and we just started seeing each other. He was wonderful to me. He took me to visit my older kids who'd been placed in a foster home. He took care of my grandmother. Howard was the only person that really cared about my well-being. We were together for about eleven years.

He died in 2006. The day before, we'd learned I was pregnant with his third child. They said it was a massive heart attack. He was thirty-eight. I loved him so much. He did so much to support me. I was depressed after Howard's death, and a whole lot started happening. I was struggling. I had my two youngest kids with me—me and Howard's children—and,

---

[3] Department of Children and Family Services.

at that time, my life wasn't stable. I'd been living in a hotel, going out, hustling to make money to pay for our room.

There was just so much weighing on me. I was tired. I was mentally tired. I was doing drugs and then I started selling drugs. I got arrested, and I went to jail July 13, 2007. I was so relieved. That's when I said to myself: *I'm going to get my life in order. I can't do this anymore. I want to raise my last two kids.* I was incarcerated for a year. I did six months in the county jail, six months in prison, and I came home right out into homelessness. There was nothing out here, no help, no resources. No nothing. I'd made a spiritual transition while I was in prison. I made a connection with God, but I didn't get help for my addiction.

Once I came out and there was nothing out here, I immediately got stressed, I was ready to go get high, and so I recidivated within two months. That's why the first two weeks upon re-entry are very crucial. If you don't have a plan, if you don't have no support, you going right back to prison. I went back and I did another year. That time, I got drug treatment, and I had to renew my mind. I had to start learning what my triggers were, know the things to look out for. I also got mental health care to heal from the things I had been through. I knew I was going to make it. I knew I wasn't going back because I had made my mind and my heart up.

I got released to a halfway house in my old neighborhood, where it all began. I went there and I was willing to do what I needed to do, like getting connected, getting outside of myself and helping people in the same situation as me, because I can't just concentrate on myself. I've learned if you focus on yourself, you focus on all your misery and problems. The first house I was in is for when you're first released. It's the one with more structure. Mandatory ninety days, according to standard arrangements through the Department of Corrections.

While I was there, I took a look at some of the things that was happening. Girls were constantly beating themselves up over their pasts, constantly grieving and not healing. They were still talking about what their momma did and what their daddy didn't do. I started thinking, *I need to volunteer.* I needed to be productive. I needed to be around people who were positive. I had been around people who sold drugs, did drugs, committing crime, and that's what I'd picked up on when I was coming up. Now I wanted to pick up on something different. Because I had children to raise.

After a couple months, the halfway house sent me out on my own. The house manager felt like I could make it by myself. Next I went to a house that was more transitional. I was in school the first two weeks I was released, getting my GED at Malcolm X Learning Center, and then my best friend was there for me. She got a house and welcomed me to stay with her for a while. I was just getting custody back of my children then. There was a lot going on.

The place where me and my two youngest boys stayed after that was a shelter out in Riverdale.[4] The house rules changed at this shelter shortly after I arrived. They were making residents come out of their rooms in the morning. We were in our own single room. You'd have to lock the bedroom doors in the mornings and go sit in the living room. It reminded me of a day room in prison. Both my kids were asthmatic. It was summertime hot. They needed to be up under a fan and they didn't have fans out there. And our meals were horrible. They'd feed us three times a day and they'd give us our meals in ounces. Three ounces of food. They would measure it out. This was the daily routine. They didn't give us enough to eat. I had a Link card. I wanted to buy our own food and bring it in the house, but they wouldn't allow it. You had to bring food

---

[4] A neighborhood in Chicago's Far Southeast Side.

for the whole house if you brought any food at all. It was twenty adults there and thirty-two kids. The way they locked us out of the rooms and how they measured that food, I thought, *Oh, my God. This reminds me of prison.* I asked them, "Where did you all get your meals from? IDOC?"[5] It was just terrible. I felt like they were getting ready to reincarcerate me again, and the only difference this time was I had my kids. I just couldn't take it, so I hit the bricks.

The thing is: I have always been homeless. I have never had an apartment for myself until 2010. That's when I moved to Twenty-Fourth and Kedzie. This was my first apartment on my own. And through the grace of God, this landlord gave me an apartment with no money down! I went and told him my story, that me and my kids was homeless, that my kids were living in this shelter and they were getting sick, my son had to have an operation on his ear from all the ear infections he kept catching. I'd met the landlord, Mr. Flores, through a mutual friend who was Latino. He told me about the apartment and he went with me when I looked at the place. Mr. Flores only spoke Spanish, so our friend was our translator. I told the landlord my story. He gave me the key that same day. So that's how I got my first apartment.

THE MORE I STARTED SPEAKING, THE BETTER I GOT

The first time I met Drea Hall, from the Coalition for the Homeless, she'd come to the halfway house where I'd stayed to talk to the residents during a rap session. She was talking about affordable housing. One thing that I always had a problem with was housing. I had barriers. I've

---

[5] Illinois Department of Corrections.

been incarcerated. She was talking about people like me, who didn't have access, who were barred from receiving Section 8 and public housing. She also introduced me to Hannah, who's in charge of the Speakers' Bureau. That's when I became a member and was given the opportunity to go out and educate about homelessness. Most people don't know how severe homelessness could be.

It's been a pleasure working with the Coalition, going to Springfield with Drea to talk to some state legislators. I attended rallies. In the beginning, being a part of the Speakers' Bureau, I was nervous talking in front of crowds. But now I've spoken to over three thousand people. The more I started speaking, the better I got. The Coalition, they gave me so much motivation. I'd never been told before, "Good job, Sonovia. Good job. You killed it. You nailed it." It made me feel good, and I wanted to do more, so I just kept it up.

I've seen some victories being with the Coalition. We had worked on an ordinance for two years. We wanted 20 percent of the TIF funds[6] dedicated towards affordable housing in blighted areas of the city. We got started on the campaign when the economy was really, really going down, and so many working-class families had started losing their homes. That initiative got adopted this year. The Sweet Home Chicago amendment. Something we're trying to make happen now is the CHA to issue housing vouchers to the formerly incarcerated. When I was released, all I knew was we were barred out. You got a background. You got a felony. You can't get Section 8. But when I sat at the table with Lewis Jordan last summer—he was the CEO over at the CHA[7]—he told me, "You would be

---

[6] Chicago's tax increment financing. TIFs allow municipalities to sequester property taxes from neighborhoods determined to be blighted into neighborhood revitalization projects such as parks, housing, and infrastructure.

[7] Lewis Jordan was CEO of the Chicago Housing Authority between 2007 and 2011.

a good candidate for our Housing Choice Voucher." He was encouraging, but this was in his last year on the job. We're just getting to know the new administration, and I still can't get housing vouchers.

I just got back from Cleveland this past summer. We went there to learn about this lease-purchase program. It's called CHN. Cleveland Housing Network. They have some kind of agreement with the banks to let them get the foreclosed houses, and they either rebuild or renovate them and they give them to less fortunate people. They set up the loans, they put you on this plan, and within fifteen years, you're gonna own this house. We met with officials and organizers, and we also met a current resident. We felt good afterwards, like, *Wow, we can take this back to Chicago.*

My trip to Cleveland was special. I had never been on an overnight trip outside of Chicago except going to prison, and I had never gotten on an airplane. This was something new. My anxiety kicked in, but I made it through my first flight. Funny thing was I fell asleep at the last minute when we were landing. I'd wanted to watch myself land and we was three minutes from off the ground, and then—bloop!—I just fell asleep. I woke up as we were pulling into the terminal. I finally got to watch my plane land on the way back into Chicago. It was dark, but I did see it. I had a good trip.

I'M JUST DOING SOMETHING DIFFERENT

I've been on the West Side all my life, but I'm staying in South Shore now. Been there for five or six months. Been there since the spring. It's different scenery compared to what I grew up with. I like the tall buildings, the trees. I'm not seeing vacant lots or abandoned buildings. I just wanted something different. I'm right off the lakefront. Right off the big old park. I was able to go to the house music picnic this year nearby, in Jackson Park. It was maybe ten thousand people out there. It was so packed. They also have reggae parties there and the Caribbeans are up there selling jerk chicken and everything. When I want to relax, I can just go out to the park. I go mingle with people I don't even know. I'm just doing something different.

The apartment I've got now—I'm very satisfied. It's spacious. I'm claustrophobic. Small spaces—I don't really get along with them. I have two bedrooms and I can make two other rooms into bedrooms. I gave my kids the master bedroom. The rooms are big. I have a sun porch. It's just beautiful. I have a walk-in closet. They told me that the apartment was vintage, but to be honest: it's just old. But it isn't that bad. I was in need. I needed to be in my own place. I want to put some work into my apartment, but my finances don't permit it right now. But I intend to stay. It's real nice. My boys have more room to run and play. This is the biggest space I ever had.

OGDEN COURTS

ASHLEY CORTLAND

AGE: *20*

OCCUPATION: *College student*

FORMER RESIDENT OF: Ogden Courts

Ashley Cortland is a junior at the University of Illinois, Urbana-Champaign, who is currently majoring in communications. After graduation, Ashley plans on going to graduate school to obtain a master's degree in social work. She hopes to become a medical social worker or work in the communications department of a hospital in Chicago. On any given day she can be spotted in the library on the Quad, in a U of I T-shirt (blue or gray), with headphones in her ears, her nose buried in a book. We meet with her at a cafe in the YMCA on campus. She is matter-of-fact about living in Ogden Courts, a public housing complex on the West Side, from 1996 through 2005. Ashley describes her mother's repeated (and often futile) attempts to have repairs made on their apartment. When rodents infested their refrigerator, it took years to resolve the problem. Ashley also describes an unannounced, unwarranted search of her apartment by the Chicago police when she and her sisters (all minors at the time) were at home by themselves. Ashley's family now lives in the West Side neighborhood of Austin. Names in this narrative have been changed at the request of the narrator.

IT WAS JUST A SPACE I COULD
GO TO FOR PEACE

I lived in Ogden Courts from when I was five until I was thirteen. Our building was seven stories, and it was T-shaped. There was a porch on each unit that was enclosed by a gate, and then there were other smaller units in the middle of our courtyard. Same thing on the other side of the street. There were actually two high rise buildings in Ogden Courts. The 2710 building and the 2650 building. Our apartment was small. Three bedrooms, one bathroom, kitchen, the living room was out in the open. And a small bathroom. It was me, my mother, and my three sisters. Most of the time we had someone staying with us, like a cousin or a family friend. My mom was generous like that. My sisters and I usually shared a room: two bunk beds. I was usually on the bottom because I was scared to sleep on the top.

During the daytime, I spent a lot of time in my mom's room. My sisters were kind of wild and rambunctious, so I went into my mom's room to get away from them. I was a nerd, so I would go in there to read, do my homework. It was just a space that I could go to for peace. She had the big bed, the big TV, and I just felt safe in there. My mother always told me, "Stay out of my room, stay out of my room." I would have to be checking out the window to make sure her car wasn't pulling up, and then I'd make sure her bed was straightened like the way she had it, make sure there was no trash left on the floor. I always snuck in there and she would always catch me.

I STARTED NOTICING THINGS HAD
REALLY STARTED TO DETERIORATE

Our housing complex had a nice playground: two basketball hoops, some benches, and these barrels that the kids used to play on. When we first moved in, the building was kept up. The grass was always mowed. We had a nice little garden in the front. The interior of the building was always nice. But as I got older, maintenance really went down. I was around ten when I started noticing things had really started to deteriorate. The walls were always dirty; the hallways were always dirty; the grass wasn't mowed. The garden just became a patch of dirt. The elevators in our building started to break down; people would urinate in them and things like that. And I know other people complained about the graffiti and the smell in the hallways and the elevator always being broke, you know, for people who lived on the top floor, doing all that walking. The refrigerator in our apartment was broken. It was kind of infested with rodents, so they moved us up to the fourth floor, but it took a couple of years for the move to finally be approved. There was a front office that I guess people went to make complaints about maintenance and things like that.

When I was little, we would go down to the front office and the next day that problem would be solved. But around the time I turned ten or eleven, the office was still open, but it definitely wasn't staffed like it was before. It was only maybe two or three people in there and they were responsible for maintaining the entire complex. I remember my mother going to that office a lot. The staff would say, "Oh yeah, we'll put the request in, we'll put the request in," and nothing would happen. My mother—she tried not to get frustrated in front of us, but we could tell that she was pretty upset. But you know, there was nothing that she could really do except go down there and keep asking. I guess I kind of got used to the lack of response after a while. At first, I was just like, *Are they ever going to do something about this?* But then after years, I just thought, *This is how it is. They're not ever going to change anything.* And I guess that's why I don't have any emotional attachment to the building itself because it was just so deteriorated.

One time, when I was very young, this girl, my older sister's friend, was playing around in the front of the building and the gate actually fell on her. It was a really big, wrought iron fence gate and it fell on her. And it messed her leg up. It's still messed up to this day. She broke her leg, and afterwards it was just a back and forth argument with the management office to try to get who was responsible for the accident. Management staff would say, "Well she shouldn't have been playing on the gate." But the gate was broke. It had been leaning for months, maybe more, and nobody ever came to fix it. We always complained about it, and nobody ever did anything. It took the gate falling on a child and her breaking her leg for building management to actually do something. They fixed it a couple days after the accident. And it was a really big deal in that neighborhood, because we always, always, always told them to fix that gate, and they just wouldn't do it.

OGDEN COURTS IN THE DAYTIME

There were other problems at Ogden Courts that were hard to get used to. I never really saw police brutality when I was growing up, but I heard about it. The people in my building knew the police by name because they were over there so much. But I remember one time, a bullet actually went through our front window. And we called the police, and it was maybe just forty-five minutes or an hour before they came and they asked us what happened, and that was it. They didn't investigate it. Afterwards, it took a while for building management to come in and board up our front-room window. They didn't even replace it. They put a cardboard panel up and my mom complained, asking that the window be replaced. The cardboard was there for years. There was police presence at Ogden Courts in the daytime because that's when people sold the most drugs. But at night, you didn't see any police. At night, it seems like they all disappeared.

I saw the police raiding people's apartments without any notice or warrant many times. In fact, they came to my apartment once. I was really young. I can't remember how old I was. Maybe nine or ten. We were watching TV and the police knocked on the door, and just opened it and a couple of them came in and started searching our apartment. And my sisters and I didn't know what was going on. We were at home with my oldest sister. She was maybe fifteen, sixteen, and my mom was at work, so we didn't really know what to do. The police talked to my oldest sister. I was washing the dishes at the time, so I was peering over to see what was going on. I didn't know what they were talking about. I just remember being very afraid and not knowing what was going on, because we were a quiet family. We had never gotten into any kind of trouble. I remember seeing them come into the living room and then go into the rooms in the back. I remember feeling scared because when I saw police officers in my neighborhood, you know, nothing good ever happened. So I didn't know if my mom was in trouble, I didn't know if my sister was in trouble, or what they were looking for. I started crying. I was terrified. Then my mother came home, and the lady who used to watch us from the first floor told her about it. I've never seen my mother that upset before. I don't know if she ever found out what they were looking for. But she never filed any complaints against the police because complaints didn't really go answered from people in that neighborhood.

Afterwards, we didn't talk about it at all. I just heard my mother talking about it to her friend downstairs and she was very angry; but she never talked to us about it. My sisters and I never discussed it with each other. It was like, *Just put it out of your mind.* I guess my mom didn't really want us to think about it. I guess she just wanted us to forget it. Before that happened I didn't really have a bad attitude towards police officers. I just knew that whenever I saw them something bad was happening. Because whenever I did see them they were arresting somebody, or searching somebody, or trying to find one of the drug dealers in the building. But my attitude kind of did change a little bit. I was more apprehensive than before.

OUR NEW HOME IS ALSO SECTION 8

We left Ogden Courts in 2006, after the city decided to tear the buildings down. We moved to Thirteenth and Kostner, in a neighborhood called K-Town: that's the affectionate name for it, because all the streets there have a K in the name. Three units in the building, three bedrooms, one bath. I didn't really see any police officers over there. The neighborhood was pretty quiet. There were more older people living in that neighborhood, so there wasn't too much drug or gang activity. We had to move from that first place after two or three years because it was foreclosed. The landlord didn't pay the taxes. That was a big deal. We were all very upset about that.

Now I live in the Austin community, also on the West Side of Chicago. Near Madison and Cicero. A three-story building. Three bedrooms, one bath still. Everyone has their own room now. The police have set up lights with cameras installed in the neighborhood. Those are pretty close to our house. My mother actually thinks they're tapping people's phones, because there's always this AT&T truck right across the street from our house in an alley, and that truck's been out there every day. And it's been a while, like two years. But the police lights and cameras aren't enough. The police should do their job. You know, to serve and protect. If you know this neighborhood is dangerous, there should be regular patrols in the morning, afternoon, and night. They should be making sure that people's rights are not violated, you know, like barging in people's houses. If you want to search somebody, make sure there's probable cause. Don't just pick some random person walking down the street just because they live in a specific neighborhood. You know, responding to police calls in a timely manner, not forty-five minutes after an incident is reported.

Our new home is also Section 8, like the one in K-town. It's definitely better. The bathroom is bigger, the living room is bigger. We actually have a fireplace—that never happened before. We have a formal dining room, a nice kitchen. But there are problems with the building, too. Now we're actually getting ready to move again because rodents are starting to get into the building. The person in the unit above us, she actually got bitten by a rat. The hardwood is coming up from the flooring in our place, so my mother's made the decision that we have to move. My sister has a son now. My nephew's one year old. We have to get out of there.

GROWING UP THERE

In high school, when my friends would ask me where I grew up, I would say "in the projects" and they would look at me with concern, like, *Oh, it must have been hard for you growing up.* Making all kinds of assumptions that there was violence and stuff like that. I really wasn't too upset about the reactions, because for the most part, it was true. It was hard growing up there.

One of the hardest things has been seeing people take the paths that they did. Like some of the girls I grew up with, seeing them go from being these happy kids to worrying about teenage pregnancy, and being in relationships with older men, and their parents being on drugs and stuff like that. That was the hardest part. Just seeing the progression, hoping that people I cared about would make it. A lot of my friends have kids now, are not in college, and have minimum-wage-paying jobs. As for the demolition of high rise public housing, I understand that the buildings are deteriorating, and it's dangerous—you know, violence, gangs, drugs— and sometimes I kind of see it as a good thing to get those buildings out of the way, and to force people out. Sometimes I feel differently. I don't know how to explain it. I'm happy to see the buildings gone because of the effects they have on people. But at the same time, you're uprooting all these people from the community they've known since they were kids. And some people don't have enough time to move and find an adequate place to stay. Can they afford these new places? Do they have to move out into the suburbs? Having to move to new schools that are far away and that they're not ready for. It's a good thing, but it's a bad thing as well.

CABRINI-GREEN, DEMOLITION

CHANDRA BELL

AGE: *39*

OCCUPATION: *Hospice caregiver*

FORMER RESIDENT OF: *Cabrini-Green*

Chandra lived in Cabrini-Green between 1972 and 1995. She now lives with her youngest child in a town home in Orchard Park, a mixed-income development blocks from where the Cabrini-Green towers stood. In fact, from the gateway of Orchard Park, the final tower of Cabrini (set to be demolished within two months of the time of this interview) is visible in the near distance, wrecking ball suspended at rest right next to it. Chandra is a spirited and welcoming host. When we get to her kitchen, she has a book about Cabrini out on the table for us to peruse. Chandra moved out of Cabrini-Green in 1995 when the demolition began, and she moved several more times before finally acquiring her current home in 2000. As a leaseholder at Orchard Park, she has experienced the CHA's one-strike policy first hand. According to this policy, a tenant can be evicted if anyone listed on a lease is charged with a criminal infraction. Chandra's youngest son was arrested a year ago (at age seventeen) on a drug charge. Chandra now grapples with the fact that once he is released from prison, he will be permanently barred from her home at Orchard Park.

CABRINI'S MY REAL HOME

All your kids play together. That's when you become a big family. One of us might get a job and be like, "Hey neighbor, can you watch my kid?" That's how it went, and it was real nice. Friends and family living there. Me, my mother, my aunties, some of the uncles, and some of my friends. Cabrini's really my home. When I was a little girl, we used to have ramps to run up and down off the balconies, we used to play jump rope and hide-and-go-seek, but we also used to be safe from the bullets. There was lots of the neighbors outside and we was on the ramps, so we were safe.

My apartment was on the fifth floor, number 509 in Cabrini. I had a three-bedroom. We had good heat because the heat came from the floor. You would never be cold. The place was pretty nice and spacious. It was comfortable. Me and my sister shared a room and my two brothers shared a room and my momma had her own room. But there were problems in the building, like water leaking from the ceiling; the hallways weren't kept up. Some of the residents was trifling. There was garbage chutes but some people used to just throw trash everywhere, all in the hallways, and that's what made Cabrini go down. Also, the maintenance was weak. My family was clean, but if you had a neighbor that had roaches, there's not much you can do. We had roaches and mice because they were everywhere. You'd have holes in the walls where the mice were coming out. We'd make work orders asking management to make repairs, but a lot of the time we'd have to take care of things ourselves. We'd get some steel wool and patch the holes, so the mice wouldn't come out and it worked okay sometimes.

THE BEST TIME AT CABRINI.
THE WORST TIME AT CABRINI.

There was a librarian that we had over there. Her name was Jackie. When I was in grammar school, I used to go to the library just to help out, just to see about the next program the library was getting together. Maybe it was *The Cat in the Hat*—reading the book and people dressed up like the Cat in the Hat. Sometimes they'd have people come out and give talks and lessons, kind of like school. We even had preachers around the projects sit us down and talk to us and pray over us.

We did talent shows about once a month at the library. Certain days we'd invite everybody to come watch. We used to do the dance off to Michael Jackson songs. Me and my friends, we had a group. Everybody did. One would dance or sing, one might recite a poem, one might model. Even had shows outside at the park. Summertime we used to play a lot of softball, jump rope, volleyball. Equipment for everything. If there wasn't enough, we shared. Everyone sat in the playground at night, even the grown people watching their kids, until they'd start shooting. We'd have to snatch our kids in order to get them out of the way of bullets.

I survived. I came close to being shot one time when I was thirteen or fourteen. I was going to the store and I had my house shoes on and I heard something going, *pow, pow*. The sound of someone sniping. I didn't stop running. I knew the majority of the gangs. Couldn't help but know them because you stayed around them. *I'm in the red building and this is the white building.* There were territories. I walked to school with my family, but they used to chase everybody. You don't want to get caught and you don't know if they got a gun. We used to be running all the time.

Christmas and the holidays—that was the best time at Cabrini. Up on the tenth floor, everybody played with each other's toys; we'd go to each house to see who had what. That was the good time. And then all of the food—all over the building. "Who's cooking today?" But on New Year's Eve, we used to have to sit back in our hallways in our house, not by no window, because it was that rough, with shooting. At ten, eleven in the morning, they'd start up. The police used to have to block the streets off. That's how bad it was. The gang-bangers was just waiting to shoot the guns off, like firecrackers. *Pow! Pow! Boom! Boom! Kapow!* That's all you hear. Bullets. And the next day, you hear people crying: "My son! My daughter!" That was the worst time at Cabrini.

I had friends who were killed when I was a girl. One was named Troy. He was going to the corner store, and they had snipers up all in these buildings and they sniped him as he was walking. From my window I just seen him fall out into the street. He was just dead. I was twelve. He was twelve, too. And I had a friend that got beat by a bat. She was probably in her twenties at that time. Some gang-bangers did it. They beat her so bad they killed her. And Dantrell Davis? Dantrell Davis got shot. That made all the news.[1] His mother was my friend. You don't know what to do in those terrible times, but you heal. And once you heal, you try not to think about it. You have to move on. But sometimes you sit back and be like, *Man, I miss my friends.*

I KISSED MY FLOOR

My mother was so strict. With all of the bad things going on, she was like, "No, you cannot stay out late." I got my last whipping when I was seventeen. I had a baby boy by then and I thought, *Oh, wow—how am I gonna get away from my mother?* Back then, you had to be at least eighteen to move into your own housing, so I thought, *I'm gonna go and fill me out an*

---

[1] Dantrell Davis was killed at the age of seven when he was caught in crossfire between rival gangs during a morning walk to elementary school with his mother.

application and maybe next year I'd be in. And I was right. The next year I was in my own apartment in Cabrini. I kissed my floor and said, "Thank you."

When I first got to my own apartment, the walls weren't painted, but I decided to do it myself because that's how rushy-rush I was, trying to get in the unit. Building management supplied me with the paint and I painted. Then I waxed my floors. I was proud. It's peaceful living on your own with your children. At that time, I had my daughter and my son. They helped me clean up even though they were one and two. We had a broom, a little broom. They were excited like, *We on our own now.*

I wasn't concerned about raising my kids in Cabrini because it was an environment I always was in and I thought it was a good environment. Plus, we couldn't live nowhere else. The only thing I was worried about was my kids' safety when the gangs shoot. Other than that, I'd never had a problem. Never. It's when I left that I got robbed. Happened when I was living out on Adams and Cicero. And you know what I said? *What if I was still at Cabrini? Would this still have happened to me?*

A LOT OF RULES AT ORCHARD PARK

In 1995, the CHA started talking about closure. Management was telling us we could move back after they tear the buildings down and build up new houses. They also said they was going to give us everything the same we had it in Cabrini, but it's much different now at Orchard Park.[2] We paid just rent in Cabrini, no light, no gas, and that helped a lot. We're struggling more now to cover all the expenses. Sometimes it's like you pay

---

[2] Orchard Park is a mixed-income development built on the former site of Cabrini-Green. Mixed-income developments include privately owned households, market rentals, and units operated by the CHA. Residents who were in good standing with the CHA before the demolition of the high rises were granted a right of return to the mixed-income developments that replaced their former homes. For more information, see glossary page 217.

double rent. Your gas, two or three hundred, your rent five, and then your check ain't but eight dollars an hour, so it's kind of troubling compared to what you used to manage, and downstairs it stays cold in the winter. It's warm in here now 'cause the heat rises.

These new units could have been made of brick, but they okay. I had an argument with one of my neighbors. She moved away now. This neighbor was a homeowner. She used to tell me, "I hear you coming down your stairs. I hear you making noise." I told her, "I think your ear is to the wall, listening to me." But the walls are thin drywall. If we had bricks, no one could hear nothing. But she was aggressive, saying, "I'll get you put out before you can put me out." And she was right. I couldn't put her out 'cause she was a homeowner. There's that difference. Homeowners can actually have parties and be wild, but when we do it's a problem, we're in trouble.

What's good here is we have a lovely washer, dishwasher, garbage disposal, mostly nice neighbors, and we have a peace of mind when we come home. Sometimes at Cabrini you got tired of the violence, the shooting and the gang-banging. This apartment is too big for me, but I don't want to give it up. You get attached even as you deal with the differences, like more bills and more rules. It's a lot of rules in Orchard Park, like no car horn blowing and no loud music, which I can understand, 'cause if my neighbors were out, I wouldn't want to disturb them and they peace. Still, all the attention take getting used to. Between the bills and the rules, that's why I'd rather go back.

I knew everybody in Cabrini. Half of the people I knew came back to the new developments in the area. Some of them stayed where they were 'cause they felt the rules around here weren't right. At Parkside,[3] you have to take drug tests if you're on public assistance. We didn't do that here. That shouldn't have been approved. Some people kept their

---

[3] A new mixed-income development in the nearby Old Town neighborhood.

Section 8 because they don't want these new homeowners in their business, like taking drug tests and screening the kids. Like my predicament. Some of them keep their Section 8, so they don't have to go through the one-strike-you're-out.

I try to be fair. I can kind of understand where building management is coming from. All the problems there was at Cabrini with drug selling, guns. They want us to change within ourselves to be better. But everybody wasn't doing bad. There was also some good people living there that kept their units up. And I was one of them. Today I'm still keeping my unit up, and my place is not a project. Sometimes I be angry because now we living in this new situation and we not getting the help that we supposed to get. CHA management knew when they moved us back in these units that our kids was going to get older. They should have done something better for them so they wouldn't get into drugs. They could make some arrangement for the children and keep them occupied, 'cause a lot of children are out here shooting, doing drugs, or selling drugs. If they'd give these kids a good opportunity to get into social and education programs like they used to, it'd be better. These older kids need a chance at jobs.

ONE STRIKE, YOU OUT

I have three kids. One child messed up. He's my youngest son. He's eighteen. He was arrested a year ago for selling, and now he's barred from my place. And I understand the rules they have, but kids make mistakes. You don't give them a second chance? One strike, you out. Everybody deserves a second chance. But my son won't ever be able to come and visit me because of a mistake he made.

They wonder why we can't raise our kids the way we want, but they making the choices for us. He's incarcerated, and it's sad to say it, but prison is a better place for him because he can't live here. He wasn't on the premises when he was arrested, but he was on the lease. I shouldn't have to get punished for what he did outside, and he's been punished; he sees his mistake now. It's sad that a child can't come and visit their mother, but I had a choice. My son or my unit. I gave my son away for my unit. Because if I gave my unit up, we could be staying in alleys and stuff. Still, it's sad.

My son knew the rules. One strike, we out. And I don't hate them for this, but it's not right. I don't regret my move. I'm mostly happy still. That's my son. That's his bed. He lie in it. And he's barred forever. Now if he comes on the premises, I could get put out. And then I'd have to ask the question like, *What if he comes to see his friends over here?* If I see him around here, I have to call the police on my son or else I'm in trouble. Them kind of rules is not right. They screwing the families up. My son could come back. What child wouldn't want to come back? But I told him, "Don't come back 'cause you can't mess it up for me." I don't think he want to mess it up for me. He messed it up for himself, but he won't mess it up for me.

CABRINI-GREEN ON THE HISTORY CHANNEL

I worked across the street at Dunkin' Donuts when they first got started with the demolitions and it was kind of sad 'cause a lot of the residents didn't want to move out of there. It's sad to see the buildings come down. I have a picture on my phone of Cabrini when they was tearing it down. Sometimes I think it's good they're gone. Because there was a lot of people got killed for nothing. A lot of people. That's what made me take the picture, remembering them.

It's history now. I want people to know that it's different looking at Cabrini-Green on the History Channel and actually living in it—it's a big difference. The difference is there was some beautiful people in there. The difference is now the building will be missed. It ain't 'cause of the bad things; we had good times in there too. You know the show *Good Times*? It's true. There were also some good times.

STATEWAY GARDENS

TIFFANY TUCKER

AGE: *21*

OCCUPATION: *McDonald's employee, student*

FORMER RESIDENT OF *Stateway Gardens*

Tiffany lived in Stateway Gardens from 1990 until 2002. Tiffany, her brother, two sisters, and mother moved out of their apartment at Stateway months before her building was razed. Their family life has been routinely disrupted ever since that move because of their difficulty finding stable housing. In accordance with the Plan for Transformation, Tiffany's mother was given Section 8 vouchers (also known as Housing Choice) to subsidize her rent. As a result of foreclosures on the buildings that housed their rental apartments, Tiffany's family had to move four times during an eight-year period. Tiffany is now a student at Daley College (one of Chicago's City Colleges) and is pursuing a nursing degree. We first meet in the bustling dining room of Tiffany's workplace, a McDonald's on the city's South Side. In the midst of the afternoon hubbub, Tiffany is serene. Finished with classes for the day, she will begin her shift in two hours.

IT WAS LIVABLE

My mom kept our household together. Sometimes I barely seen her because she had to work all the time. She's worked at Wendy's most of my life. For a while, she was a manager, but then she fell out one day from too much stress. The doctors kept her in the hospital for about a week after that and then she went back down to working crew at her job. Growing up, my two sisters, my brother, and me had to be there for each other. A lot of times we'd have to babysit ourselves.

We had a three-bedroom apartment in Stateway Gardens. Wasn't big, but it was livable. We had a front room, big kitchen, no dining room. My auntie, my cousins, and us, we all stayed in the same building. We cousins spent time playing with each other, got each other up in the mornings, walked to school together.

We had close connections at Stateway Gardens. We knew everybody. We had our ups and downs, but it was mostly fun. A lot of people say, "Well, you from the projects, you're ghetto, you're gonna be this, you're gonna be that." But it's not that simple. Stateway wasn't all negative. There was a lot of gangs, a lot of shooting, but that didn't mean we couldn't come outside. It was a bad place to live, but there was community, too. The adults would organize parties for us. Cook a lot of food, give away school supplies and try to encourage young people to do something better.

My grandmother used to hate coming to Stateway Gardens because a lot of the times when she came by, they'd be shooting outside. She spent maybe two nights over at our house. But she always used to pick us up and take us shopping. She visited, but she never stayed. She hardly ever came up the stairs. As little kids, we'd go stay in her neighborhood. We didn't know how to use public transportation, so my grandmother would come pick us up and we would go over to her house and spend the night. Sometimes that was our getaway.

I HATE MOVING

Our school was across the street from the building where we stayed. Benjamin Wright Raymond. Raymond School is still there, but it's closed now. I was at Raymond from kindergarten until sixth grade. We moved out in the summer of '02. I was twelve years old.

When I first heard about the plans to demolish Stateway Gardens, I was like, *Oh my God, we have to start something new. I'm not ready for this.* I hoped that we'd be able to keep attending our school, but my mom said, "I don't wanna keep giving you guys bus passes for you to keep going down there. You're just gonna go to a different school in our new neighborhood." I was so scared that I cried. My siblings were mad, especially my older sister, she's one year older than me. It was her last year at Raymond and she wanted to graduate with all of her friends. All of us were upset, really, but we learned to adjust.

The way it turned out, we ended up moving a whole lot. The buildings where we stayed went into foreclosure again and again. Each time we got notice, we'd only have a few months to relocate. The law is strict on people with Section 8 vouchers. Moving took steps. We'd have to go to the CHA headquarters, inform them that we had to move, and then request our moving papers. We'd go see different apartments. A lot of places don't take Section 8 vouchers, but we found some options on the South Side. I was always there for the viewings because I wanted to check out what kind of space I might have. We'd try to find a house—that was our main issue: finding a house that was big enough. A lot of places were pretty nice, but sometimes my mom wouldn't like the neighborhood, or we'd be too far from public transportation, or there'd be a problem with the landlord. You want to move somewhere where you're comfortable with the landlord. Some of them would ask my mom a long list of questions, like, "How old are your kids? Are they going to have boys over? Are they going to have people hanging off the front porch?"

When the questions got to be too much or if I felt someone looking us up and down funny, I'd be like, *Nah. That landlord's going to be there all the time watching us.* We learned that the hard way, with our first place at Sixty-Fifth and Yale, in Englewood. A lot of the houses we went to, we got that bad vibe. We'd talk afterwards and agree, "No, we're not going to move here." Because we didn't want another situation like before.

Our first apartment outside of Stateway was at Sixty-Fifth and Yale, by St. Bernard Hospital. I went to Parker Community Academy for seventh and eighth grade. I didn't make many friends and we didn't know many of our neighbors because a lot of them were freshly moving in. We were strangers to each other. No one was really conversing with neighbors. Our landlord there was difficult. He lived downstairs from us and he'd always be crowding us, invading our privacy, coming in without notice, even when we wasn't there. Once it came time to move, my mother was serious about finding us somewhere else where we'd be appreciated. We stayed in Englewood and moved from Sixty-Fifth and Yale to Sixty-Third and Carpenter.

By that time I was in high school, going to Dunbar. I traveled by CTA bus. It took an hour or two to get there, so I learned how to get around. We stayed on Carpenter for almost three years, and then we moved again because that building was getting foreclosed, too. We moved to Seventy-Fifth and Emerald, where we stayed for a good year, but then the person who owned that building couldn't keep it up. Another foreclosure. We had to move again. I hate moving.

Each move since we left Stateway Gardens has been different. The first one was okay because the CHA helped arrange and pay for it. The rest we had to pay for ourselves, and my mother would have to take off from work to handle everything. Each move took time. Each move took so much. It was never our fault when there were foreclosures, but we still had to get out. It was worrisome.

We'd always try to leave when it got warm outside. Too much trouble with snow and ice on the sidewalks. I hated packing. I'd stay around late after school to avoid it. But I helped with other things. The day of our third move, I got off work at McDonald's about five in the morning and me and my little brother, he was in grammar school then. We cleaned the whole house. I covered the bottom floor and he covered the top. We vacuumed, mopped, scrubbed everything down, threw away things we weren't taking with us. I can't count how many garbage bags we filled. We had to make so many trips outside to take out the bags and we were forgetting about stuff because we were exhausted. After we finished, we both fell asleep on the porch.

WORKING HARD

We've been in our current place in West Englewood since 2008, since I graduated high school. We have a four-bedroom, two-bath. We really like that house, and the landlord is pretty laid back. He comes by and checks on it, but he doesn't come every day to make sure we keep the apartment well. It's well kept. My mom loves it. She doesn't want to go anywhere. Actually, she wants me to stay there as long as I can, but I'm like, "Mom, once I get myself together, I gotta go!" She said, "You don't have to move, you don't have to go." But, you know how it is when you get older. You want your own stuff.

My mom is a kind of person that's always to herself; she really doesn't go to other neighbors' houses and things like that. She works and comes home, and takes care of our sick grandmother. My older sister does a lot of the helping, too. My grandmother had a stroke two years ago and she moved in to this house with us. We're taking care of her now, making sure she gets her medication and everything. She needs twenty-four-hour-a-day care.

My grandmother was very hardworking. She worked at a factory way far out of the city, where they made detergent bottles. She'd be there all the time. Worked there for thirty-five years, stayed at the same house for thirty-five years, had the same phone number for thirty-five years. She came from Mississippi, so working hard and making her own money, she always wanted to do that. But weekend come, I'd relax with her. We were shopping buddies. She's had three strokes now. She can't talk, and so I don't remember how she used to talk. It's been a long time since I heard her voice. It's tough, but we manage every day.

I've wanted to be a nurse ever since I was a little girl. Now I'm trying to get my bachelor's degree. When I started college, I was full-time and working forty hours a week. It's a big load. Since I was at McDonald's full-time through high school, I learned how to manage my studies with work, but once I get into the nursing program I may not be able to have a job at all. Becoming a nurse is what I have to do. After I graduate and start my career, I might stay in the city, but I'll probably move out to the suburbs. It's not bad to try new things. I'll see how I like it out there and then if I don't, I'll come back. You know how you get when you're homesick.

VIEW OF THE DAN RYAN EXPRESSWAY
FROM STATEWAY GARDENS

LLOYD "PETER" HAYWOOD

AGE: *48*

OCCUPATION: *Bus driver, activist*

FORMER RESIDENT OF. *Stateway Gardens*

Peter grew up in Stateway Gardens, on the city's South Side. He lived in Stateway for most of his life (from the late 1960s through the early 2000s), surrounded by an extended network of family. He worked for several years doing construction and restoration projects in his neighborhood, and he lived at Stateway when the Plan for Transformation was announced. Catalyzed by his great-grandmother's grief at losing her home there, Peter became increasingly active in community organizing, advocating for collaboration with the CHA as they made plans for demolition and mixed-income housing. He now lives in Park Boulevard, a new mixed-income development blocks away from his former address. His relocation experience has been a turbulent one, as he summarily lost his lease from his first (replacement) apartment and was redirected to Park Boulevard, where he has faced particular scrutiny as a tenant with a Housing Choice Voucher. In our conversation, Peter speaks vividly of life and family in the high rises. He speaks with equal passion about life since the high rises have come down. For Peter, as for many former residents of high rise public housing in Chicago, the Plan for Transformation has not been an easy transition.

THE SQUARE MILE

My family had been in that area forever. The square mile: from Federal and State Street over to the lake; from Thirty-Fifth over to Thirty-Ninth Street. That was what I knew was my neighborhood. Some of my relatives were in Stateway, some were at Ida B. Wells Homes, some over on Michigan around Twentieth. A lot of family all in the vicinity. My first home was in Stateway, living with my brother and my grandparents. My grandmother raised us. And my great-grandparents were nearby.

My great-grandmother was Osieola Haywood and my great-grandfather was Edward Haywood. They met as young adults, got married, moved to Thirty-First and Wentworth, then relocated to Stateway a few years later, after it was first built. They stayed there up until they passed. My great-grandfather came from Tennessee. My great-grandmother came from Alabama. She said Alabama was a place she never wanted to go back to. She really didn't like to discuss her childhood. She said some bad events took place that led her to leave Alabama and travel up here to Chicago. My great-grandfather would talk about his childhood, but not in any real detail that I can remember.

Me? I wanted to play. I didn't really want to hear any stories about down South. My great-grandfather would get you. He'd get home from work and you'd have to pull off his shoes. He'd say, "Boy, you want to make these two bits? Come over and take off these shoes." And he'd have on those black dress socks and his feet would be stinking! First, he'd start off playing a game. You spelling words. *Spell this. Spell that. What's this math problem? What's that one?* And he'd have you massaging his feet. I would try to stay away but there was no way of escaping it. All that for *two bits*. Two bits was a quarter. He'd give you that quarter and you'd be like, *Man, two bits should be more than this!*

For a long time my great-grandfather worked as a porter for the railroads. I was told he always wanted to be a policeman, but he was too short, so he finally settled for being a security guard. He'd be in the house in full uniform. Me being little, I didn't know the difference. I thought he was a policeman. He worked security until his health began to fail him. He passed of bone cancer in 1978. I was in eighth grade. My great-grandmother lived another twenty years. She was strong. She'd probably still be here today—I think she would have lived to be a hundred, but she fell and broke her hip. That was the beginning of the end. She was ninety-something when she passed.

She never wanted to be put in a home. That was something she always stated. Don't ever put her in a home. She also didn't want to be somewhere with only a bunch of seniors. She wanted to live around young people. Just hearing little children outside, calling them, giving them candy—she just loved it. It kept her going. And family wanted to stay with her. She simply loved to cook for us. Breakfast, lunch, and dinner. "Boy, get out my pots!" You get up in there, you smelling lamb chops and Brussels sprouts.

When the sheriffs brought her the news, it was the way they knocked at the door that scared her. She never had no police coming and beating at her door. She thought they were looking for somebody. The sheriff's department was going door to door and they had a lot of police cars pulled up around the building. They gave notice in a letter about court appearances for eviction. When they served her the papers that the building was going to court with the closures, she thought for sure that she was being put in a nursing home. This was the beginning of summer in '97. The thought of losing that apartment was more than she could bear. You could have put a new apartment on that same floor and said, "Hey, Mrs. Haywood, move here." No. She wanted to be in *that* apartment.

I remember the day vividly. We were sitting at the kitchen table with her—me, my brother, my great uncle, and a couple of friends—and she was crying. We were saying, "We're going to fight for this. It's going to be all right." But she just went numb on us. After that, she just went into her own little world. She shut down because that's where she wanted to be until her last day: in that house where she lived with my great-grandfather. A couple of weeks later, she went into the hospital, and that was the last time I saw my great-grandmother alive.

WE NAMED IT RABBIT TOWN

I was raised in Stateway from infancy. Then I moved with my grandparents from Stateway to 3601 Lake Park Avenue in 1977. We were in a three-story connected to a twelve-story high rise. In the square mile. I loved the old Stateway, so I'd go back over all the time to visit my old friends. Of course, my great-grandmother was still there. I was twelve. The building we moved into on Lake Park was fairly new. The management there had lots of rules. You couldn't do this. You couldn't do that. They had carpeted hallways. I liked to shoot marbles and you couldn't hang out in the hallways. If you shot marbles, that meant you were in somebody's hallway and they'd be complaining. I didn't want my grandmother getting in trouble with the management office and have them talking about eviction.

When we first moved to Lake Park, we started exploring the lakefront. Some friends from Stateway would come over. After school and in the summertime, we'd go and venture along the shoreline, walking the rocks on that terrain, from McCormick Place back down to Sixty-Third Street Beach. A couple of years went by and when we entered high school, I started cutting classes. During the elementary school years, I'd gone to grade school every day. My grandmother worked in the cafeteria at Raymond School, where me and my brother went. She kept tabs on us. But when I got to high school I could stay out of sight.

Wendell Phillips High School was part of my family's tradition. My grandparents went there. My aunts and uncles. When it came time for me to go, I heard stories: "The P., if you go there, you gonna have to fight." And man, I was scared. *I gotta go to this school here.* You know you graduate eighth grade and your friends all have that same look of concern and worry. "We going to the P. now, it's going to be like this." Your mouth saying, "Yeah," but your heart is just thumping. But it worked out. Upon getting there, I was lost in the school. It was big and new, and because I was so busy looking for my classroom, I really didn't have time to take in all the people. And before you know it, the people that you know from Stateway came up to you. "Hey, Pete." So now you walking around with them and they showing you around.

Now I got my little chest stuck out and got my head held high. It was like a hand in glove. I hit the classes for a second, but I'm looking at my friends hanging out in the hallways. I don't make that period class, and since I don't make that period class, I'm thinking the school's going to call home. But when they don't call home, I miss the next one. *Wow. Didn't no one call home.* And before you know it, it's just an everyday thing. I'd get up in the morning to go to school to meet up with my friends and hang out.

Me and my friends spent lots of time on the lakefront. It's nine degrees, but we don't care. We're out on the lakefront at eight o'clock in the morning. We found this little isolated piece of land around Thirty-Seventh and we named it Rabbit Town. We'd go to that part of the lakefront because we knew the rocks were jagged. We'd be out there walking the rocks and I'm thinking I'm Jacques Cousteau, and I guess everybody else is feeling the same way, and that's how we stumbled upon it. Wild, weeds, ragged trees, and rocks. We'd see rabbits and little critters around there that I'd never seen in the city. We'd be over there and in the winter, water would come up over the rocks and freeze up. A thick layer of ice would form out there and we would be out there playing hockey with sticks and chunks of ice, just running around. We didn't have any ice skates. We'd just go out there and do mischievous things. You could smoke some weed and the police ain't coming. It was a little retreat. When it was warm, we'd get the marijuana seeds and just throw them on the ground and then the plants would eventually grow because everything out there grew wild and on its own.

We all knew to meet up in Rabbit Town. We'd venture out to Dunbar High School, get in trouble there, and then you might have the police chasing you because of truancy. And we'd run to the lake and we'd know where to go. When I went out there with one of my girlfriends, she'd be afraid because of the isolation of the place and the rocks being all jagged. I'd be out there showing off. She'd be amazed. I thank God that I didn't fall in no water, because if I had, I would have drowned.

Now they've built a whole marina down there. They took all the fun out of it. One day about a week ago, me and my step-son Darryl went over to that part of the lake and I didn't like it. They should have left it like it was, with the smaller beach. There used to be a big tunnel that was an underpass at Thirty-First where you cross over to the lake going underneath the traffic. You could holler in that tunnel and hear your voice echo off the walls. That underpass—they took it out. There's a little tunnel there now.

Wendell Phillips High School had an attendance office. They'd put me on probation. I'd go to school for about a week straight and then slip off again because my friends would be waiting. So I'm not going to class. I'd tell my grandmother that I did homework in study hall. I'd get up, find my notebook, grab the same books I'd grab every day and just head out. My friends, my brother and me, we'd get away from all the streets around Stateway because we had to avoid people who knew our parents. We can't go that way 'cause his mom will see him. My uncles and them, they're hanging on State Street. We'd go on adventures. We'd go to Pershing School down near Lake Shore Drive and shoot ball. In the wintertime, when there wasn't a ball to shoot, we'd be out there dunking

LLOYD "PETER" HAYWOOD

ice chunks. We'd go downtown to the movies or to the Treasure Chest game room. I hung out like that until I finally got kicked out of high school in 1982 when I should have been a senior.

I woke up this one particular day and everything was going as usual—I was getting myself so-called ready for school and my grandmother asked me to go get her purse off of her bed. I thought she was about to give me some extra spending money, but it turned out she pulled out a letter they'd sent her from school. When I saw it, my heart just sank. I was expelled. My grandmother was mad and hurt. She told me, "I've been supporting you going to school, but you haven't been." And by that time, I was also a father. She said, "You want to act like a man, you'll have to go through with it then." I had to leave her house. I knew I'd messed up, I had some sense of pride for my family, but at the time, I didn't value tomorrow. I couldn't see myself saying, *I'll be thirty, thirty-one, thirty-two.* I never looked at life like that. It was what this counselor once told me: the Peter Pan syndrome. You're young and you think you're gonna just be young forever. After I got expelled and left my grandmother's house, I ended staying with my baby's mother and my great-grandmother, and then other relatives. I went back and forth like that. I stayed connected to my grandmother, though. She raised me since I was a baby. We were close all my life.

I COULDN'T COME HOME EMPTY-HANDED

My grandmother would give me and my brother this money to go play lottery. She'd give us the money and we'd keep it, thinking, *All those numbers, hers ain't gonna fall.* We'd get to keep a few extra dollars. Unfortunately, on this one day, this number she bet on actually fell! And it was like, *Oh, wow. This number popped this time!* She was supposed to win a little over $500. I was thinking, *Oh man, I can't go home. How am I gonna get this money for her?* This was summertime, so you could stay out all night. I happened to come up on this dice guy, and the Lord knew that I had to have this lady's money. I got in this dice game and then I was pitching pennies, two for a dollar, and I got her money back. I was thinking, *Now I can finally go home and eat me a good meal.* I was making plans. *I'm gonna get me a bag of weed and a drink for me and my friend.*

So I went up to my friend's house and there was a girl outside named Peaches, she was someone who I grew up with. She had run into some guys we all knew. They'd been drinking and they were smacking on her. I knew the guys who were giving her a hard time. All of us, including Peaches, had grown up in the same building. My friend's momma, she said, "You all go walk her home." And he was like, "No, momma," 'cause we had just got that weed. I sat there on his porch, looking out at what was happening, and I thought, *Well the Lord just blessed me, I guess it'd be a good thing to help out.* So I said, "Come on man, let's go and walk her home."

We had a few other friends with us, and we all walked her home. Seven of us altogether. Peaches lived about three blocks away. The building she lived in at the time—we weren't thinking about it—but these guys there were starting a gang war. So we went in the building, got in the elevator, and before it could go up, it kind of jerked to a stop. That elevator had been rigged so it would go off track. While we were trying to get the door all of the way open, I heard a woman outside saying she was going to call the fire department to help us. And then I heard a young man's voice threatening her, telling her she'd better go away. Right after that, one of my friends was starting to slip through the opening we'd made, prying the door open, and then *bang!* There was a flash of gunfire across his face. He cried out, "Oh, my eyes!" And then a shotgun barrel poked through the elevator doors and fired right at me. The guys outside were taking turns shooting at us. First one arm moving around with a gun, shooting around. And then another arm would stick in with another gun, and the shooting kept going like that. All of us moved into the farthest corner of the elevator, trying to fight to stay on the bottom of our pile. Four of us got shot. And finally it got quiet. The shooting probably only ended because the guns had been emptied. By the grace of God, no one died. Me and this younger guy were the most critically injured. I was shot in the chest and the hip. But I didn't know it at first. After we got off the elevator, I ended up running up eleven flights and then my back got to feeling funny. I didn't even know I was hit until I stopped moving.

It was an experience. A life-changer. I lost my grandma's money, too, but it wasn't the guys who shot me that took it. I think it was the paramedics that did that. I remember when they came for me, I had a half pint of Canadian Mist in my pants pocket and I also had my grandmother's money in there. They took the bottle right away and when I asked for it back, they said, "You can't have this." Never got my money back. Got my clothes and shoes, and that was it. But in the hospital, all I could think was, *I got some money, I got it. I'm gonna bring it home.* I couldn't come home empty-handed.

HE HIT THAT GAVEL, AND I JUST KNEW THAT LIFE WAS OVER

There were quite a number of years after high school when all I basically did was gang-bang. It's a period I don't really like to talk about because I don't care for it. I had lived running the streets. On top of gang-banging was baby-making. I'm not thrilled about the outcomes of the situations because I haven't been what you would call an ideal or complete father figure. Now I'm trying to build relationships and mend them bridges.

After I was shot, I was trying to just find a way to be normal. CHA had come up with this program called the Step-Up Program around '93.

They were teaching some of the young men in the neighborhood how to do minor building maintenance, renovate apartments, stuff like that. It's bittersweet to think about it now. It was the first program in my life I ever completed. I was looking forward to getting a job, my first full-time job, but I ended up going to jail after the Bulls won the championship and I got arrested. I was twenty-eight. The arrest was supposed to have been for looting. Right after the Bulls won, people were going into the stores in my neighborhood, tearing the stores up, and I actually went into this one store to go get my little cousin. Ready to tell him, "Get up out the store and go home." But when I got there, he'd left and the police was coming right in. They were saying, "Put your hands up."

I thought I'd be charged with some little misdemeanor. There were thirteen of us in all in the store. They took us to the police station and the police told us we were being charged with burglary, and I was wondering, *How could you charge someone with a burglary when the door of the store was wide open?* And I asked the officer that. He was a sergeant. He said, "Since this one's so smart, we gonna put this other murder charge on him." And I was like, *Whoa, wait a minute.* I said, "Charge me with the burglary. I'd rather have a burglary. Please don't put no murders on me." Yeah, that was a humbling experience.

Before all this happened, I'd spent a night in lockup, but I'd never spent time in a jail. I didn't know anything about the judicial system, how it worked inside. Upon getting charged, we took a bench trial, which I think was totally bogusly done. The judge asked the police what evidence they had that I'd broken into the store, what I had in my possession. They said I didn't have anything. The store owner said he was in the store and then he said he wasn't in the store. I was this close to beating the charges, but then one of the guys who got arrested with me, he sort of snickered. This happened as the judge had been listening to all these false stories from the prosecution and then we're telling the judge we don't even know who this arresting officer is. When this guy snickered, the judge said, "I'm gonna find you all guilty because *he* finds this funny." And the judge hit that gavel, and I just knew that life was over as far as me being a productive member in society.

I tried explaining to the judge, "Your Honor, if you look at my record, I haven't been to jail. And I didn't wait to get twenty-eight to start being a burglar." But it didn't matter.

I thought I was gonna get three years, but since I'd never been in prison before, they gave me two years probation. And 122 hours of community service. I did time at the county jail. I was incarcerated for about five months and I did my community service. At the time, I just wanted to have a good name. I didn't want to be a disgrace to my family. I really wanted to have a good name with the community, with people in general, because even though I've done dumb things, I always felt I was an honest person. I was a person that you could trust.

I wish I could redo that whole thing. I had a friend who I grew up with in the early years, we'd been best friends, and he went on to retire from the armed services. Back then, he was trying to help me get into the National Guard and that opportunity just folded after all of that, just crumbled.

IT WAS AN EDUCATION.
TRIAL AND ERROR.

A lot of us guys want to do good, but with no employment, what you going to do? And when I came up, it was like guys hanging under the buildings all day. You go to school, they outside, you come home from school they outside, all through the night. When I was young, I thought that was just really the way of life, you know. You had some working people there, but with the majority of people who seemed to be the cool people, ain't nobody working. Once you get going with work, you see your own vanity, it's like, you've been lied to. People call you *slick* and *player* and it's all lies, for nothing. Because not only are you *slick* and *player*, everybody else is *slick* and *player*. I got to looking at guys who came up before me, and how these guys was ending up in and out of jail, half of these guys would be homeless, or were starting to be homeless, and living under the L tracks. I just thought, *Wow, I don't wanna be like this.*

Before I formally met Jamie Kalven, I had sized him up. Here was this white man carrying this big cell phone, walking around freely. This was back in the time when it was a dream to have a cell phone, back when they first came out.

When I finally met Jamie, it was right around the time I was focusing on serving my community. The local advisory council had called for volunteers for building clean-ups: sweeping, mopping, getting graffiti off the walls. The whole nine yards to make the buildings look inhabitable. Since my building was the first one slated for demolition, there was special focus on fixing what the court said were violations. Jamie was working in the community and he'd set up a construction and preservation crew. That day, his crew came to work my building, 3617-3615 Federal. It was a fairly hot day, but I was doing a little sweeping around, even while everyone else took a break. Jamie told me he liked my work ethic. I told him I was behind about $600 in rent from housing. I had a great-aunt who'd lent me the money and when I saw Jamie was hiring, I thought, *I can make the money to pay her back now.* He instilled a trust in me and gave me some employment. You'd see a lot of guys always around him saying, "Could I work for you? I wanna work for you." They were trying to escape their life.

Jamie put trust in me. The first job I worked on was a building across the street from Stateway. The Overton Building.[1] We did a complete interior demolition, saving the outside of the building. It was the first piece of work that kept me truly honest. When you get through at the end of the day, you might drink a couple beers with the guys, but you basically tired. We did the work by hand. Channel that negative energy, make it positive. We'd have sledgehammers and axes. The only thing electrical that we had was a Sawzall, but other than that we would do it by hand.

I learned some skills being in the Step-Up Program, and I also learned skills growing up in the apartments. Housing would hardly fix the things right, if you waiting for them, you'll be waiting forever. You'd experiment with things and see how it works. Trial and error. When we worked in this building, there was no power, so we had a chance to work things out. Some people make these big deals about constructing work, "You have to go to school for carpentry." You're gonna understand the point of reading a ruler or whatever, but you can learn what goes where just by trying to build it up. It was an education. Trial and error. It was a good master to me, it brought me up to speed. Since then, I've been into some other building maintenance programs and completed them. That first work was always the backbone of what I learned how to do.

After working on the Overton, we would do small odd jobs, anything from A to Z. I worked for about five years doing that labor and then, of course, I was trying to get into heavier things with the CHA, trying to get work for guys in the neighborhood, getting employment to do demolition. But the first work was a cleaning program. CHA was letting the buildings deteriorate and people were keeping garbage in their apartments. There were rat and rodent infestations. Jamie got a little contract for the crew. We'd go into the building and clean up the apartments and

---

[1] The Overton Hygienic Building is a registered landmark.

then he was also starting this other project, working with the residents, getting information from them to see what their needs were. Advocacy work. Once I did that, Jamie pulled me over to that project because he knew I knew my way well through the community, and on top of that, I was a pretty good reader, could do things: clerical and administrative work, work on computers. It was pretty cool. It was my style, and Jamie instilled a trust in me, and he done it. You had people looking at you, noticing you. I got onto the local advisory council at Stateway, and people take a look at you, they see what you can do. Some managers from the public housing development were taking notice of what I was doing and how I treat people and talk with people.

The people in management had me supervise several projects for them, to be in relationships with contractors who they would have come in and renovate apartments. Later on, I'd help prep the high rises before the demolition crews come in to tear the buildings down. It was a very good experience.

On that note: I'd like to thank Miss Adrienne Lawson, Miss Francine Washington, as well as Jamie Kalven and Patsy Evans. Another person, Danielle Walters, she was instrumental in helping me. When I got kicked out of high school I would go register for the GED, I'd pay for it, but I would never go take it, because I took it once and I failed by like eleven points. I'm still no good in math. But Danielle Walters took the time to give me encouragement, and she would take me to a couple of these little restaurants over here in Hyde Park. We'd be eating at the table and she'd take coins out of her purse and have me doing math in front of all of these people! She was serious, you know, and she helped me out. She took me to the testing center, waited outside in her car, intercepted me when I tried to leave, and turned me right back around. I got my GED.

I met Danielle Walters through Jamie. And it was part of the reason that my employment ended with Jamie because there was some things going on and I got into an argument with her and Jamie told me, "Pete, I'm sorry. I have to let you go." It was bitter, you know. It was a learning experience. I apologized to Danielle afterwards, a couple months later. I apologized and made amends. Repairing that with them, I started coming to the idea: *I have to try to repair the relationship with my children.*

My oldest son had been going in and out of prison. I told him, "You touched places I haven't." And I want to teach him, *Don't be like me, but break the chain.* One chain that I was able to break was my father's. He was a user of heroin. He'd pleaded with me, "Promise you'll never use this." And I promised I wouldn't. Unfortunately, he died from complications from his addiction. So there are lessons I try to share with my son. He has two children by this young lady, my first two grandchildren, and she stated she didn't want to deal with him going back and forth to jail, so she took up and left him. I'm trying to convince him. "Find your children, still be a part of their lives, because you see what happens." He's started to listen, but he's still running through something else 'cause he young and he got that energy, you know. He could use a sledgehammer in his hand. *Go hit on this rock!* A few years ago, he almost lost his life as well. A guy shot him six times. Once he recovered, he sort of mellowed it down. He needed a change of venue and so he moved to Iowa. When I last spoke with him he said he was doing okay—him and his fiancée had just got an apartment.

I have another son in Milwaukee who I need to go and see. That's what I have to do when I get my car running right. He and his brother have been living in Milwaukee for a while. His brother, my other son, he's deaf, but he accepted my apology for not being there like I should have. He accepts it. But the one I need to go and see—he won't. I know he has his displeasure, so I have to understand because I'm the root cause of that. I have to try to fix that. I tell him, "Your other brother, he's deaf, but he do try to get in contact with me. You can talk. You won't say two words, and I'm not a mind reader." But the Lord, he'll find a way. I can fix that.

I wish that every male could sort of think on this time because we could fix our communities, but all these babies we went and made, we gotta go and correct them wrongs of not being involved. It didn't take me being in penitentiary, locked up for the rest of my life, to come to that conclusion. I've been working this thing with my oldest son, the one in Iowa. I've been trying to bridge the gap. When it's finally working is when they give you a call. "Hey, how you doing?" With my daughters, I've pretty much been there, but I haven't been the breadwinner, I haven't been the supporter of my children. But I love them all, and I love no one better than the other. No divisions. When I was young, I thought that was an excuse. I'm the black sheep of the family. I was the black sheep because of the things I was doing.

"STATEWAY GOT MEN IN THEIR GROUP"

The work I did in the community gave me a sense of responsibility. It gave me the ability to step up and be accounted for—for the things I should have done and shouldn't have done. It gave me the opportunity to know that everything my elders said—my aunts and uncles—everything they said was true. *If I do it this way, this and this and this will happen.* It came to pass. I'm doing it this way and I was shot up, almost dead, in jail, like they said I'd be.

Unfortunately, my grandmother and my great-grandmother never got a chance to see me complete some little accomplishments that I made in life. My great-grandmother didn't see the turning point. The day when the sheriff knocked at everybody's door in our building, and they was passing out these letters about court appearance for eviction, that's when my great-grandmother just took sick from thinking that she had to go. This was the beginning of summer, '97. The thought of losing that apartment was more than she could bear. A couple of weeks later, she went into the hospital, and that was the last time I saw her alive.

I was about thirty-three when all that happened. And I got into community politics because I was mad. I was hurt by what happened to my great-grandmother. I wanted to be assured that this plan for so-called transformation included the people from Stateway Gardens living in the newer places.

There was a hurting feeling realizing what we were up against. You go into court and you have these lawyers and officials who've never lived in a development, lived on the property, or even set foot on the property, and they're saying that bricks was falling off of the building. It wasn't true. They dreamt up these cockamamie, fabricated stories, and they bought scaffolding and put it around the building to protect people from debris or whatever they say was falling from the building, but it wasn't falling from the building, and I just thought, *Wow.*

When I was working community organizing, I started getting other males actively involved. Not older guys, but younger, educated brothers. Getting them more involved in the community politics at that public housing development. And people were taking notice of that when we go to these meetings. "Stateway got men in their group who are concerned about their community." It wasn't only women, like people got used to. And I think that was really stirring up something. With CHA, they'd be putting these women off with vague promises, but these guys gonna want more specific answers and action. It was the same thing when I went to that last program the CHA organized. They paying for us, they putting us through a program with no substance and no clear outcome in mind. I been through these building maintenance programs and have certificates, and this thing is designed for everyone to fail. It led to nothing. We getting some little worksheets to fill out, but there's nothing that a person can go on to do. I been in several programs where I seen the difference. I told everybody in that class, including the instructor: "You know when everybody leave here they ain't going to know not a bit more about hanging a piece of drywall."

The program I participated in was called *Pathway to Green*. This was last year. This was supposed to been a six-week program with some employment at the end of it. It was just for show. People got paid, some money got swept under the rug, and then they moved onto the next agenda. But they're not even thinking about the fact that you have some people here *really wanted to work*. There was supposed to be jobs on the construction sites after you finished this program. That's the way it was advertised. But once you get through it, you just go get a job working out at O'Hare Airport at a Sbarro's or some other fast-food place, just like nothing ever happened. It didn't amount to nothing but empty promises. And then you have people with the hope and desire of getting into the program watching you go through it. Men came from all over the city. All over the city. The outcome with CHA programs has always been this way. It was just set up to say, *Something's happening.* Somebody's intention may be good in the beginning, but it all ends up in corruption.

A SCARED FEELING

When I first heard that they were planning to tear down the buildings at Stateway, I was hurt. It was a scared feeling. And it's still a scary feeling because everything is uncertainty. You couldn't trust CHA or something they were saying in the beginning. *How do I trust you that this will go on as you say it will?*

When I first moved from the CHA development, back in 2005, I wasn't too thrilled or pleased about it because I basically wanted to stay there on the land at Thirty-Fifth Street, where Stateway was. Once

I moved to my first place, near Washington Park,[2] I adapted to it and got comfortable with it all, real quick. For a change, I'm on the first floor, so no stairs and no elevators, which I thought was great. I don't have to walk up anything but these five steps. In the apartment at Stateway, I lived as high as the twelfth floor. When you carry your groceries, them stairs are tedious. I was walking flights as a routine because the elevators would be broke. I couldn't believe it when I first moved to the place near Washington Park. Five stairs! The apartment was nice. It was just cozy for myself and my daughter. The park had a water slide just east of us. I could take my daughter and my granddaughter there. We were there about a year and a half.

I just started accepting the fact that Stateway is torn down, gone, so I just tried to move on. I didn't speak to the neighbors at the Washington Park apartment too much. I'd come into my apartment and leave out the next day and maybe go sit at other friends' houses or something like that. One day, I went to take my portion of the rent to the landlord and the landlord wouldn't take it. I was wondering why. The landlord told me to call the management company that was over at CHA. It turned out that the CHA quit paying the rent to the landlord, and so I had to hurry up and move. I was told, "You have to take this other apartment or you gonna be on the street." It was an forced move and there was no explanation for it.

Then the CHA moved me to Park Boulevard, a mixed-income development. When I went to the apartment where they sent me, I'm looking at the ceilings first. Twelve-foot ceilings, and I have to pay light, gas. Heat travels upward. I could show you my light bill. At first, my kilowatt hour usage chart was down, but as of November, December, January, February, March, the bars they're way up. But I don't even use these lights. I don't

---

[2] Washington Park is a South Side neighborhood; the 380-acre park itself, on the neighborhood's southeast edge, was designed by Frederick Law Olmsted and Calvert Vaux.

even plug up no Christmas lights or nothing. I'm barely at home. I have some kin who loaned me money to help pay the light bill, because if I can't even keep my lights on, the gas on, that's cause for an eviction. When I moved into the apartment, they wanted to evict me because I wouldn't get the gas and light cut on. I think that the Plan for Transformation is designed like everything else. It's designed for you to fail. And they can say, "See we did this for them, but they didn't want it," without logically or economically looking at it.

The new development—the place I live now—I don't like it. It's called Park Boulevard. I never liked the idea of restaurants and apartment buildings in conjunction. Or a storefront and apartment buildings in conjunction. Because with the restaurants, it's a vast amount of food that they cook and dispose of daily, which makes for rodent infestation. Then you have rat bait boxes, but the rat poison is out on the property, and you've got children playing on the property. It makes no sense whatsoever. I'm right on top of Starbucks, so that's at Thirty-Fifth and State Street. Smelling coffee forever, and I don't even like coffee. And there's a pizza place and popcorn place. I don't even care to walk around. I was never happy about the location. I want to live back on the 3600 block. Since I've been here, my car's been broken into. I can't park my car under my window to keep a watch on it because of city meters. You have to pay all night. What business has the coffee shop got that you park that long to have a parking meter? I have to park in the lot behind where I live. I can't see my car, I can't hear my alarm.

RULES ARE STRICTLY ENFORCED
WITH THE CHA TENANTS

I always wanted my home to be a place of serenity for me and my children. One of my sons went to prison for fighting dogs, and when he got out, he didn't have nowhere to go. I live in a place, this apartment, where I can't have my own son come live with me to get him off the streets. So, what's left for him to do? They're saying, "No, he can't come stay with you." I think that's stupid, that's a stupid law that they put on us: that one-strike policy. It's frustrating and it hurts.

Right now my brother's homeless. He keeps up with me and calls every other week to say, "Pete, I'm okay." I don't always know where he's in, I just know he's in Chicago. And I figure there was nothing wrong with him having his mail come to my address, but there was. I can't help him out that way because he's had trouble. And there have been little instances where he gets arrested for stupid stuff. Homeless people use the rest room outside and he got caught doing that. He jumped the turnstiles at the L to try to get on there to sleep, and so they arrest him and he gives my address as his address. And so CHA tries to pull me off for lease violation. CHA sends the management a notice that this person has been arrested and is using this address. Building management knows he's not staying there. I told one of the landlords, "I can't help control whether mail comes here for him. He's not doing anything over here." It's just crazy.

Even a homeowner is not gonna see their son or their daughter on the street, it come down to little pitty-pat things, which are really great slaps in the face. These rules are strictly enforced with the CHA tenants, and it's altogether different for the homeowners. When I first moved into my building, there was a guy of a different class, different income. He was a white guy. He looked at me and said, "Can I help you?" He was asking me one thing, but he was meaning another. What he meant was, *What are you doing here? Who let you in here?* "No, you can't help me." It seemed he was figuring out that CHA people were going to be living there and shortly after he approached me, he got a For Sale sign in his window.

You had tenants with video cameras outside on their balconies recording the places where they figure people are living with public housing vouchers, and it was apparent to me from the first day. One day I was right outside changing my flat tire, and I'm looking at the people peeping out their windows. I'm thinking, all these people looking out the window about to call 911, but didn't nobody see nobody when my car got broken into. I had gone to the building management after my car was broken into and they told me they couldn't really see anything on the footage from their cameras, but let something happen to the homeowner, then they gonna see everything. Someone going to jail. I'm coming to the conclusion now with CHA and even with this country today: the laws they make is not the laws for us, the laws they make are to be exercised on us. Expediently.

One of my biggest fears, you know, is gun rights laws. CHA tenants can't have a gun their apartments. The homeowners, they can have these guns. What if the homeowners turn out to be the people like this guy who did the shooting in Aurora, Colorado? How am I supposed to protect myself? Just grab a frying pan and stand beside my front door and hope?

IT WAS JUST FOREVER CHANGING

When CHA was holding the first meetings about Stateway being demolished, the first proposal was: they take a building down, they build another one on that spot. That was the initial proposal. Then it changes. *We're gonna take another building down and another two buildings, then three buildings down, and we'll build on them spots.* But finally it was, *Take all but one down. This building we'll leave. People who want to stay here, here in this building, this one building, we'll build around it.* So they started building on Thirty-Fifth and then the final change, *We want this building gone too.* It was just forever changing. Forever changing.

At Stateway, it was people helping people in the buildings. Like there was a lady, Miss Millsap. If I was hungry, I could go over to her house and eat breakfast, or I could go to this building, to Miss Wells's house, and eat lunch, and really that's how a lot of us were living. People were taking care of each other. Every building had those cooks, they was older, their children got older and moved out, but they loved to cook, they loved to feel a part of doing something. If someone was homeless, they would bring food that they had left over to feed them. It was just a sense of love from the neighbors. Everybody got food stamps and some was blessed who had work and others were retired off their jobs. A lot of the ladies will caring for people's children, going to a thrift shop and getting clothes for boys and girls. I'll never forget those people. They'd say, "Pete, you want something to eat?" Sometimes I would, sometime I wouldn't, but I was just always thankful to know that they were willing and able to do that.

Miss Millsap, she was funny 'cause she get mad if you don't come. "You see I cooked all this food and you ain't come?!" She would cook soul food. Good, nutritional soul food. Black-eyed peas, fish fries, whatever, and this was every day of the week. Miss Millsap was steady making meals. Not a day goes by. "I got this breakfast." Sausage and eggs. Pancakes. People might offer her some change. "Miss Millsap, I got my stamps." When I moved out to Fifty-Sixth Street, near the park, they'd moved Miss Millsap on Fifty-Seventh. Today CHA won't let her move back into one of the apartments where Stateway was, saying something about her income is too much. It's crazy. I don't feel that connection with the people where I live now—people looking at you as if you gonna do something to them.

They closed the last building in 2006. I moved out of there in 2005. Being at Stateway as people were leaving was sad. It was a sad feeling, it was a hurtful feeling. All of the acquaintances that you had over the years, to see 'em go, it's like, they gone. You try to move on. In moving on you know, you don't forget the people, but a few months removed from someone, your conversations change, certain things change. You try to talk, but eventually the connection slips away. You talk sparingly. We don't have the camaraderie, that thing in common. Now you start socializing with people who you didn't know before but also used to live in Stateway. Everyone's sharing the same fears—*We gonna be displaced, we gonna be out here. They putting us out of here, since we don't have no jobs.*

I haven't been to school. I don't have this, that, the other, and there are particular criteria that they were saying we needed for the right to return to live in the neighborhood where Stateway had been. You saying we supposed to work thirty hours a week for a right to return? I can't get a job for *eight* hours a week! You volunteer and you do this and you do that. I'm getting credentials and can't get anything with them.

As people were leaving, it was always changing. *Oops, we didn't mean that.* The pendulum would swing. *We said this, we said that, but this is what we gonna do.* This is at the end of the day, at the end of you sitting and attending meetings and planning, or thinking you planning and negotiating. It was nothing but the waste of our time and energy.

The 3651–3653 building on Federal. This final building was sitting a block and a half away from construction. It's not in the way of anything. You still got roads to the building, and roads to the area where you working. And now we had to move. You dug and you blew plumes of dust, tearing down buildings around us all that time. We breathed in all the asbestos, all of whatever you could possibly be breathing in. If I could breathe in that dust when these buildings coming down, why not let me breathe in the dust of something coming up? "It's unhealthy." Wasn't it unhealthy that you tearing these older buildings down and we gotta breathe this? I've been breathing the dust in from them buildings coming down for all them years, and you done dug all in the ground, sideways, from the other part of the planet, maybe. I breathed all that in, I took all that in. Shouldn't I want to be here? It's the dust of something new. It's still unhealthy, but I breathed that in, so let me breathe this in.

APPENDICES

I. TIMELINE OF HOUSING AND CIVIL RIGHTS IN CHICAGO

1865—Thirteenth Amendment to the United States Constitution abolishes slavery in the United States.

1865—The Illinois Negro Code, which made it a misdemeanor for African-Americans to move to Illinois, is repealed.

1868—Fourteenth Amendment to the United States Constitution guarantees equal protection under the law to all citizens.

1874—Illinois state law forbids segregation in education.

1885–1911—A series of statutes forbids public accommodation segregation in Illinois. However, African-American Chicagoans continue to face discrimination.

1890–1908—Ten of eleven southern states rewrite their constitution to restrict African-American voting rights.

1910—The start of the Great Migration. Due to the collapse of the cotton economy, the oppressive Jim Crow system in the South, and the North's need for labor, especially during the World Wars, approximately seven million African-Americans migrate from the South to the urban North. More than 500,000 of these migrants move to Chicago.

1914–1918—World War I. As the U.S. enters World War I in 1916, cities in the North and Midwest face labor shortages due to the enlisting of 5 million men and the U.S. government's decision to halt immigration from Europe. Many African-Americans are enticed to leave the South by the opportunity to work in Northern cities.

1917—The U.S. Supreme Court rules in *Buchanan v. Warley* against publically enacted racial zoning ordinances. The decision creates a rise in privately established racially restrictive covenants to hinder African-Americans from settling in white neighborhoods.

1919—Chicago Riot of 1919. Ethnic tension runs high due to economic competition amongst different immigrant groups after World War I. After African-American youth Eugene Williams is struck with a stone by white men and drowns at a segregated beach, a riot breaks out that results in the deaths of dozens and the injuring of hundreds of Chicagoans, most of them African-Americans.

1927—The Chicago Real Estate Board (CREB) drafts a standard restrictive housing covenant to ban African-Americans from renting or purchasing housing. The first clause of the covenant is an agreement that "no part of said premises shall in any manner be used or occupied directly or indirectly by any negro or negroes, provided that this restriction shall not prevent the occupation, during the period of their employment, of janitors' or chauffeurs' quarters in the basement or in a barn or garage in the rear, or of servants' quarters by negro janitors, chauffeurs or house servants, respectively, actually employed as such for service in and about the premises by the rightful owner or occupant of said premises." Approximately 85 percent of Chicago property falls under covenant restrictions, limiting African-Americans to a handful of neighborhoods.

1929—The Great Depression begins with the stock market crash of October 29. The consequences of massive unemployment and homelessness spur Federal and municipal agencies to innovate new forms of public housing and other forms of economic assistance.

1933—Illinois state statute bans employment discrimination on account of race in work for public buildings and public works.

1934—Intellectual and housing activist Catherine Bauer publishes *Modern Housing*, a call to replace urban slums with planned housing modeled after European urban reconstruction following World War I. Bauer's writing shapes plans for public housing for decades.

—Congress passes the National Housing Act. In response to widespread foreclosures and evictions at the height of the Great Depression, the National Housing Act launches the Federal Housing Administration and puts programs in place to make housing more affordable.

1937—Congress passes the Housing Act of 1937, also known as the Wagner-Steagall Act. The law grants funds to municipal housing agencies to provide housing assistance to low-income citizens.

—The Chicago Housing Authority (CHA) is founded to provide housing for low-income households. The CHA's first director is Elizabeth Wood, a visionary housing advocate and friend of Catherine Bauer.

1938—The first three CHA public housing developments—Jane Addams Houses, Julia C. Lathrop Homes, and Trumbull Park Homes—are constructed.

1939–1945—World War II. The expansion of industry during the war induces many Southern African-Americans to move to Chicago. During the war, the CHA is redirected to build housing for workers in the war industry and returning veterans. This includes a housing development built for African-American war workers—Altgeld Gardens.

1940—The U.S. Supreme Court rules in *Hansberry v. Lee* that a housing covenant barring Carl Hansberry and his family from living in the Washington Park neighborhood of Chicago is illegal. Hansberry's daughter Lorraine would later draw from the experience in penning her play *A Raisin in the Sun*.

1941—Construction is completed on the Ida B. Wells Homes, the first CHA public housing development for African-Americans. It houses 1,662 families. The complex is named after the iconic journalist and activist who helped form the NAACP.

1942–1962—Beginning with the Frances Cabrini row houses and extending through the William Green high rises, the Cabrini-Green housing development is constructed over a twenty-year period.

1946—Airport Homes riot. The Airport Homes are a public housing development designed as transitional housing for returning veterans. White veteran residents riot when

African-American vets and their families try to move into the housing development.

—Future Mayor Richard J. Daley runs for Cook County Sheriff as a progressive, anti-covenant reformer.

1947—Fernwood Park Homes Riot. White veterans in transitional housing again riot when African-American war veterans and their families try to move into the housing development.

1948—In *Shelley v. Kraemer*, the United States Supreme Court rules that all racially restrictive housing covenants are unconstitutional.

1949—U.S. Congress passes the Housing Act of 1949, providing additional funding for public housing. The CHA proposes housing developments to be built all over the city, but white alderman in the city council reject plans for public housing in their wards. For decades, CHA policy is to build housing developments only in mostly African-American residential areas or adjacent to existing public housing developments.

1949–1950—Dearborn Homes constructed. It is the first CHA building to have elevators.

1951—The Chicago City Council approves the Duffy Commission to build eight public housing sites in overpopulated African-American neighborhoods, and an additional seven public housing sites on vacant land outside those neighborhoods.

—Cicero Race Riot. A mob of thousands of white residents of the Cicero neighborhood attack an apartment building that houses Harvey E. Clark, Jr., an African-American war veteran, and his family.

—Ogden Courts and Loomis Courts constructed.

1953–1954—Trumbull Park Homes Riots. The first African-American family to move into Trumbull Park is attacked by a mob. For weeks after, crowds throw stones at the family's apartment. More African-American families moving into the housing development is followed by more violence.

1954—In *Brown v. Board of Education*, the U.S. Supreme Court disallows state sponsored school segregation.

—The CHA board strips Elizabeth Wood of her powers after she battles the Chicago City Council over her plans to integrate public housing. She later resigns.

1954–1955—Harold Ickes Homes constructed.

1955—Richard J. Daley becomes mayor of Chicago.

—Grace Abbott Homes constructed.

1955–1958—Stateway Gardens constructed.

1956–1958—U.S. Commission on Civil Rights reports 256 cases of racial violence in this period, including a race riot in Calumet Park in July 1957. A majority of incidents take place in Park Manor and Englewood, while more than a dozen incidents occur near Trumbull Park.

1957–1969—Henry Horner homes constructed.

1961—Rockwell Gardens and Robert Brooks Extension constructed.

1962—The CHA completes construction on Robert Taylor Homes, a 4,321-unit public housing development on the South Side at the edge of Bronzeville, Chicago's historic African-American neighborhood. At the time, Robert Taylor is the world's largest public housing development.

1963–1966—Raymond Hilliard Homes constructed, containing two towers for elderly housing and two towers for low-income family housing. The complex includes lawns, playgrounds, and an open-air theater.

1964—Congress passes the Civil Rights Act, ending legalized segregation of schools, workplaces, and public facilities.

1965—Congress passes the Department of Housing and Urban Development Act, establishing the Department of Housing and Urban Development (HUD). A cornerstone of Lyndon Johnson's Great Society program, HUD is designed to reform and administer federal housing and urban development programs. The distribution of Section 8 housing vouchers is one of HUD's earliest functions.

1965–1967—The Chicago Freedom Movement/Chicago Open Housing Movement draws together Martin Luther King, Jr. and the Southern Christian Leadership Conference in Chicago. Mayor Daley and King have a summit meeting. The CHA promises to build public housing with limited height requirements, and the Mortgage Bankers Association agrees to make mortgages available regardless of race. Daley promises to lobby for more open housing legislation and build housing developments all over the city. After the meeting, Daley declares the agreement an unenforceable "gentleman's agreement." King's aide Ralph Abernathy later writes that Daley is "a fox, too smart for us."

1966—CHA resident and housing activist Dorothy Gautreaux becomes the lead respondent in a lawsuit against the CHA that claims that Chicago public housing violated the equal protection clause and the recently passed Civil Rights Act. Litigation following the suit would last for three decades and result in landmark public housing reforms.

1968—Martin Luther King, Jr. is assassinated on April 4 in Memphis, Tennessee. Violence begins that night in cities across the U.S. In Chicago, riots affect neighborhoods predominately on the West Side, with some violence on the South Side and Near North Side as well. More than eleven people are killed, hundreds injured, two thousand arrested, and entire city blocks are destroyed by arson and looting. In high rises such as Cabrini-Green, snipers begin shooting indiscriminately from upper stories, a practice that continues sporadically for decades. Many business districts and services decimated by the riots never recover.

1969—The Supreme Court rules in *Gautreaux et al. v. CHA* that Chicago public housing is substandard and in violation of the equal protection clause and the Civil Rights Act of 1964. The CHA is barred from building additional high rises and from segregating public housing developments in predominately African-American neighborhoods. The ruling begins the decades-long dismantling of Chicago's high rises.

1970—Chicago police officers James Severin and Anthony Rizzato are shot and killed while on patrol in the Cabrini-Green housing development by two snipers from a nearby high rise. The incident increases tension between police and high rise residents throughout the city.

1976—The Supreme Court rules in *Gautreaux v. Hills* that HUD bears some responsibility for the CHA's discriminatory housing policies. The decision results in the disbursement of thousands of Section 8 vouchers to CHA residents and movement of many high rise residents away from areas of concentrated poverty. Many residents, however, choose to stay in public housing. The ruling leads to similar changes in metropolitan areas across the country.

1981—Mayor Jane Byrne moves into Cabrini-Green to draw attention to the high crime rate. Police presence is increased during her stay and she leaves after just three weeks.

1988—Operation Clean Sweep. CHA guards and Chicago police raid housing developments searching for guns and drugs. The American Civil Liberties Union later files a suit on behalf of residents that allege civil liberties violations related to warantless searches,

1992—A ten-year old Dantrell Davis is on his way to school when he's killed by a gang member's stray gunshot.

1993–2000—In an attempt to de-concentrate poverty, newly appointed HUD Secretary Henry Cisneros takes up an ambitious plan to replace high density public housing throughout the U.S. with mixed-income housing and Section 8 vouchers. The HOPE VI program developed in Congress provides grants to modernize public housing and demolish distressed public housing.

1995—Declaring that "public housing is on trial in Chicago," Henry Cisneros and HUD begin procedures to take control of the administration of the CHA. Fourteen thousand of nearly 40,000 housing units are condemned, and the city begins to formulate what will soon be called the Plan for Transformation.

1995–2011—Cabrini-Green high rises demolished.

1997–2000—Robert Brooks high rises demolished. Some Robert Brooks row-houses reconstructed and renovated.

2000—The CHA officially launches its Plan for Transformation. By the end of the ten year plan 25,000 units of housing are to be renovated or built new, and the CHA administrative staff is to be reduced significantly. The plan focuses on a shift to lower-density mixed-income communities and housing vouchers to replace the bulk of public housing units. The 25,000 households in good standing with the CHA as of October 1, 1999 are granted "right of return" to their former neighborhoods when reconstruction is complete or offered Housing Choice Vouchers (formerly Section 8 vouchers) instead.

2001–2008—Henry Horner Homes demolished.

2001—Phase I of redevelopment at Henry Horner Homes site is completed. The new community is a mixed-income development known as Villages of Westhaven.

2002–2003—Ida B. Wells Homes demolished.

2003–2006—Rockwell Gardens demolished.

2007—The last of the ABLA high rises, Robert Taylor Homes, and Stateway Gardens demolished.

2009—Some of the Frances Cabrini row houses redeveloped.

—Initial renovations completed on Dearborn Homes.

2009–2010—Harold Ickes Homes demolished.

2010—After ten years, approximately 80 percent of the 25,000 units budgeted under the Plan for Transformation are complete. Of the 16,500 non-senior households awarded right of return, only 9,300 (56 percent) remain in the CHA system as CHA leaseholders or recipients of Housing Choice Vouchers. The remainder (44 percent) live in homes without subsidy or have died, been evicted, or gone missing. Thirteen percent have fallen out of contact with the CHA, and seven percent await finished construction of new units in their old neighborhoods in order to satisfy the right of return.

2013—The CHA plans to have completed 88 percent of the planned 25,000 housing units by the end of the fiscal year.

II. GLOSSARY

Chicago Housing Authority (CHA): Established by the state of Illinois in 1937, the CHA oversees all public housing programs in the city of Chicago. The CHA owns more than 20,000 units that it provides mostly to seniors and families. At its peak, the CHA owned and rented out 40,000 units throughout the city. The authority also administers nearly 40,000 Housing Choice Vouchers (formerly Section 8).

CHA Police Department: A dedicated police force monitored CHA housing from 1989 to 1999, when the city began the Plan for Transformation. District offices were built directly in developments such as Robert Taylor Homes and the CHAPD provided twenty-four hour patrolling.

Community policing: An approach to crime prevention that focuses on a high level of cooperation and coordination between police and civilians within affected communities.

Dan Ryan Expressway: A freeway that runs through the south side of Chicago. Until their demolition, public housing high rises including Robert Taylor Homes and Stateway Gardens ran parallel and to the east of Dan Ryan Expressway for nearly four continuous miles from Garfield Boulevard to Cermak Road.

Folks Nation: A group of affiliated gangs throughout the Midwest and South that includes the Gangster Disciples, La Raza, and offshoots. Rivals of gangs that comprise the "People Nation." The Folks Nation represents with symbols such as a six-pointed star, a trident, and the color blue.

Gangster Disciples: One of the most prominent gangs in Chicago. The Gangster Disciples were formed by an alliance of smaller gangs through the 1960s and developed a notable presence within the high rises. Part of the Folks Nation and rivals of the Vice Lords.

***Gautreaux v. Chicago Housing Authority*:** A case brought against the CHA by the ACLU and residents such as Dorothy Gautreaux that charged the housing administration with violation of the equal protection clause due to substandard conditions and racial segregation within Chicago public housing. The case, decided in 1965, forced the CHA into receivership and marked the beginning of the end of high density, racially segregated urban housing in Chicago and other cities across the U.S.

Group home: Shared public housing institutions made up of residents who are deemed unable to take care of themselves, such as minors without guardians, the mentally ill, those with disabilities, and the elderly. Many U.S. cities, such as Chicago, provide some access to shared living spaces for low-income mothers and their children.

Halfway house: A shared living space designed to lower recidivism rates amongst recovering addicts and those recently released from prison. Halfway houses can be public and privately run, and residents are often remanded to halfway houses as part of criminal sentencing or on the recommendation of prison officials.

***Hills v. Gautreaux*:** A 1974 decision by the U.S. Supreme Court that resulted in the distribution of Section 8 vouchers to residents of many of Chicago's distressed public housing developments. The lead respondent was Dorothy Gautreaux, a housing resident and activist.

HOPE VI: Also known as the Urban Revitalization Demonstration program or Housing Opportunities for People Everywhere, HOPE VI was first enacted by Congress in 1992 as part of a broad plan to redevelop distressed public housing by providing block grants to municipalities. Over two decades, HUD has distributed nearly $7 billion to more than 130 municipal housing authorities, resulting in the demolition of distressed high rises and the construction of mixed-income housing developments.

Housing Choice Voucher Program: A program under the auspices of HUD and the CHA that distributes Federally funded vouchers (formerly known as Section 8) to low-income Chicago residents, allowing low-income households to rent private housing.

Housing and Urban Development (HUD): The U.S. Department of Housing and Urban Development was formed under the Johnson administration in 1965, replacing the earlier Roosevelt-designed Federal Housing Administration. Among numerous other functions, HUD distributes public housing development grants and Section 8 vouchers to municipalities.

Mixed-income housing: An approach to public housing that integrates apartments, row-houses, and condos targeted to all income levels—some publicly supported, some market-rate—within single city blocks or neighborhoods. Mixed-income housing is designed to de-concentrate poverty and attendant effects such as poor educational opportunities, dysfunctional local economies, and high crime rates. Cities across the U.S. have shifted toward mixed-income models since federal initiatives in the 1990s.

One strike policy: Sets of rules adopted by housing authorities starting in the mid-1990s by housing authorities across the country, including the CHA, to determine eligibility for public housing and Section 8 vouchers. Under the policy, applications for public housing assistance are turned down if the applicant or a member of his or her household has ever been convicted of one of a broad range of crimes.

Operation Clean Sweep: A city-wide program launched in the 1980s to combat crime and gang activity in the city's housing developments. The program featured planned raids that targeted illegal drugs and guns through massive apartment-by-apartment searches.

People Nation: A group of affiliated gangs that includes the Latin Kings, Vice Lords, Four Corner Hustlers and offshoots. Rivals of gangs that comprise the "Folks Nation." The People Nation represents with symbols such as a five-pointed star, a cane, and the color red.

Plan for Transformation: A massive, multi-billion dollar realignment of public housing in Chicago that began in 2000 under Mayor Richard M. Daley. Prominent goals of the Plan have included demolition of population-dense high rises, issuance of housing vouchers, slashing of CHA staff, and the construction of 25,000 new or renovated housing units. As of 2013, construction of new units has not kept up with demolition of old units, leaving many former high rise residents without replacement housing.

Restorative justice: A philosophy of justice that focuses on support for victims of crime and rehabilitation of perpetrators of crime rather than punishment and retribution. The aim of restorative justice is to heal damage done to individuals and communities by criminal activity.

Section 3: A provision of Federal HUD grants that requires participating municipalities to provide training, employment, and contract work to low-income residents, especially those who live in public housing.

Section 8: A federal voucher program that authorizes direct federal payments to independent landlords on behalf of over three million low-income citizens across the country. With Section 8 vouchers (now called Housing Choice Vouchers), recipients generally pay around 30 percent of their gross income toward rent and the remainder of their rent is covered by the federal government.

TEC-9: The Intratec TEC-DC9 is a 9mm semi-automatic handgun capable of supporting magazines of fifty rounds or more. The gun is popular with street gangs across the country because it is small enough to conceal but supports high capacity magazines.

Vice Lords: A prominent national gang with roots in Chicago. The Vice Lords are rivals of the Gangster Disciples. As with the Gangster Disciples, the Vice Lords played a prominent role in the violence that took place amid the high rises.

NOTABLE CHICAGO PUBLIC HOUSING DEVELOPMENTS

ABLA Homes: A group of four separate housing developments (Jane Addams Homes, Robert Brooks Homes, Loomis Courts, and the Grace Abbott Homes) on the West Side that contained 3,500 total units. Resident population peaked at 17,000, though the mix of low rise and high rise structures were designed for a much lower density. Most of the ABLA Homes, including all of the high rises, have been demolished to make way for mixed-income housing and the expansion of University of Illinois–Chicago, University Village, and a mixed-income development called Roosevelt Square.

Altgeld Gardens: Low rise public housing built in 1945 in the Far South Side and made up of two-story row houses spread out over 200 acres. At its peak, Altgeld housed 3,500 residents. Lower density than the high rises, much of Altgeld has remained intact through the Plan for Transformation. Still, concerns about asbestos and high cancer rates linked to industrial pollution have led to numerous reconstruction developments over the past few decades. The CHA has plans to redevelop or demolish up to 600 units through 2013.

Cabrini-Green: Perhaps the most iconic of Chicago's housing developments. A mix of high rise and low rise buildings containing nearly 3,600 units, Cabrini-Green housed more than 15,000 people. Though not the largest of Chicago's housing developments, Cabrini-Green was perhaps the most visible in the city's Near North Side, close to the city's central business district. Cabrini-Green has been the subject of countless news articles, editorials, and opinion pieces and fictional representations in novels, movies, and television shows such as *Good Times*. Almost all of Cabrini-Green has been demolished, with the last of the high rises brought down in 2011.

Dearborn Homes: Located on the South Side, Dearborn Homes was one of the earliest high rise housing developments in Chicago, the first to include elevator buildings, and one of the few high rises to survive the Plan for Transformation. Dearborn Homes consists of 800 units spread out over sixteen acres of mostly six- and nine-story buildings.

Henry Horner Homes: A housing development of high and low rise structures on the Near West Side completed in 1969. At its peak Henry Horner was made up of over 1,600 units. The last high rise in the development was demolished in 2005 and the last low rise in 2008. The Henry Horner Homes are being replaced by mixed-income housing development such as Villages of Westhaven.

Ida B. Wells Homes: One of Chicago's earliest housing developments and the first built specifically for African-American residents, initial construction was completed in 1941. Ida B. Wells was located in the Bronzeville neighborhood not far from Robert Taylor Homes and Stateway Gardens and was adjacent to later housing developments such as the Clarence Darrow Homes. The Ida B. Wells homes were made up of mostly low- and mid-rise buildings, with some high rises, totaling more than 1,600 units. Most demolition was completed by 2003. Currently a mixed-income development called Oakwood Shores.

Robert Taylor Homes: One of the largest, most iconic, and population dense high rise developments in Chicago. Robert Taylor Homes was completed in 1962 and was made up of twenty-eight sixteen-story residential buildings that ran for two miles parallel to the Dan Ryan Expressway. At its peak, Robert Taylor Homes housed more than 27,000 people in over 4,000 units. The homes were cleared of residents by 2005 and demolished in 2007.

Rockwell Gardens: A housing development on the West Side that consisted of over 1,000 units covering sixteen acres. Rockwell Gardens was demolished in 2006, and they've slowly been replaced by 750 housing units, with 264 units reserved for former residents of Rockwell Gardens as part of a mixed-income development called West End.

Stateway Gardens: A high rise development contiguous to Robert Taylor Homes. Together, Stateway Gardens and Robert Taylor Homes made up the largest continuous block of public housing in the world. Like the Robert Taylors, Stateway Gardens was completely demolished by 2007.

III. THE LAST TOWER: THE DECLINE
AND FALL OF PUBLIC HOUSING

In an article originally published in Harper's *in May 2012 and printed below in full, Ben Austen captures the historic scope of the CHA's high rise developments, from the construction of the buildings to their demolition and the plan to replace them.*

Forty years ago, when U.S. cities began abandoning high rise public housing, blasting crews would fill a tower with explosives and in a few monumental booms all would be reduced to rubble and rolling clouds of dust. It was as swift as it was symbolic. Now the demolitions are done by wrecking ball and crane, and the buildings are brought down bit by bit over months. This gradual dismantling seemed especially ill-suited to the felling, in March 2011, of the last remaining tower at Cabrini-Green. Described almost unfailingly as "infamous" or "notorious," this Chicago housing project had come to embody a nightmare vision of public housing, the ungovernable inner-city horrors that many believe arise when too many poor black folk are stacked atop one another in too little space. For the end of Cabrini-Green, I imagined something grandiose and purifying—the dropping of a bomb or, as in *Candyman*, the 1992 slasher film set in Cabrini's dark wasteland, a giant exorcising bonfire. Instead, as I watched, a crane with steel teeth powered up and ripped into a fifth-floor unit, causing several feet of prefabricated façade to crumble like old chalk. Water sprayed from inside the crane's jaws to reduce dust.

The fifteen-story high rise was known by its address, 1230 N. Burling. Already stripped of every window, door, appliance, and cabinet, the monolith was like a giant dresser without drawers. The teeth tore off another hunk of the exterior, revealing the words I NEED MONEY painted in green and gold across an inside wall.

Chicago was once home to the second-largest stock of public housing in the nation, with nearly 43,000 units and a population in the hundreds of thousands. Since the mid-1990s, though, the city has torn down eighty-two public-housing high rises citywide, including Cabrini's twenty-four towers. In 2000, the city named the ongoing purge the Plan for Transformation, a $1.5 billion, ten-year venture that would leave the city with just 15,000 new or renovated public-housing family units, plus an additional 10,000 for senior citizens. Like many other U.S. cities, Chicago wanted to shift from managing public housing to become instead what the Chicago Housing Authority (CHA) called "a facilitator of housing opportunities." The tenants of condemned projects were given government-issued vouchers to rent apartments in the private market, or were moved into rehabbed public housing farther from the city center, or wound up leaving subsidized housing altogether.

The centerpiece of the plan, though, was an effort to replace the former projects with buildings where those paying the market rate for their units and those whose rents were subsidized would live side by side. Since 1995, when the federal government rescinded a rule that required one-to-one replacement of any public-housing units demolished, the U.S. Department of Housing and Urban Development has awarded billions of dollars to cities nationwide to topple housing projects and build in their stead these mixed-income developments.

During his twenty-two years as Chicago's mayor, Richard M. Daley had moved Lake Shore Drive and created Millennium Park, but he believed the Plan for Transformation represented his most sweeping effort to reshape the city's landscape. Daley proclaimed that mixed-income housing would reconnect shunned sections of the city to services and investment, and that these developments would allow poor African-Americans who had lived in social and economic isolation to reap the rewards of a middle-class lifestyle. "I want to rebuild their souls," he said.

In 1995, residential property sales in the two-block radius around Cabrini-Green totaled around $6 million. By the start of the Plan for Transformation, according to an analysis by the Chicago Reporter, annual sales had reached $120 million, and total sales from 2000 to 2005 neared $1 billion. The neighborhood looked like nothing I remembered from my years growing up in Chicago in the seventies and eighties. Down the street from 1230 N. Burling stood a mixed-income development of orange-bricked condos and townhomes called Parkside of Old Town. Its squat buildings were outfitted with balconies and adorned with purple ornamentation and decorative pillars. There was a new school, a new police station, a renovated park, and a shopping center with a Dominick's supermarket and a Starbucks. A Target was expected on the site the last tower would soon vacate. Later, I would warm up two blocks south in @Spot Café, where employees from Groupon's nearby corporate headquarters streamed in to pay full price for lattes and panini.

Today, what seems harder to fathom than the erasure of entire high rise neighborhoods is that they were ever erected in the first place. For years the projects had stood as monuments to a bygone effort to provide affordable housing for the poor and working-class, the reflection of a belief in a deeper social contract. And although that effort had by most accounts failed, the problems represented by the likes of Cabrini-Green persist, and nothing remotely adequate has been built to replace what has been demolished. Chicago has yet to complete the Plan for Transformation's 15,000 family units, and even that number would fall woefully short of need: when the CHA opened its public-housing waiting list in 2010, more than 215,000 families applied. Since only about a third of the units in the mixed-income buildings are reserved for public-housing tenants, hundreds of these developments would have to be built all across Chicago—in a market glutted with foreclosures and short on buyers. In numerous cases the cleared sites that public-housing residents hoped one day to repopulate were still vacant lots. Only 2,100 former public-housing residents, and fewer than 400 from Cabrini-Green, currently live in mixed-income buildings citywide. Most of the others were uprooted and replanted in unfamiliar areas no less uniformly poor and black—though now they had to manage without the support networks and extended family that had surrounded them in public housing.

The night before the wrecking ball got started on 1230 N. Burling, I joined fifty former Cabrini residents who had gathered outside the building. The tenants huddled around a marching band of local teens, the tack-tack-clap of drums and cymbals ringing in the air, the flag-waving majorettes visible from blocks away. Carol Steele, a stout woman in her sixties who was bundled in a large black coat and Cossack hat, asked me, "If you get rid of the high rises, where is there going to be enough land to put all the people?" Steele was the president of the tenant board for the Cabrini row houses, a group of two- and three-story buildings that is the final surviving portion of Cabrini-Green. She said, "You don't get rid of the neighborhood for the crime, unless it's a land grab." A man in his early twenties named Will, who wore a red windbreaker and a red White Sox cap and didn't want to give his last name, had relocated to the city's Far West Side, "where nobody talks to you, and you don't know your neighbors." He nodded toward the condemned tower. "A lot of stuff went on over there," he said, somewhat apologetically. "I know it played a part in it coming down. But it ain't quite as simple as that. It's a place you been your whole life. It's like the memories and families just scrubbed."

Mike McClarin, a 1230 N. Burling tenant of thirty-five years, explained to me that the residents there had been poor but mostly did the right thing, that they wanted no more and no less than other citizens. McClarin went on to say that he had a message for the mayor, for President Obama, for all of America, and if we stepped away from the others at the vigil, he'd recite it to me. "It's not just buildings. It's not a place, it's a feeling," he began in verse, his eyes locked on the vacated high rise, where on top floors windblown ceiling fans spun eerily. "Since we all confess, to be raised in Cabrini was a blessing. . . . Cabrini is down but not out. Have no doubt, Cabrini is God's goods stretched out."

I visited Carol Steele—or Miss Steele, as everyone called her—one afternoon at a Cabrini row house that had been converted into the tenant-board offices. Up until 2010, the CHA's redevelopment plans had earmarked the row houses for preservation. Having passed the viability tests that condemned the neighboring high rises, the row houses were, if not New Urbanist showpieces, passable low rises with stoops, yards, and public gathering spaces. By 2010, the city had reno-vated 146 of the nearly 600 units and begun clearing out the remaining homes, but then suddenly stopped work, allowing blight to spread. White shutters and hanging flowerpots decorated the rehabbed homes, but they were outnumbered by column after column of boarded-up units. Last year, the status of the row houses was changed to "to be determined," and in September the CHA evicted an additional thirty-five families living in un-rehabbed units. Julia Stasch, an architect of the Plan for Transformation under Daley and now the vice president of U.S. programs at the MacArthur Foundation, which has pumped $61 million into the plan, said of this change: "Pockets of poverty on the perimeter of the mixed-income make it that much harder to create new norms, to create new community. It diminishes the potential of what we're trying to achieve." When I asked Steele about the future of the row houses, she said, "We're going to be going to court here in a few minutes."

Steele grew up in the neighborhood soon after the row houses were built. Named for Mother Francesca Cabrini, the first American to be canonized, the row houses were constructed to provide affordable living for World War II veterans who came to this industrial area along the Chicago River in search of factory jobs. An early experiment in integrated housing, Cabrini quickly filled with working-class families. In a book about this era, tellingly called *When Public Housing Was*

Paradise, a white resident recollects, "With an integrated project we were all one big family. . . . It was a real village." "It was the United Nations over here," Steele told me. In 1958, when the Cabrini Extension towers were built on the south side of Division—fifteen cherry-colored high rises known as the "reds," with nearly 2,000 apartments—Steele and her family were among the first tenants. Four years later, the William Green Homes (named for a former president of the American Federation of Labor), eight "whites," among them 1230 N. Burling, went up on the north side of Division, bringing the project's total to 3,600 units, with an official peak population of 15,000.

Unlike the low rises, Chicago's tower-and-garden projects were built primarily for the rush of black migrants from the South. There were 278,000 African-Americans in Chicago in 1940; by 1960, there were 813,000. White aldermen refused to allow public housing construction in their wards, so the new projects were set within the city's existing "black belt." Elizabeth Wood, the progressive head of the CHA, saw an opportunity to replace the area's things with settlements. The projects, she said, would be "bold and comprehensive," forming more than mere "islands in a wilderness of slums." Even the austerity of their modernist designs—now an emblem of the impersonal warehousing of the poor—then heralded all the promise of a refreshingly new age.

But Chicago's projects were underfunded and poorly maintained almost from the start. The ratio of children to adults in these developments was ruinously high, and well intentioned laws regarding maximal allowable income for public housing residents ultimately forced out the most stable rent payers in the population. The projects were further undone by gangs, crack, and a federal drug policy that turned many residents into felons. By 1995, Chicago housing projects made up eleven of the country's fifteen poorest Census tracts.

That Cabrini-Green became a symbol for the worst of these system-wide—and, really, nationwide—failings has much to do with its prime location, just a few minutes' walk from Michigan Avenue's Magnificent Mile to the east and tony Old Town and Lincoln Park to the north. Cabrini residents called their home the Soul Coast on the Gold Coast. Although white Chicagoans were unlikely to pass through black neighborhoods on the South and West Sides, they probably drove or even walked past Cabrini Green. The city's news teams needed only to head into their own backyard to report on project life. The heinous crimes that occurred there—by neither type nor frequency unique to Cabrini—became causes célèbres. Snipers in a Cabrini high rise killed two police officers crossing a nearby baseball field in 1970. After a few deadly months at Cabrini in early 1981 in which eleven residents were murdered and thirty-seven wounded, Mayor Jane Byrne moved into one of the towers to promote new safety initiatives. For her three-week stay, Byrne brought along a massive security detail, and residents say she welded shut one of her apartment's two entrances. In 1992, a stray bullet killed seven-year-old Dantrell Davis as he and his mother walked hand in hand from their Cabrini building to the nearby school. The murder prompted the Chicago *Tribune* editorial page to demand: TEAR DOWN THE CHA HIGH RISES. The housing authority sealed off four of the towers, including the one from which the shot was fired. President Clinton's housing secretary, Henry Cisneros, declared, "The national system of public housing is on trial in Chicago."

As Steele recounted Cabrini's history for me, we were joined by Charles Price, who had managed several of the high rises. Price, a nattily dressed man of late middle age, with a handlebar mustache, a pinstripe suit, and green alligator-skin boots, brought Steele a lunch of Chinese food. While they ate, they talked about the many pop-culture depictions of Cabrini-Green, which, they felt, misrepresented life there. Steele rolled her eyes as she mentioned a 1975 dime novel called *The Horror of Cabrini-Green*, narrated by a sixteen-year-old high rise resident named Bosco who shoots up, fights, rapes, and murders his way through the book. During one brutal stretch of pages, a boy playing atop an elevator is cut in half, a police officer is set on fire, and Bosco and his buddies break into the local church and kill the priest. Steele and Price brought up the movie *Cooley High*, sometimes called the black *American Graffiti*, about students at the vocational school of that name that once stood beside Cabrini, and also *Good Times*, the 1970s sitcom ostensibly set in the "reds" (the buildings are shown in the opening and closing credits, but the project is never named). Thirty years later, on *The Bernie Mac Show*, the comedian protagonist is forced to take in his sister's kids because she's a crackhead from Cabrini. "I should have left y'all at Cabrini-Green," Bernie Mac says of his nieces and nephew. "A bunch of animals. Like you ain't got no home training."

The scary "Cabrini-Green" vision of project life certainly plays some part in the now widespread sentiment that public-housing residents are undeserving of government "handouts." This disdain helped ensure that Chicago's projects really did become unlivable, as the CHA neglected to repair and refill many units when they became vacant (what a successful lawsuit filed against the agency in 1991 called "de facto demolition"), which allowed gangs and squatters and decay to settle in.

Price recalled how on a Jamaican vacation not too long ago an Australian man spotted Price's Bulls cap and declared that he knew just two things about Chicago: Michael Jordan and Cabrini-Green. Price revealed that he actually worked at the housing project, and the Aussie's eyes just about popped out of his head. "Oh my God! Do they walk on all fours there?" Steele cried, mimicking a half-wit's surprise.

Shortly before the demolition of 1230 N. Burling began, the CHA held its rotating monthly board meeting in an old field house that sits in Seward Park, within sight of the condemned tower. I heard about the meeting from a former Cabrini resident, Willie "J.R." Fleming, who told me he had helped organize a protest of the day's proceedings. What Fleming called the Plan for Devastation could be considered a success, he said, if the metric was forcing poor people off prime real estate and moving them to areas where there were even fewer jobs and transportation options, where crime, gang activity, and schools were worse. Between 2000 and 2010 the city's African-American population decreased by 181,000, or 17 percent. Fleming saw the housing fight at Cabrini as part of a much larger battle, and he'd started an organization called the Chicago Anti-Eviction Campaign, which partnered with other groups across the city "to enforce our human right to housing." (Months later, he would train Occupy Chicago protesters to take over foreclosed homes.) Fleming doffed a fedora, revealing long cornrows with a patch of snowy white on top. "This is what activism gets you," he said.

At 8:30 a.m., when the board meeting was scheduled to start, two dozen protesters marched into the gymnasium. Carrying signs, they sang a refrain: *Like a tree that's standing by the water / Black, white, and brown, we shall not be moved.* They were residents and supporters of a housing project called Lathrop Homes, a development in a well-off section of the North Side that was next in line to be demolished. Unlike other condemned projects, however, Lathrop consisted solely of low rise buildings with gardens and front porches; its tenants included not just the very poor but also a range of lower-income earners. The residents didn't want to be forced into the private market or into temporary housing, especially since they doubted they'd be able to return to whatever replaced Lathrop; nor did they agree that market-rate apartments were needed in the redeveloped community, as the surrounding area was already full of market-rate condos. William Wilen, a public-interest lawyer who has represented CHA residents for nearly forty years, summed up for me the pervading distrust in the "transformation" process: "If you were going to plan redevelopment from a tenant point of view, what are the odds you'd say, 'What I want you to do is force me out, even though I may not want to go, then tear my building down, then make me wait fifteen to twenty years for a replacement unit'?"

Despite the Lathrop group's dramatic entrance, the meeting didn't get under way for another two hours, when the CHA board members finally arrived. Lewis Jordan, the CEO of the housing authority, took his position at the center of a table at the front of the gym. There were several procedural matters, and then the floor was opened for public comments. A few people held forth passionately within their allotted two minutes. Carol Steele brought up the future of the row houses, saying it was about time to rehab all the units there. A teenage girl from Lathrop announced that she was being displaced from her community and made to feel like less of a person and young American. Most speakers, however, seized their moment at the microphone with far more dramatic élan, the two-minute mark being merely a prompt to shift rhetorical gears. *My time's up? You should start on time!* A well-heeled Lathrop neighbor yelled at the officials seated a few feet in front of her—"Your mandate is to provide public housing, not to transfer public land to private hands!"—while audience members loudly echoed her cries. Another speaker charged the CHA and its developers with racial racketeering, inside dealing, and refusing to put black folk to work. "Train us!" someone behind him demanded. One man called out the board member to Jordan's left, Myra King, a twenty-year resident of a low rise housing development on the South Side and the chairwoman of the group that oversees all the city's remaining tenant boards. He said few tenants had been given construction jobs or other work as promised in the Plan for Transformation, and yet somehow "your daughter and boyfriend got jobs. So we asking you to step down." King nodded, her face a clenched mask. Jordan and the other commissioners stared ahead, glassy-eyed.

Outsiders to Chicago, a city known for its indomitable political machine, might not expect its operators to subject themselves to such lashings from the rabble. But this restive theater has long been commonplace at public meetings there, even those chaired by Mayor Daley (and now the city's new mayor, Rahm Emanuel). These eruptions may actually be part of the mechanism, a relatively benign outlet for an underclass that often feels acted upon by larger, intractable forces. Later, when I met with Lewis Jordan at the CHA's downtown offices, he shrugged off what he considered the performance piece of the board meeting, assuring me that Lathrop residents already were included in the planning process and that some of the loudest screamers were themselves on the working group determining the development's fate. Jordan, affable and attentive with me, was the fourth CEO under the Plan for Transformation. He had dutifully carried out the marching orders of the plan, tweaking them little even as the housing market in Chicago collapsed. Having grown up in Chicago public housing himself, he described the job he inherited in terms of a relay race. "I can't question how the guy behind me handed off the baton. I just know I got it now and I'm running like hell, and if I get the chance to cross the finish line I will."

For many years the CHA was one of the least efficient and worst-run city agencies, a sinecure for the bottom rung of patronage appointees. In 1995, federal officials took over the city's mismanaged housing system, ceding control only once Chicago began drafting the Plan for Transformation. But in 2003, an independent monitor determined that relocation under the plan had gone too fast and was underfunded. Each of the counselors contracted to find tenants new homes handled more than a hundred cases at a time. Of the thousands of residents relocated from public-housing high rises in the plan's early years, the majority had ended up in areas of highly concentrated black poverty. The CHA has since improved its relocation process, reducing counselors' caseloads, hiring a new social-services provider, and adding job-training opportunities. Even in 2009, though, the CHA had to place a full-page advertisement in the *Chicago Sun-Times* announcing that it didn't know the whereabouts of some of the former residents it was supposed to be tracking, and would the following 3,200 people please get in touch.

I visited Peter Holsten, the developer who built and managed most of the mixed-income housing around Cabrini-Green, at his offices just west of 1230 N. Burling. Photos of Mayor Daley, Barack Obama, and Clint Eastwood as Dirty Harry hung over his desk. In addition to the new developments, Holsten operated rehabbed public housing around the city. "I'm a believer that with strong management you can have any kind of housing," he told me. The architect Holsten hired to design some of the mixed-income housing at Cabrini, Peter Landon, had presented a proposal to the CHA years ago that would have preserved sections of high rise Cabrini-Green. His low-cost rehab, in 1999, of Archer Courts, a then-blighted project of seven-story buildings in Chicago's Chinatown, replaced the chain-link fencing that surrounded the open-air walkways on each floor with frosted glass, creating spaces where residents now look out at the Chicago skyline and at their children in the playground below. The redesign transformed how tenants and neighbors conceived of the building, without displacing a single resident or expensively overhauling the layout of the individual units. It was a public-housing success story. For a Cabrini rehab, Landon looked at the "reds," the towers south of Division, and suggested a more varied, less densely populated "infill" design in which a couple of the buildings would be replaced by gardens and two- or three-story structures. But the mandate from Washington at the time was for wholesale demolition, for putting an end to failed housing projects. "The political will was not there to do it," Holsten said.

Holsten described the building of affordable housing as his life's work. "I want all the kids in my developments to go to college," he said, "and the heads of the households to be employed, and for the cycle of poverty to be broken." One of Holsten's employees is a woman named Niki Clay, who had grown up in a Cabrini high rise and, in 2002, relocated to a Holsten mixed-income apartment. While I was speaking with Holsten, Clay brought him a stack of papers to sign, and he introduced her as a public-housing resident with a surprising work ethic and a promising future. He asked her to tell me what it was like to live beside market-rate families. She definitely felt safe in mixed-income housing, she said, but it was a strangely quiet place. She had to learn to be more reserved. "I'm used to a community where you ring someone's doorbell and say, 'Hi, I'm Niki, I'm your neighbor, I have two children.' That isn't this environment." I asked whether she ever celebrated her kids' birthday parties at home. No, she went to Chuck E. Cheese's. What about a get-together with friends? Nope, neighbors might complain. A family gathering? A cookout? "I don't want any trouble," she explained. "I just stay low-key."

Clay was part of the grand experiment of mixed-income housing. Pressed into the same building, and even the same floor, were conflicting American ideologies of self-sufficiency and social obligation, home ownership and public assistance. (Never mind that the entire HUD budget last year was just over a third of what the federal government loses annually on mortgage-interest tax deductions, the vast majority of which are claimed by the nation's top 20 percent of earners.) To qualify for the few available spots, families needed to be drug free and have good credit, no police record, and no lapsed payment on rent or utilities. The acceptance rate has been incredibly low.

The families that made it in are required by the CHA to work thirty hours a week or enroll in job training or school for a comparable amount of time (the housing authority arranged for city colleges to be free to tenants). Public-housing residents found other rules applying to them but not to the condo owners next door especially onerous: regular home inspections and drug tests; restrictions on owning dogs, barbecuing, gathering in public areas, and hosting guests. Last year the CHA discussed requiring all parents in public housing to submit their children's report cards to the agency. Condo boards tended to set policies that affected every resident, including those who didn't own their units and who had no voice in the condo association. At Westhaven Park, a mixed-income community that replaced the Henry Horner Homes on the city's Near West Side, market-rate families felt threatened when their new neighbors hung out in groups in the lobby, so the condo board simply removed all the furniture from the area. Linda Jones, a former Cabrini resident who was awarded a unit in a mixed-income development, said that the double standards sometimes made her think she was living in a prison. "*They* can get buck wild, but as soon as we get buck wild, they want to send an email blast to the CHA to complain," Jones said. "You can't have two different sets of rules."

Holsten acknowledged that some of the condo owners in his buildings weren't cut out for the eclectic mix of inner-city Chicago. He said it would have been better if some had stayed in the more "homogenous" areas they came from, but now they were underwater on their mortgages and stuck. "To be real honest with you," he added after collecting his thoughts, "I've met some of the owners over there and they're assholes, fucking assholes. I've got owners, and they're great. But there are some assholes. They're prejudiced." Nine years into the social experiment, Linda Jones felt better about the dynamic in her community. "They used to think we were nasty, but we proved them wrong," she said of her white neighbors. Now these neighbors often asked her to regale them with stories about Cabrini-Green in the bad old days.

Deborah Hope lived in the Cabrini row houses for nearly twenty years before moving to a fourth-floor unit in the newly built Parkside of Old Town. Her tidy apartment overlooks the 1230 N. Burling plot. Hope is almond-eyed and smooth-skinned, and on the day I visited her she wore her thick braids tied up in a red, yellow, and black scarf. Her eight-year-old grandson had professed illness that morning and had been allowed to stay home from his charter school. He disappeared into a back room as Hope sat across from me in her living room and launched into a two-hour uninterrupted account of "all the horrible things."

It all began, Hope said, when she was ten years old and her mother moved the family into the projects, to Rockwell Gardens on the West Side. That was the start of the disasters for them, the murders and drugs and alcohol and what they call the felonious society. Her sister was stabbed to death in the elevator, and Hope, at thirteen, took charge of raising her eight-month-old nephew. She pointed to a portrait of her sister on the wall above the dining room table, a pretty girl of eighteen, heavy-lidded, seated in a rattan lounge chair. A photograph on top of Hope's television showed a brother who had died of AIDS. She counted off fifteen family members—including the sister, another brother, an aunt, and two of her own children—who got killed by guns or knives.

Hope later moved into an apartment on the North Side, in an all-white neigh-borhood. Yuppieville, she called it. They paid full rent, $1,500 a month, no assistance, food stamps, or medical card. She was raising four kids at the time, working three jobs, one for American Airlines at O'Hare, another at a skating rink, and the third as a school crossing guard. Hope would come home to drop off money and head right back out, riding the train or a bike. Then her mom died, at the age of fifty-two, Hope's age now. And her brother went to prison, for being a "menace to society," the court said. He got twenty years for selling drugs. Hope said there were weak men and strong men, and her brother was strong. He taught her about drugs, meaning that if he caught her doing any he would fuck her up, break her legs. He kept her scared straight, and even today she didn't smoke or drink any hard stuff. But her landlords found out about her brother and said they didn't want that kind. They raised the rent up so high Hope couldn't manage, and she ended up in eviction court. She was given two weeks to get out and either head into emergency housing or be homeless. She didn't want to go back to the projects, but she had no other choice.

She thought it was 1990 or 1991 when she moved into the row houses, because her son died in '93. He got killed hanging out in the old neighborhood, in Yuppieville. He was standing in the wrong place, someone's drug turf. Hope was in Texas at the time, and when she got back her son was dead.

Back then the row houses were cleaner than the other projects. Bullets used to fly through her window, but at least the streets were swept. Hope talked about all she had to do to raise her children there. She mentored them, volunteered at their schools, sat with them at tutoring, found a way to buy them the right clothes and books. Then they'd walk out the front door and the beatings would start. They'd get busted in the head, punched in the eye. She had BlueCross BlueShield, but it still cost extra to pay for stitches or buy medicine. She couldn't take them to the emergency room if the rent was due, so she sewed them up herself. She learned how to do all that. Her children, the ones still living, were now thirty-four and twenty-five, and she thought the beatings they got at Cabrini permanently messed them up. You can get only so many beatings and keep on saying, "I am somebody," Hope said. She'd like to blame someone for the attacks on her kids, and if she could sue someone, it would be the people who didn't manage the property right, the city that allowed the violence to go on in the street. But the police were down there now, security walked around right when her children were attacked. The city was always in charge of Cabrini, Hope said, but it just didn't enforce anything. She believed the projects were designed for more black people to get murdered, for more black-on-black crime, for AIDS and lupus and heart attacks and diabetes to kill people off. And most of the rest were sent to jail. You could count on your hands and toes how many survived all that drama.

Then the rehab thing started in the row houses, and Hope was moved from her upstairs unit to the ground floor. That's when they started breaking into her house. She couldn't sleep because of all the crackheads and dope fiends outside her window. You never knew when they were going to come in. One day they stole everything they could steal. They even took a couch, walking down the street in the middle of the day and supposedly no one saw it. Plenty of times she cried to the managers, who told her she could move into the projects, meaning the towers. Those buildings were coming down first, so she'd be relocated sooner or have a chance for the new developments. But to her, everything about the projects stunk. So she stuck it out in the row houses. In the projects, she thought she would have been trapped, or forgotten. She was glad the change came, the Plan for Transformation, because how it was before was horrible.

When she was accepted into Parkside of Old Town, she had to undergo a background check and a drug test. At that point she didn't care if they wanted to draw blood. She understood that mixed-income housing couldn't accept everybody. Inspectors visited her new place about six times a year, sometimes without warning. With so many of her people dead, she made the inspectors sit and talk. "Okay, Miss Hope, gotta go," they'd tell her, and she'd say, "Let me tell you something else, honey," with them already halfway out the door. Her son was barred from visiting her there after he was put on probation for a drug charge. If Hope wanted to see her son now, it had to be somewhere other than her apartment. She wasn't about to play games with the new developers.

Recently two families on her floor had large gatherings. One was a wake for a child who died of asthma. The other was a wedding celebration. Both events were crowded and got a little rowdy; beer was drunk and bottles were broken. The next day, Hope said, the public-housing family with the dead child got an eviction notice slipped under its door. The market-rate unit with the newlyweds got nothing. They even made a rule that public-housing people could have parties only between eight in the morning and eight at night. "Where do parties end at 8 P.M.?" Hope wanted to know. When she saw her white neighbors in the hallways or foyer, she always greeted them. "Have a tremendous Thursday! See you on fantastic Friday!" It was how she spoke to everyone. But none of them ever spoke back. Sometimes their dogs would run up to her, Hope said, but that's because animals can always tell when a person is nice.

Before, when she lived in the row houses, she had floods, rats, roaches, undesirable people. She couldn't stand to deal with all that. Where she lived now was better. But it was lonely. She didn't see it as a home. She wanted me to understand that. She was trying to make it feel like a home, but it mostly felt like a hotel.

One afternoon I met Mark Pratt at Jenner Elementary, the Cabrini-Green school rebuilt as part of the Plan for Transformation.

Pratt had worked a variety of jobs at Jenner and was a producer of the documentary *Cabrini Green: Mixing It Up*, about the decades-long redevelopment of the project. Pratt moved to Cabrini-Green as a child, in 1972, and, until March 2012, his mother lived in a row house, surrounded on each side by vacant units, mold spreading in the shared walls. In the 1990s, he served on Cabrini's tenant board, consulting with architects and lawyers about the possible redevelopment plans. But in 1999 he secured a bank loan and moved with his wife and young children to a single-family house on Chicago's South Side. "I tried to do what was right for the people in the buildings and the neighborhood," he told me. "But a rift formed in our leadership. I started seeing promises broken. I just wanted out."

A basketball tournament was taking place in Jenner's new gym, and middle-school teams from around the city had come to the former Cabrini-Green. Pratt hoped the tournament would showcase Jenner, which was still at less than half its capacity. He took me on a tour of what was left of the neighborhood, showing me a picture of Cabrini-Green by what had been cut away from it. One lot was where a cluster of nineteen-story "reds" once stood, including one the Cobra Stones gang had renamed the Palace. Nearby was an empty field that had been the site of the elementary school Pratt attended. Pratt pointed out the ghost town of the boarded-up row houses; a recently rehabbed baseball field where students from Walter Payton magnet high school were practicing; a forest of gleaming high rises leading to the lakefront, thrown up just as the projects were starting to go down; the most elaborate Parkside townhomes, some unsold and unin¬habited; and the more humble mixed-income units from which friends of his had been evicted. "It's all surreal to me," he said.

This winter, a few months after Rahm Emanuel inherited a budget deficit of $636 million, and as the foreclosure crisis showed no signs of ending, the CHA said it would "recalibrate" its twelve-year-old Plan for Transformation. When I spoke with Charles Woodyard, the new head of the CHA, he said he was going to continue to invest in the existing mixed-income communities. He also mentioned the possibilities of a higher proportion of low-income families filling up mixed-income buildings and of public-housing residency coming with a time limit. What the CHA wouldn't be able to do, he assured me, was construct new units for the 40,000 families who made it on the agency's waiting list, to say nothing of the hundreds of thousands of other Chicagoans in need of affordable housing. Money for social safety-net programs nationwide has disappeared. "In America, housing is not a fundamental right," the MacArthur Foundation's Julia Stasch told me.

Mark Pratt and I circled back to Jenner's main entrance, where he warmly greeted a former student and spoke excitedly to a mom about his favorite television show, the biker-gang drama Sons of Anarchy. Just before we parted, I brought up a scene in the Cabrini-Green documentary, filmed in 1999, where he explains his decision to leave the project to his then eleven-year-old son, Trevonte. "Why are you quitting?" Trevonte demands, pleading with his dad to keep the family at Cabrini. Looking back, Pratt thought it silly to believe he should have listened to an eleven-year-old. Yet when they moved, Trevonte ended up traveling to and from school on his own, returning to an empty house. He skipped classes, got involved in gangs and drugs. At Cabrini, Pratt believed, none of that would have happened. Trevonte's grandmother, his uncles and aunts, they would have all watched out for him. His older cousins would have seen him hanging out and ordered him to get his butt back home. "That's community," Pratt said. "I didn't think it through. I thought we were in a nice house, a new community. I made a terrible mistake." He shook his head. "Leaving Cabrini was the worst decision I ever made in my life."

IV. HIGH RISE ARCHITECTURE

The following is an excerpt from Blueprint for Disaster, *D. Bradford Hunt's 2009 ground-breaking exploration of the Chicago Housing Authority, from its creation and policy choices to the Plan for Transformation. Here, Hunt discusses the political, cultural, and economic forces that led to the construction of high rise public housing: fashionable modernist ideas of urban architecture, federal mandates, visionary ambitions of city planners, and a lack of communication with public housing residents.*

For many, public housing's failure in Chicago and elsewhere can be blamed on its architecture, especially the stark elevator buildings built from the late 1940s on. Few defended these designs, even in their early years. Catherine Bauer[1] in 1954 privately called early postwar projects "monstrous barracks blocks," while the *Chicago Defender* in 1957 labeled Chicago's first wave of postwar high rises "prison bins."[2] Criticism mushroomed in later years, especially after St. Louis imploded its 2,700-unit Pruitt-Igoe project in 1972 (after a mere seventeen years of operation). Postmodernists condemned the minimalist, repetitive, concrete towers of Pruitt-Igoe and the Robert Taylor Homes on aesthetic grounds as sterile and unfriendly environments. They heaped criticism on the intellectual forefathers of architectural modernism, including Swiss-born theorist Le Corbusier and his 1932 "Radiant City," which proposed leveling central Paris and replacing it with "Towers in the Park" in an effort to impose rational order on the perceived chaos of that city. Le Corbusier's ideas and the equally influential teachings of Walter Gropius at Harvard's Graduate School of Design elevated high rise forms to futuristic inevitability and greatly influenced a generation of architects. But once applied to real cities, critics maintained that modernism produced rigid buildings in undifferentiated spaces that lacked "human scale." Modernism was supposed to put functionality and efficiency first, but later observers found the buildings dysfunctional when it came to the essential tasks of creating community and policing social

---

[1] Influential housing activist whose work led to the creation of the national public housing program during the 1930s.

[2] Catherine Bauer, "Comments on 'The Search for the Ideal City,'" January 9, 1954, box 4, Warren Vinton Papers, Cornell University; *Chicago Defender*, December 2, 1957.

space. Building residents were unable to "defend" their communities because of such misguided designs.[3]

Some contended that factors beyond the architects' control were the source of public housing's dysfunction, including the program's restrictive limitations, urban racism, and the poverty of residents. Architectural historian Dell Upton asserted that projects had to be Spartan "to reinforce the economic principle that only those who can pay should have pleasant physical surroundings: anything more robs the industrious."[4] But many critics pointed to the design professions for public housing's debacle. As Paul Gapp, the *Chicago Tribune's* architecture critic in the 1980s, declared, "Overall, much of the blame for the Chicago Housing Authority's failures must be attributed to architects. The influence that began with Le Corbusier has persisted, and ugly, oppressive buildings have multiplied."[5]

While Corbusian ideas swayed planners at many housing authorities and while the CHA's high rises did function poorly because of a host of design choices, blaming architects for public housing's failure exaggerates their importance. Such arguments assume that the complex social problems of families and cities could be solved merely by proper design—a variant of the environmental determinism that plagued the logic of progressive slum reformers. Instead, architects operated within planning assumptions and policy restrictions that tightly constrained

---

[3] Newman, Oscar. *Defensible Space.* New York: MacMillan, 1972. On various criticisms of Corbusier and Gropius, see Charles Jencks, *The Language of Post-Modern Architecture* (New York: Rizzoli, 1977); Jane Jacobs, *Death and Life of Great American Cities*; Tom Wolfe, *From Bauhaus to Our House* (New York: Farrar, Straus, and Giroux, 1981); Pearlman, *Inventing American Modernism*; Nicholas Dagen Bloom, "Architects, Architecture, and Planning," *Journal of Planning History*, 7, no. 1 (2008), 72–79.

[4] On Pruitt-Igoe, see Mary C. Comerio, "Pruitt-Igoe and Other Stories," *Journal of Architectural Education* 34, no. 1 (1981): 25–31; Roger Montgomery, "Pruitt-Igoe: Policy Failure or Societal Symptom," in *The Midwest Metropolis: Policy Problems and Prospects for Change*, edited by Barry Checkoway and Carl V. Patton (Urbana: University of Illinois Press, 1985); and Katherine G. Bristol, "The Pruitt-Igoe Myth,"*Journal of Architectural Education* 44, no. 3 (1991): 163–71. All three authors make the crucial point that architecture is less important than other factors in public housing's downfall, and their work is influential to this chapter. See also Lee Rainwater, *Behind Ghetto Walls: Black Life in a Federal Slum* (Chicago: Aldine, 1970). Dell Upton, *Architecture in the United States* (New York: Oxford University Press, 1998), 239; and Sam Davis, *The Architecture of Affordable Housing* (Berkeley and Los Angeles: University of California Press, 1995), 11–13.

[5] *Chicago Tribune*, April 14, 1982.

design possibilities. As we've seen, progressive planners wanted large-scale projects, and USHA regulations limited room sizes to minimal levels. The continued cost obsessions of Washington administrators—more than any other factor—forced the CHA to build upward. Using the market-failure logic that had justified public housing in the 1930s, administrators in the 1950s believed that public housing projects had to be less expensive to build than private ones. Otherwise, justification for the program—and congressional support—would vanish. Federal officials operated in a fragile political environment in the 1950s, and while blatant McCarthyism played only a small role, public housing was continually attacked on ideological grounds. Thus, bureaucratic anxieties and cost concerns, far more than modernist architecture, led to high rise construction in large cities, including Chicago.

The CHA began "experimenting," in the words of Elizabeth Wood,[6] with high rise buildings soon after the war. In 1945, the CHA proposed multistory buildings for its first postwar project, Dearborn Homes, located on a black belt slum site recommended by neighborhood groups and the area's African-American state senator. A distinct choice was available for the Dearborn design: the CHA could use three-story walk-ups, as at the earlier Ida B. Wells Homes, or it could venture into new territory and build six-story elevator buildings with roughly the same number of apartments and cost per unit. Elizabeth Wood defended the latter choice by claiming that elevator structures "achieve a more attractive pattern for the use of the land" and "gives us wide-open spaces, larger playgrounds, and a general effect of a park that will not be possible if the land were developed as three-story walk-ups."[7] Following the ideas of Corbusier and Gropius, high rises offered the best of both worlds—ordered housing and more park space—thereby rationalizing the urban environment.

Corbusian logic, however, was only one element of the CHA's thinking; practical concerns influenced choices. Issues of cost weighed heavily on planners,

---

[6] The first executive director of the CHA, a position Wood held from 1937 to 1954.

[7] Elizabeth Wood to alderman George D. Kells, September 21, 1945, City Council folder, CHA Subject files; Wood to PHA administrator Orvil Olmsted, October 14, 1946, CHA Development files, IL 2-9; People's Welfare Organization of Chicago, *History of Dearborn Homes*, 1950, CHM.

and the CHA carefully studied the experience of the New York City Housing Authority, which had begun rebuilding the Lower East Side of Manhattan in the late 1930s with six- and eleven-story buildings. The CHA considered New York's high density designs to be the "most economical" at keeping construction costs low. Although it seemed counterintuitive, the CHA recognized that high rise buildings were less costly on a per-apartment basis than walk-ups, with savings in mechanical systems and other design features outweighing additional costs related to foundations and elevators.[8] Further, elevator buildings offered the flexibility of increasing the number of apartments at a future date without sacrificing green space. When additional funds became available in 1948, for example, the CHA added three extra floors to half of the buildings at Dearborn, creating a density one-third greater than the Chicago Plan Commission's guidelines. Wood dismissed concerns, saying the increased density would "change the picture of the future community little . . . and the present serious overcrowding in the Negro areas indicates the need for an augmented supply of housing for Negroes."[9] This same urgency to address the housing shortage also pressured planners of the 1948 relocation projects. The CHA proposed a "Tower in the Park" plan for the ill-fated McKinley Park site and slated mid-rise buildings for seven of its nine relocation sites, believing higher-density elevator buildings could address the housing shortage with little apparent damage to urban space.

To design the CHA's earliest high rises, Elizabeth Wood convinced the CHA board to hire prominent and rising Chicago architectural firms with modernist bents, including Skidmore, Owings, and Merrill and Harry Weese. She hoped their reputation and abilities could assuage the nervousness of many regarding the high rise form. Skidmore produced designs that strongly resembled Mies van der Rohe's 1948 Promontory Point apartment building in Hyde Park, with exposed structural elements, concrete frames, and minimal ornamentation. Promontory Point was designed under strict cost restraints by its developer, and its relatively

---

[8] See Elizabeth Wood to Loebl and Schlossman, February 16, 1946, and Wood to Orvil Olmsted, October 14, 1946, both in CHA Development files, IL 2-9; Robert Taylor to alderman William J. Lancaster, October 28, 1948, CHA Subject files. On St. Louis, see Alexander von Hoffman, "Why They Built Pruitt-Igoe," in *From Tenements to Taylor Homes*, edited by John F. Bauman, Roger Biles, and Kristin Szylvian (University Park: Pennsylvania State University Press, 2000), 189–91.

[9] CHA, "Development Program for IL 2-9," CHA Development files.

low cost made it attractive as a prototype for numerous CHA projects, including Ogden Courts and later the Cabrini Extension.[10]

Not until January 1952 did high rise design in public housing receive a more thorough discussion, when *Architectural Forum* devoted eighteen pages to the subject. The editors featured Elizabeth Wood as the only voice favoring low rise over high rise apartments. In a reversal of her earlier thinking, Wood acknowledged that her "experiment" with high rises in Chicago was a mistake, and she argued for the superiority of low rise designs on gendered grounds. She began with the premise that "the design of a dwelling unit must make possible the fulfillment of other than mere shelter needs." A child, she explained, has a "need for nearness to his mother." These assumptions led Wood to call the row house "simple and natural. The indoor-outdoor activity takes place close to where the mother is at work. The child can keep in touch with her. She can hear him if he cries or gets into a fight." By contrast, in high rises the playgrounds are awfully mingled at some distance, vertical as well as horizontal, from the family supper table," resulting in "much less parent-child play." Further, she had changed her views on the green space created by Corbusian layouts and was no longer convinced of their utility:

> It is argued that by piling families up in the air you have much more ground available "for use." . . . But it is also interesting that when architects and planners lay out a low coverage high rise project, they almost immediately will lay out a large and beautiful mall and other fenced and grassed areas, all of which will promptly be labeled with "keep off the grass signs." . . . No matter how many uses the landscaper and planner allot to the usable areas, they are essentially less personal, less capable of creative use by man and child, than are row-house areas.

Wood added that she had attempted to recreate the benefits of low rises by using gallery designs but admitted they were a "poor substitute" for low rise grounds.[11]

---

[10] Phyllis Lambert, "Mies Immersion," in Lambert et al., *Mies in America*, 356–57; Eric Mumford, "More than Mies: Architecture of Chicago Multifamily Housing, 1935–1965," in Waldheim and Ray, *Chicago Architecture*, 85.

[11] Elizabeth Wood, "The Case for the Low Apartment," *Architectural Forum*, January 1952, 02.

The modernist *Architectural Forum* framed the debate between low and high designs as one between the "sociologists," represented by Wood, and the "architects," represented by Douglas Haskell, the journal's editor. Haskell used his editorial power to shape the issue to his liking. Whereas Wood began with gendered observations of family living patterns and the desires of tenants, Haskell presented the architect as master of spatial realities to which tenants must conform. Working from the premise that "increased density of population and building" was an urban fact, Haskell declared the preference of tenants was "unimportant" and that "a public not used to elevators or play corridors must learn to use them, just as new car owners must be taught to drive." Haskell criticized "idealists" like Wood who cherished private play space, and he championed Corbusian thought. Disparaging a New Orleans walk-up project for producing only "useless shreds and patches" of grass, he concluded that high rises "yielded acres [of grass] in big sweeps." While conceding Wood's point that these open spaces needed to be available for play, he reasoned that competent management could make "imagined perils disappear" and "new advantages learned until they become natural." To prove the point that with a little "imagination" high rise forms could be perfectly functional—and to undercut Wood's argument—Haskell then devoted three pages to the CHA's relocation projects, using them against her by deeming them a success.[12]

Next to Haskell's vision of architects as practical problem solvers in the "real" world of high density and high urban costs, Wood's "idealist" and gender-based defense of the low apartment appeared quaint and weak. The *Architectural Forum* series exasperated Catherine Bauer, and she belatedly entered the fray in opposition to her "old friend" Haskell in the May 1952 issue of *Progressive Architecture,* a competing publication. Bauer raged against the high rise form and the architects who pushed "Le Corbusierism" and "showy structures and slick technocratic 'solutions'" to urban problems. She objected to high rises on a host of grounds, including Elizabeth Wood's child-rearing concerns as well as their high density.

But her main objection was that families with children did not want to live in such buildings. "When every survey ever made in the United States to my knowledge, from the crudest market study to the most refined piece of intensive field research, seems to indicate an overwhelming preference for ground-level

---

[12] Douglas Haskell, "The Case for the High Apartment," *Architectural Forum,* January 1952, 103–106.

living, this fact can hardly be tossed aside with contempt," she wrote in a slap at Haskell. Retreating from some of her collectivist impulses of the 1930s, Bauer maintained that high rises were rigid and "impersonal"; they failed to allow the necessary privacy and personal freedoms that families craved, often in the form of an enclosed backyard.

High rises could work for certain groups, namely, the rich, the old, or single individuals, but they were "least suitable" for those on "whom we are now foisting it wholesale: families with very low incomes, from slums, mostly with children." As an alternative, she returned to her theme from the 1930s that slum clearance should be abandoned for the time being and low-density vacant land projects should be developed instead.[13]

But Bauer's ideas met a cold reception from the architects most involved in designing public housing. In a speech to public housers shortly after the appearance of Bauer's article in May 1952, Minoru Yamasaki, a leading modernist and the architect of St. Louis's Pruitt-Igoe project (and later of the World Trade Center), disparaged her views and offered a blend of slum reformer and Corbusian logic in response. Yamaski asked, "How can anyone say—as one eminent low riser did recently—that we should put off building in slum areas until a better time? Now is the time, today, not tomorrow; for every year until we have eliminated all the slum areas from all our cities. Slums are the cancers of our cities, and the only time to stop a cancer is now." He renounced vacant land construction, stating that "building large projects on the outskirts further overextends our already inadequate transportation systems and by-passes our major problem—that of eliminating slums." Yamasaki insisted that high rises were the future of the city and defended his designs for Pruitt-Igoe, regretting only that Egan's Public Housing Administration[14] had required a density of fifty-five units per acre, "almost double the thirty-five per acre which we were trying to attain and which we believed desirable."[15]

---

[13] Catherine Bauer, "Clients for Housing: The Low-Income Tenant—Does He Want Supertenements?" *Progressive Architecture*, May 1952, 61–64.

[14] The Public Housing Administration was the federal agency in charge of the public housing program and became part of the Department of Housing and Urban Development (HUD) in 1965.

[15] "Address made by Minoru Yamasaki in Pittsburgh at the MARC of NAHO Conference on Friday, May 23, 1952," outgoing correspondence, box 4, Bauer Papers.

The PHA's regulations also forced the CHA back to the drawing board on its federally funded projects. In a compromise between cost and design, Wood had hoped to build a mix of two-story row houses, mid-rise buildings, and high rise buildings on the CHA's 1950 slum sites, but the new rules on density and total development cost meant scrapping the row houses and using only elevator buildings. Federal officials then compelled multiple redesigns of several projects. The Cabrini Extension rose from a collection of seven-, nine-, and sixteen-story buildings to its completed form of seven-, ten-, and nineteen-story structures. Density increased only slightly, from fifty-one units per acre to fifty-four, but cost savings were found by deleting one entire building while adding floors to the remaining buildings at a relatively low marginal cost, driving down the all-important total development cost per unit to acceptable levels. The CHA's original plans for the Cabrini Extension easily met the per-room construction cost limits in law; row houses and high rise apartments both cost close to $2,000 per room to build, well within the statutory limit of $2,500. But clearance expenses added another $2,000 to $3,000 per unit, depending on density, pushing plans beyond arbitrary total development cost guidelines. The easiest way to reduce total development cost, then, was to build higher. Years later, Elizabeth Wood recalled, "We hated the federal agency with a passion since it was so absolutely inflexible in every aspect of design."[16]

However, provisions in the 1949 Housing Act championed by Catherine Bauer offered a way around the high cost of slum land. Federal Title I urban redevelopment funds could be used to purchase and clear land that could then be sold to public housing authorities at their write-down cost on the same terms that might go to private builders. This, in essence, would dramatically lower the cost of slum land to public housing authorities and allow for lower-density row

---

[16] CHA, Official Minutes, April 13, 1953; CHA, "Addendum no. IV to Development Program for Project IL 2-20," CHA Development files, IL 2-20. The PHA forced similar changes in other cities, including Buffalo in 1952 and Baltimore in 1953. See Gilbert Rodier to Charles Slusser, December 18, 1953, and Rodier to John Taylor Egan, January 7, 1953, box 5, "Correspondence of the Commissioner of Public Housing," RG 196; Wood, "Ideals and Realities in Subsidized Housing since 1934," 67. Data for "Construction Cost per Room" and "Total Development Cost per Unit" from CHA, Actual Development Cost Statement, a report to the Public Housing Administration found in CHA Development files for individual projects.

houses and walk-up projects. Philadelphia was the first city to use Title I money to support its public housing program, but few cities followed its lead. Warren Vinton[17] pushed the Urban Redevelopment Administration and the PHA to cooperate more, but incentives in the 1949 law, unforeseen and left uncorrected, worked against coordination. Slum clearance using Title I funds required a direct cash contribution from cities (equal to one-third the federal contribution). If Title I slum clearance was used for private projects, this cash contribution would be recaptured in the form of property taxes on the new privately owned structures. But if Title I money was devoted to public housing, then cities would still have to layout a direct cash contribution and would recapture only a modest PILOT payment. Moreover, the public housing program had long absorbed its own slum clearance costs under Vinton's generous 1937 formula with no cash subsidy from the city (only tax exemption). Given the choice of spending its cash for urban redevelopment for public or private ends, cities rationally chose to devote urban redevelopment money exclusively to private projects. This meant the public housing program had to absorb slum clearance costs within its total development expenses, thereby forcing higher densities and hence high rise buildings.

By 1954, the CHA had sufficient experience to confirm Wood and Bauer's thinking that high rises were detrimental for public housing. Families with children preferred row houses, as the two women understood, and, overshadowing everything, the CHA's early high rises had become managerial headaches. Trash chutes, heating plants, and elevator systems proved difficult to maintain. Even more than the preferences of families, ballooning social disorder, serious security concerns, and escalating maintenance costs at the new high rises drove the CHA to seek ways to build low rise, walk-up buildings within acceptable costs.

---

[17] Warren Vinton was a longtime senior federal housing administrator from 1938–1957.

V. WHERE ARE THEY NOW?

In 1995, HUD took control of the CHA and condemned over 14,000 of more than 36,000 existing CHA housing units. By 2000, many high rise complexes were only half occupied due to poor living conditions. The Plan for Transformation was originally billed as a decade-long realignment of Chicago public housing set to begin in 2000 and end in 2010, with the goal of using federal funding to construct 25,000 new or refurbished housing units for the 25,000 CHA households in good standing with the administration.

In April of 2011, shortly after the tenth anniversary of the Plan for Transformation, the CHA released a report detailing the progress it had made through the original length of the plan, focusing on the movement of former public housing residents who had been displaced to prepare for demolition of old units. Though virtually all of the high rises had been torn down by 2010, only 80 percent of the planned replacement housing had been constructed (as of 2013, that number is not yet 90 percent).

The CHA's report, with excerpts reprinted here, highlights some of the setbacks that the plan has faced, particularly after the housing crash of 2008. Of the 16,500 non-senior households that were granted the right to choose between private housing vouchers or return to newly constructed mixed-income housing units, only 9,300 (56 percent) remained on the CHA's books by the end of 2010. The rest had died, been evicted, lost contact with the CHA, found unsubsidized private housing, or were still waiting for construction on new units to be completed.

BACKGROUND

In 1999, when Mayor Richard M. Daley agreed that the city would take back control of CHA from the U. S. Department of Housing and Urban Development (HUD), properties were in disrepair, with many residents living in substandard conditions. Moreover, CHA developments constituted 11 out of 15 of the nation's poorest census tracts. Of the more than 38,000 units owned by CHA, less than 25,000 were habitable and HUD had condemned 14,000 outright. While HUD had originally called for the simple demolition of the housing and the "vouchering-out" of all residents, Mayor Daley insisted instead that the housing be either repaired or rebuilt—this time as mixed-income developments that would anchor communities and end the isolation of residents in definable pockets of poverty.

The Plan for Transformation formally began on February 6, 2000 when

CHA and HUD signed an agreement (known as the Moving to Work (MTW) Agreement) that committed HUD to providing:

- $1.5 billion in capital funding, subject to congressional appropriation each year, for the restoration or replacement of 25,000 units for public housing eligible residents;
- A Housing Choice Voucher (formerly Section 8 voucher) for every unit demolished and not funded by HUD for replacement; and Greater flexibility in use of capital funds and greater regulatory flexibility.

In return, CHA would:

- Demolish 14,000 CHA public housing units which did not satisfy HUD's 202 Viability Rule requirement;
- Provide all new housing in mixed income communities; and
- Provide services to the existing lease-compliant households on October 1, 1999 (known as original 10/1/99 residents) to help them relocate and strive for self-sufficiency.

THE POPULATION

This report is based on CHA's comprehensive tracking data on the status of all original 10/1/99 residents:

At the beginning of the Plan, there were approximately 25,000 households in good standing who lived in CHA housing. Of those, nearly 8,300 were residents of senior housing and approximately 16,500 resided in family or scattered-site developments. Twenty-eight percent (28 percent) of the 8,300 seniors still live in CHA housing or with a Housing Choice Voucher (CHA voucher) in the private market, and the vast majority of these reside in the properties where they lived in 1999. The balance of the original seniors have either died or moved away without CHA subsidy.

On the other hand, among the original 16,500 households in family and scattered-site housing (10/1/99 family housing residents), there has been great movement over space and time. This report provides an in-depth look at those families who in 1999 lived in one of the developments that had been slated for demolition or rehabilitation and who, since that time, have moved to another development or into the private market using a CHA voucher. It is important to note that while CHA aims to be accurate and inclusive with this report, residents of CHA housing and those using vouchers move often and the information captured in this report is subject to constant change.

As part of the Plan for Transformation, all original 10/1/99 residents are guaranteed a choice of permanent housing. Each household that was (and remains) lease-compliant has the right to choose where they wish to live on a permanent basis, be that in a new or rehabilitated public housing unit or in the broader community using a CHA voucher. In fact, these 10/1/99 residents are guaranteed first choice of any rehabilitated or redeveloped property and their claims take precedence over any person on the general wait list. That said, 10/1/99 residents are obligated to make that choice only once and when they do, their "right of return" is satisfied under the law.

WHERE ARE ORIGINAL RESIDENTS NOW?

As of the end of 2010, excluding seniors whose buildings were rehabbed without the need for tenants to move outside of their developments, of the original 10/1/99 family housing residents granted a right of return, more than 9,300 remain in CHA's system. The reasons for the decrease in number are varied. Seven percent (7 percent or 1,240) of residents are currently living in the private market without CHA subsidy but remain in contact with CHA, having expressed a desire to return to CHA housing. Another 8 percent (1,307) are living in the private market without subsidy who left CHA housing after their Right of Return was satisfied. Seven percent (7 percent or 1,221) of residents have died, 9 percent (1,488) have been evicted and 13 percent (2,202) have not responded to CHA outreach and thus their location is unknown. Residents who are non-responsive have an option for reinstatement should they ever contact CHA. Looking at the more than 9,300 original family housing residents who still remain in the system, either by renting in a CHA development or renting through CHA's voucher program, we know that 36 percent or 3,395 of these residents currently live in traditional family developments, 20 percent or 1,896 live in the newly created mixed-income communities, and 44 percent or 4,097 are renting in the private market using a CHA voucher.

By tracking the addresses of those current 4,097 original family housing residents relocating with CHA vouchers (known as relocatees), we also know that the vast majority reside in Chicago, with only 60 residents currently using a CHA voucher in the suburbs and only 11 residents currently using a CHA voucher outside of Illinois. While in the first years of the Plan residents who left developments clustered nearby, today former 10/1/99 family housing relocatees who now have CHA vouchers reside in 71 of the city's 77 neighborhoods.

NEAR NORTH REDEVELOPMENT AREA (FORMERLY CABRINI-GREEN)
WHERE ARE THEY NOW?

At the start of the Plan for Transformation, there were 2,625 public housing units at Cabrini-Green, of which 1,282 (49 percent) were occupied. Due to updates since 1999, 1,770 Cabrini-Green families were granted a Right of Return. Of those, 10 percent (171) of residents have moved to the private market without CHA subsidy but remain in contact with CHA and have yet to make their final housing choice. Another 4 percent (66) are living in the private market without subsidy and already made their final housing choice, seven percent (129) have died, 10 percent (172) have been evicted and 10 percent (179) have not responded to CHA outreach and thus their location is unknown. Residents who are non-responsive have an option for reinstatement should they ever contact CHA.

At the end of 2010, 1,059 original Cabrini-Green households were still living in CHA housing or renting in the private market with a CHA voucher. Of those remaining households, 35 percent (372) currently live in mixed-income housing, 20 percent (215) live in other public housing, and 45 percent (472) are living in the private market with a voucher. Four hundred forty-four (444) original families are currently living in Frances Cabrini Extension North mixed-income replacement housing or Frances Cabrini Row-houses.

The largest concentration of former Cabrini-Green households is in the Near North Side community area, indicating that many residents still live near their original development. Today, former Cabrini-Green residents reside in 58 community areas throughout Chicago.

BROOKS HOMES AND ROOSEVELT SQUARE (FORMERLY ABLA HOMES)
WHERE ARE THEY NOW?

At the start of the Plan for Transformation, there were 3,235 public housing units at ABLA, of which only 1,079 (33 percent) were occupied. Due to updates since 1999, 1,153 ABLA families were granted a Right of Return. Of those, 5 percent

(58) of residents have moved to the private market without CHA subsidy but remain in contact with CHA and have yet to make their final housing choice. Another 6 percent (64) are living in the private market without subsidy and already made their final housing choice. Twelve percent (12 percent or 133) have died, 11 percent (125) have been evicted and 10 percent (113) have not responded to CHA outreach and thus their location is unknown. Residents who are non-responsive have an option for reinstatement should they ever contact CHA.

At the end of 2010, 660 original ABLA households were still living in CHA housing or renting in the private market with a CHA voucher. Of those remaining households, 25 percent (or 166) are currently living in mixed-income housing, 50 percent (or 328) live in other public housing, and 25 percent (or 166) are living in the private market with a voucher. Four hundred thirty-seven (437) original ABLA residents are currently living at Brooks Homes or in the Roosevelt Square mixed-income community.

The largest concentration of former ABLA households by far is in the Near West Side community area, indicating that many residents still live near their original development. Today, former ABLA residents reside in 44 community areas throughout Chicago.

VILLAGES OF WESTHAVEN AND WESTHAVEN PARK
(FORMERLY HENRY HORNER HOMES)
WHERE ARE THEY NOW?

At the start of the Plan for Transformation, there were 1,743 public housing units at Horner, of which 682 (39 percent) were occupied. Due to updates since 1999, 699 Horner families were granted a Right of Return. Of those, 3 percent (18) of residents have moved to the private market without CHA subsidy but remain in contact with CHA and have yet to make their final housing choice. Another 8 percent (56) are living in the private market without subsidy and already made their final housing choice. Five percent (32) have died, 11 percent (76) have been evicted, and 9 percent (63) have not responded to CHA outreach and thus their location is unknown. Residents who are non-responsive have an option for reinstatement should they ever contact CHA.

At the end of 2010, 454 former Horner households were still living in CHA housing or renting in the private market with a CHA voucher. Of those remaining households, 87 percent (394) are currently living in mixed-income housing, 1 percent (6) live in other public housing, and 12 percent (54) are living in the private market with a voucher. Three hundred eighty-eight (388) 10/1/99 Horner families are currently living at Villages of Westhaven or Westhaven Park. By far the largest concentration of former 10/1/99 Horner households is in the Near West Side community area, indicating that the majority still live at or near their original development. Today, former Henry Horner residents reside in 25 community areas throughout Chicago.

OAKWOOD SHORES (FORMERLY MADDEN PARK, IDA B. WELLS
AND WELLS EXTENSION, AND CLARENCE DARROW HOMES)
WHERE ARE THEY NOW?

At the start of the Plan forTransformation, 2,891 public housing units remained at Wells and Wells Extension, Clarence Darrow, and Madden Park Homes, of which 1,426 (49 percent) were occupied. Due to updates since 1999, 1,621 original families from these sites were granted a Right of Return. Of those, 8 percent (128) of residents have moved to the private market without CHA subsidy but remain in contact with CHA and have yet to make their final housing choice. Another 5 percent (75) are living in the private market without subsidy and already made their final housing choice. Eleven percent (174) have died, 8 percent (129) have been evicted and 16 percent (266) have not responded to CHA outreach and thus their location is unknown. Residents who are non-responsive have an option for reinstatement should they ever contact CHA.

At the end of 2010, 849 original Madden/Wells/Darrow households were still living in CHA housing or renting in the private market with a CHA voucher. Of those remaining households, 24 percent (205) are living in mixed-income housing, 15 percent (126) live in other public housing, and 61 percent (518) live in the private market with a voucher. One hundred fifty-four (154) original Madden/Wells/Darrow families are currently living at the Oakwood Shores mixed-income community.

The largest concentrations of former Madden/Wells/Darrow households are in communities in proximity to their original development, including Douglas, Oakland, and Grand Boulevard. Today, former Madden/Wells/Darrow residents reside in 50 community areas throughout Chicago.

WEST END (FORMERLY ROCKWELL GARDENS)
WHERE ARE THEY NOW?

At the start of the Plan for Transformation, 1,136 public housing units remained at Rockwell Gardens, of which 439 (39 percent) were occupied. Due to updates since 1999, 519 families from Rockwell Gardens were granted a Right of Return. Of those, 10 percent (50) of residents have moved to the private market without CHA subsidy but remain in contact with CHA and have yet to make their final housing choice. Another 4 percent (23) are living in the private market without subsidy and already made their final housing choice. Eight percent (40) have died, 9 percent (45) have been evicted, and 15 percent (79) have not responded to CHA outreach and thus their location is unknown. Residents who are non-responsive have an option for reinstatement should they ever contact CHA.

At the end of 2010, 282 former Rockwell residents were still living in CHA housing or renting in the private market with a CHA voucher. Of those remaining households, 25 percent (72) currently live in mixed-income housing, 10 percent (28) live in other public housing, and 65 percent (182) live in the private market with a voucher. Forty-three (43) original Rockwell families are currently living at Archer Courts, One South Leavitt, or West End mixed-income replacement sites.

The largest concentrations of former Rockwell households are in communities in proximity to Rockwell Gardens on the west side of Chicago. Today, former Rockwell residents reside in 40 community areas throughout Chicago.

THE PERSHING AND PARK BOULEVARD (FORMERLY STATEWAY GARDENS)
WHERE ARE THEY NOW?

At the start of the Plan for Transformation, there were 1,644 units at Stateway Gardens, of which 689 (42 percent) were occupied. Due to updates since 1999, 696 families from the development were granted a Right of Return. Of those, 8 percent (55) of residents have moved to the private market without CHA subsidy but remain in contact with CHA and have yet to make their final housing choice. Another 9 percent (60) are living in the private market without subsidy and already made their final housing choice. Seven percent (46) have died, 8 percent (55) have been evicted and 13 percent (88) have not responded to CHA outreach and thus their location is unknown. Residents who are non-responsive have an option for reinstatement should they ever contact CHA.

At the end of 2010, 392 former Stateway residents were still living in CHA housing or renting in the private market with a CHA voucher. Of those remaining households, 18 percent (71) currently live in mixed-income housing, 7 percent (29) live in other public housing, and 75 percent (292) live in the private market with a voucher. Sixty (60) families are currently living at the Pershing or Park Boulevard mixed-income replacement sites.

The largest concentration of former Stateway households are in Douglas, where Stateway Gardens was formerly located, and in nearby communities. Today, former Stateway residents reside in 41 community areas throughout Chicago.

LEGENDS SOUTH (FORMERLY ROBERT TAYLOR HOMES)
WHERE ARE THEY NOW?

At the start of the Plan for Transformation, 3,784 public housing units remained at Taylor Homes, of which 1,559 (41 percent) were occupied. Due to updates since 1999, 1,564 families from Taylor Homes were granted a Right of Return. Of those, 8 percent (121) as residents have moved to the private market without CHA subsidy but remain in contact with CHA and have yet to make their final housing choice. Another 7 percent (103) are living in the private market without subsidy and already made their final housing choice. Six percent (88) have died, 6 percent (92) have been evicted and 12 percent (189) have not responded to CHA outreach and thus their location is unknown. Residents who are non-responsive have an option for reinstatement should they ever contact CHA.

At the end of 2010, 960 former Taylor residents were still living in CHA housing or renting in the private market with a CHA voucher. Of those remaining households, 15 percent (140) are currently living in mixed-income housing, 7 percent (69) live in other public housing, and 78 percent (751) live in the private market with a voucher. One hundred twenty-two (122) original Taylor residents are currently living at Langston, Quincy or Legends South (Coleman Place, Hansberry Square, Mahalia Place, and Savoy Square) mixed-income replacement sites.

The largest concentration of former Robert Taylor households are in Douglas, where Robert Taylor Homes was formerly located, and in nearby communities throughout the near and far south sides. Today, former Robert Taylor families reside in 49 community areas throughout Chicago.

254254254

254254

VI. PLAN FOR TRANSFORMATION
AFTER TEN YEARS

In 2010, with a grant from the Chicago-based John D. and Catherine T. MacArthur Foundation, MIT professor Lawrence J. Vale and research fellow Erin Graves released a report on progress made by the Plan for Transformation over its first decade. Their wide-ranging study synthesized findings of researchers who had followed the plan from its inception. After its release, Vale said of the report, "Overall, we see a mixed picture. Some research shows that for one set of residents, the plan has truly transformed their lives . . . But for another set of residents, especially those remaining in non-rehabbed housing, there has been an increase in crime and these residents show higher levels of stress. And many residents have lost vital social networks due to relocation." In April 2013, the University of Chicago Press published Vale's book, Purging the Poorest: Public Housing and the Design Politics of Twice-Cleared Communities *about the dismantling of public housing in Chicago and Atlanta.*

The following question and answers are excerpted from section three of the report, "Consensus Findings, Unresolved Debates, and New Research Directions," that addresses three broad topic categories: the process of the plan itself, outcomes for residents, and outcomes for neighborhoods. To access the full report, visit dusp.mit.edu/faculty/lawrence-vale.

1. PROCESS

How many 10/1/1999 residents will benefit from moves into mixed-income developments?

Some scholars question ultimately just how many CHA leaseholders will live in mixed-income housing. The Plan was presented to the public as an initiative that involves, "demolishing the old projects and replacing them with fewer units that are higher quality and serve a wider mix of income levels." Given this goal, some scholars question the number of original residents who will live in mixed-income developments, and, more generally, question the relative paucity of hard units serving those with extremely low incomes. According to Boston, just 1,035 of the 10/1/1999 households lived in the 2,472 subsidized units in the CHA's new mixed-income housing developments as of 2007. While construction of mixed-income housing is only about one-third complete, the low return rate as calculated by Boston suggests that few of the 10/1/1999 residents will ultimately live in mixed-income developments, implying that most of those who do gain places in the 'public housing eligible' portion of the new mixed-income communities will not be 10/1/1999 families with a Right of Return. However, 2010 data from the CHA indicates that 2,198 households (including 35 seniors) eligible for a right of return currently occupy a unit in a mixed income development, out of a total 2,977 completed units (CHA, personal communication, May 25, 2010). Thus, given the discrepancy between Boston's analysis of CHA data and the data supplied by the CHA directly for this report, it remains an open question how many original residents have benefitted from mixed-income redevelopment. According to Joseph (2008), developers are having difficulty finding 10/1/1999 residents to move into the available units in mixed-income developments, sometimes because such residents elected to become permanent voucher holders or sometimes because the tenant selection criteria in the new mixed-income developments is a major deterrent, "even to those who are currently eligible." Alexander (2009) adds that the implementation of the mixed income housing Initiative "may preclude large numbers of original public housing residents from returning to the new developments." It is worth reiterating that the Plan intended that only 7,697 of the 25,000 public housing units planned for revitalization would be located in mixed-income housing developments. That relatively few 10/1/1999 residents will end up in the new mixed-income communities is therefore not a failure of the plan; it is, rather, a premise of the Plan. Still, it remains an open question how many 10/1/1999 residents will ultimately occupy those units.[1]

---

[1] CHA figures for the return of public housing residents to mixed-income developments are within the range of HOPE VI returns nationwide. As of September 30, 2008, HUD figures showed that 24 percent of "the total households relocated" had returned to HOPE VI sites, though this figure may overstate the return rate since it doesn't take account of those households lost to the public housing system before they could be temporarily relocated (Cisneros and Engdahl 2009, 302). Return rates vary significantly. The Urban Institute's HOPE VI Panel Study that has followed five developments over time in different cities that received HOPE VI grants in 2000, found that only an average of 5 percent of households had returned as of 2005 (with additional returnees expected in subsequent years). At another extreme, however, some housing authorities have brought back up to 75 percent of former public housing residents, although those sites tended to be among the few where the housing was merely rehabilitated, rather than demolished and rebuilt for a mixed-income constituency (Popkin and Cunningham, 2009, 194–195).

*How should the CHA balance the goal of finding affordable housing
with the goal of reducing racial segregation?*

Research on the Plan for Transformation suggests not a declining significance of race (Wilson, 1978), but rather a changing one. Many of the evaluations of outcomes for residents assess the racial concentration of residents' new neighborhoods, and there appears to be little change in the racial concentration of movers' destination neighborhoods. The assessment of racial concentration originates in part from the Gautreaux cases, which law professor Lisa Alexander (2009) called the "Brown v. Board of Education of public housing reform." The landmark cases made the construction of public housing units in racially segregated areas illegal and rendered the racial diversity of public housing tenants' neighborhoods a salient variable. Yet scholars and practitioners debate the relevance today of restricting the construction of public housing (or voucher use) in predominately black areas (Boston, Pattillo). The situation has been made even more complex by the growth of Chicago's Latino population since the Gautreaux cases were first litigated, all part of a larger racial and ethnic diversification that calls into question the relevance of basing policy on the assumption of a black-white political demographic. Moreover, Pattillo (2007) underscores growing class diversity within what is often represented as the monolithic "black community." She identifies various interest group struggles among black public housing residents, middle-and working-class black homeowners, black city officials, black developers, and black community organizations, as well as white city politicians. Pattillo uncovers what occurs when these forces intersect in neighborhoods that house both black public housing residents and black middle class residents. In some ways their interests coalesce and in other ways their interests diverge. Consequently, the debate remains unresolved about how the location of public housing in black neighborhoods affects poor black residents. Court action reflects the changing class dynamics in African-American neighborhoods. A 1981 federal court order in the HUD portion of the Gautreaux case held that public housing in Chicago could be built in so called "revitalizing areas" (Polikoff 2006, 240). Revitalizing areas contain a substantial minority population but are undergoing sufficient redevelopment or revitalization to indicate that the areas will become more economically integrated in a relatively short time period. The introduction of the standard of revitalizing areas, then, reflects an ongoing ambiguity about the import of low-income minority households living in racial minority-dominated neighborhoods.

Has the Plan for Transformation caused more residents to lose their housing assistance sooner than without the Plan?

To date, half of the original 10/1/1999 residents are no longer active tenants of CHA housing and we know little about how that other half now lives (except in cases where we know that they are by now deceased). Thus, if one uses Boston's figures, the long-term outcomes for nearly 8,000 former CHA households[2], all of whom were CHA residents when the Plan for Transformation began, remain unknown. And, perhaps more importantly, it is still unclear if the Plan for Transformation caused residents to lose their housing assistance sooner than would have occurred without this Plan. Boston attempts to adjudicate this matter by determining the expected attrition rate. As Boston (2009) puts it, "we will find that the percentage of families who exit housing assistance is stable from year to year. They exit for the following reasons: some families fall behind in rent and therefore are evicted; some heads of households become seriously ill and are not longer capable of living unassisted; some die; some are evicted for various lease violations; some secure housing in the private sector; some are evicted for engaging in criminal activity; some move away from the Chicago area. . . .[T]he correct question therefore becomes, by how much has revitalization or rehabilitation increased the normal rate of attrition" (p. 100). Boston then seeks to calculate the expected rate of attrition using CHA historical data. This is somewhat problematic, given that he calculates the 'normal' or 'baseline' attrition rate for the seven years prior to the start of the Plan for Transformation (October 1992 to

---

[2] This is the sum of 10/1/1999 residents who, as of 2007, had moved out of the area (1,668), received a Section 8 transfer (1,588—although a transfer was received, the individual still exited housing assistance), skipped (1,279), gave no notice of intent to move out (1,146), were evicted for delinquent rent (860), had no termination reason indicated on their record (831), or were evicted for other reasons (568). This number totals 7,940 and does not include those residents who died (Boston, 2009). However, preliminary figures supplied directly from the CHA to the authors of this report in December 2009 suggest that far fewer 10/1/1999 households have lost their right of return—only 4,378. Therefore, the CHA and Boston figures remain unreconciled at this time.

October 1999). As documented by Jacob and others, a significant amount of demolition of CHA housing occurred in the 1990s, so these demolitions could well have skewed the 'normal' rate of attrition upward, thereby raising questions about what constitutes a reasonable baseline rate. More seriously, even using this baseline to compare the pre-2000 attrition rate to that of the first seven years of the Plan for Transformation, Boston found that attrition rates during the Plan for Transformation exceeded the expected rate of attrition. He reports that in addition to the expected rate of attrition of 6.6 percent (p.80) "attrition was higher in the years following the plan by 2.5 percentage points yearly" (p.100). This additional attrition, Boston notes, can be considered an effect of the Plan for Transformation. Yet Boston's Draft report does not discuss this finding further, and thereby appears to dismiss its significance. 2.5 percent is indeed a small number, but this is an *annual* difference that accumulates across many years. From 2000 to the end of Boston's data set in 2007, there have been seven full years of accumulated excess attrition. This suggests that, cumulatively, about 17.5 percent of CHA 10/1/1999 households with a Right of Return may have lost their housing assistance due to the Plan for Transformation; this is the number beyond the 'expected' rate of attrition. It remains important for researchers and policymakers to know more about why these additional households left. There are CHA administrative codes that ostensibly provide a reason why most households had their assistance terminated or chose to depart, but these data have not yet been systematically analyzed by independent researchers. How many left voluntarily and how many left for other reasons? If most of the excess attrition from CHA housing during 2000-2007 was involuntary (and not due primarily to death or serious illness), is the non inclusion of that segment of the cohort data sufficiently significant to skew Boston's analysis of the outcomes for the overall CHA population? That is, will omitting 17.5 percent of the data from the analysis—households that presumably fared worse than most—cause the findings to overstate the overall improvement for CHA residents resulting from the Plan for Transformation?

Related to this, researchers should study whether the Plan for Transformation has increased homelessness in Chicago. Moreover, if it has, it will be important to know whether this is this because legitimate CHA tenants have lost housing assistance or because illegal tenants (those not on the CHA lease) have been displaced.

How have 10/1/1999 CHA residents with a Right of Return
experienced the housing choice process?

The research to date reveals that the Plan for Transformation's net impact on the original 10/1/1999 leaseholders may not be quite as significant as the architects of the Plan intended. In part this is due simply to the length of time that it has taken to implement the Plan. As of 2007, just over half of the 10/1/1999 residents were still active CHA households and thus able to benefit from the potential positive changes the Plan sought to make in their lives. To date, there are also very few families who have moved into mixed-income developments, and researchers have documented a decreasing likelihood that 10/1/1999 residents will choose to (or be able to) exercise their Right of Return to move into mixed-income developments. While scholars note that the prevailing assumption of the Plan for Transformation was that most non-senior residents would be able to move out of public housing and into either mixed-income housing or the private market through vouchers, for most 10/1/1999 residents this has not been the case. Yet, as noted earlier, Boston's analysis of CHA administrative data shows that, as of 2007, there were just over 3,400 voucher holders, while 3,345 households remained in public housing (excluding senior housing), suggesting that for the many of the 10/1/1999 households, the benefits from living in the private market have been inaccessible.

In any case, over the medium and long-term, the benefits derived from the Plan for Transformation will increasingly benefit future residents, rather than the 10/1/1999 residents that had suffered through the worst conditions. This is to be expected from a long-term plan premised on a transformation of Chicago's entire public housing system. In the short-term, though, there is an issue of which 10/1/1999 families are able to pass the selection criteria to get vouchers. The increasingly stringent criteria for voucher use brings into question just how much "choice" residents truly have in availing themselves of the Housing Choice Voucher option. Do relocated residents really feel that they had a choice about type of housing? What constrains their choices?

What are CHA residents' perspectives on the Plan for Transformation?

Many researchers have questioned whether the CHA residents affected by the Plan for Transformation actually support it, and this has certainly been a popular question for Chicago journalists. According to Pattillo (2007), the vision for mixed-income redevelopment was developed in private meetings in Chicago between largely private institutional actors such as developers, university representatives, financial intermediaries, and lawyers. Public housing residents were all but excluded from these private meetings. While the CHA and other agencies held some formal meetings, many of the most important decisions that determined which public housing residents could ultimately return to the new developments were made in private settings and these decisions were not subject to public review. "The evolution and implementation of the mixed-income policy reveals that it did not emerge from the 'bottom up.' Mixed-income housing was not necessarily a solution for the public housing problems voiced by public housing residents. In fact, the Central Advisory Council (CAC), a representative body made up of representatives from each public housing development was not systematically included in the initial goal setting and development of the Plan. Rather, the CAC was only asked to vote to approve the Plan after it was fully developed by the CHA . . . Mixed-income in Chicago, thus, contributes to the gentrification of public housing neighborhoods and to the displacement of, rather than the empowerment of, many former residents" (160).

*How will the Plan for Transformation change the
self-identity of the CHA?*

The CHA has also transformed its role in public housing provision from an owner to an incentive creator. As Smith (2006) explains, "[a]s laid out in the original 'Plan for Transformation,' the CHA no longer positions itself as a housing provider, but rather now is a 'facilitator' of housing." Prior to creation of the Plan, the CHA owned and managed over 20 large multi-family public housing developments and an even larger number of senior properties in inner-city neighborhoods. Now the CHA only owns the land under the new mixed-income developments; it does not own the buildings or other improvements on the land. The new mixed-income developments are owned by private developers who lease the land under the developments from the CHA under a 99-year ground lease for one dollar per year. Despite the reduction in family units under ownership and management, as noted earlier, the CHA has increased its holdings for seniors. What do these shifts in mission and clientele mean in terms of a change in the identity of the housing authority?

2. PEOPLE

How have residents fared when they moved into the private housing
market with vouchers?

Researchers generally conclude that residents who have moved into the private market using HCVs have shown a variety of improvements. For those residents who remain clients of the CHA and have moved into the private housing market using vouchers, moving out of distressed public housing into a place that is safer and lower poverty has had a positive impact on residents' quality of life. Both the NORC studies and the Urban Institute studies confirm that there have been improvements in movers' mental health. These studies also show that neighborhoods are also safer than their former public housing neighborhoods. Finally, studies concur that most movers enjoy better quality of housing. Reports from voucher holders indicate that they feel safer and live in safer areas (Popkin, 2010; NORC, 2007). Importantly, contrary to popular lore, there appears to be little crime impact from the influx of public housing residents into the private housing market (Boston, 2009; Hartley, 2008).

How have residents fared who have remained in traditional
CHA public housing?

The research suggests that thus far there have been few benefits for non-movers: those households who have remained in CHA conventional public housing, especially that which has not yet been rehabilitated. While research shows dramatic improvement to residents' mental health when they use vouchers to move to the private market, residents who remain in family public housing show elevated levels of stress. The cause of this remains unknown: it may be caused by the hyper concentration of disadvantaged households left behind in public housing units. It may also be a reflection of the trend for more high functioning households to move into the private market.

*Do those who move with vouchers continue to show improvements over
time after moving into the private market?*

Although there is some research consensus about the benefits of moving away
from conventional public housing developments with the assistance of a Housing
Choice Voucher, most of these studies only assess movers a year or two after they
move from public housing, so longer-term outcomes remain unknown, especially
in cases where voucher-holders move multiple times.

Researchers have speculated that movers will become more socially integrated
into their new neighborhoods and that this can be beneficial, as residents make
gains from productive social ties. But other researchers speculate that increased
social integration could be detrimental, especially for youth, for whom early social
isolation may be protective.

What have the outcomes been for CHA youth?

Adults and, especially, adult heads of households, have received the bulk of the
scholarly attention when assessing the impacts of the Plan for Transformation.
Consequently we know less about how the Plan has affected youth. The existing
research on children and youth is limited. The Panel Study includes youth and
offers some intriguing findings about differences in behavior between movers
and non-movers and between boys and girls, but the sample size is small. The
Chapin Hall Center for Children at the University of Chicago has conducted
research comparing educational outcomes for children who have remained
in CHA housing to those who have relocated from it, but this has remained
unpublished. Additionally, the NORC Residential Satisfaction Survey includes
questions about youth, but the analysis of the data is limited and the findings
are entirely quantitative. NORC researchers expect to conduct further analysis of
their data on youth outcomes.

Meanwhile, as the Metropolitan Planning Commission highlights, current
service strategies focus on job readiness and self-sufficiency for adults, yet
more than 11,000 of CHA residents are age 20 and younger (Chicago Housing
Authority, 2008b).

Do residents who leave public housing experience gains in employment?

The CHA has identified self-sufficiency and increases in employment and income levels as a prime goal for the Plan for Transformation. Numerous debates about outcomes remain unresolved. There are contradictory reported findings regarding employment gains, resident health, and outcomes for movers vs. non-movers. Reported research findings on employment outcomes also vary. Buron (2004) found little or no improvement in employment rates for voucher holders. Barriers to employment include residents' poor physical and mental health status and low levels of education, as well as the poor status of the economy (Popkin and Theodos, 2008). Unpublished research from the Chapin Hall Center for Children at the University of Chicago found that, for those households reporting earnings from employment during 2000, 2001, and 2002, the median incomes of households and household heads were higher for CHA residents than for those that had relocated away from CHA properties. However, both Danilin (2009) and a joint study by the Chicago Housing Authority, The Partnership for New Communities and The Mayor's Office of Workforce Development (2006) found increases in employment income for those who left traditional public housing. While Boston's findings passed his tests for statistical significance, the MPC (2006) drew a more cautious conclusion from the Chicago Housing Authority's joint study, citing a number of alternative explanations that would minimize the impact of the increase in employment income for movers.

There is a clear disconnect in the research between Danny Boston's findings in his draft report that show gains, and most other work—in Chicago and nationally—that has not found employment gains from voucher use. Further research needs to take place on this issue. A key question may be, if gains to employment status and income do take place, how many years does it take for positive results to appear? And, in Chicago, what has been the effect of the CHA's new system-wide work requirement?

*Are residents with HCVs moving into mixed-income
(or opportunity) neighborhoods?*

The Housing Choice Voucher (HCV) program aims to move residents into mixed-income neighborhoods as part of an overall strategy to deconcentrate poverty.

However, the research shows that residents have had limited success moving into units in low-poverty opportunity neighborhoods. While maps created by Boston for his draft report (2009) claim to show that, increasingly, the HCV movers are moving to 'better' neighborhoods, the maps also appear to reveal that few of these moves (even the recent ones) have been to the top "Community Attribute Index" quintiles. However, the data presentation and analysis in Boston's draft report do not allow readers to make these calculations with sufficient detail, since early version of the report does not provide tabular data about how many HCV holders have moved into neighborhoods with particular poverty characteristics, and does not then provide these tables over time so that the trend can be assessed for statistical significance. Since the CHA has redoubled its efforts to move residents into opportunity neighborhoods, the question of mixed-income residency also remains an urgent matter to resolve. Yet there is no standard definition for a "mixed-income neighborhood," making it difficult to assess whether the HCV moves are to "mixed-income neighborhoods" and whether options such as scattered site housing qualify. Can a neighborhood be considered "mixed-income" if it is also still 40 percent poor (and, therefore, still designated as "high poverty"), for instance? Once a standard for what counts as a desirable form of mixed-income neighborhood is reached, it may finally be possible to answer the question: How many CHA clients will live in neighborhoods that qualify as mixed-income?

What have the outcomes been for seniors?

There appears to be almost no research on the senior population, a fact made even more surprising because a greater number of post transformation CHA holdings are in senior developments. According to the CHA (2002), in the inventory of Chicago Public Housing units, 7,063 of the senior units were occupied. Yet the Plan for Transformation called for 9,382 senior units to be developed. This is the only category of housing where the CHA planned to increase the number of units (by restoring the stock to full occupancy). Perhaps some of this increase reflects the number of residents who have aged in place, or perhaps this increase reflects a desire to deal with a less complicated constituency and/or set of buildings. The question of why the CHA chose to increase the number and percentage of housing units for seniors remains undiscussed in the research literature. Under the current Plan for Transformation, 37.5 percent or 9,382 of the 25,000 planned public housing units will be senior housing (and these will house many more seniors than were offered a Right of Return). This is the single largest category of CHA properties under the Plan, so it is particularly surprising not to be a setting for research. What impact has the Plan had on seniors? For example, do they show the same improvements in mental health measures that the working age adult population has when moving with vouchers or to mixed-income communities? Or do they fare less well, more like younger households who have moved into other CHA properties? How has the Plan affected the networks of seniors, especially those offering social support? What has the impact of relocation been on this population? What kinds of support have been most helpful to assisting this vulnerable population? How have seniors fared in different settings: In senior-only developments? In mixed-income communities? In other communities where they are raising grandchildren (grandfamilies)?

How have residents fared in rehabilitated public housing?

The prospects for CHA residents moving to rehabilitated family public housing remain uncertain. Additionally, researchers find that because the lease compliance rules are more strict now than they were in the early years, the remaining population has become "doubly disadvantaged": they were unable to move when standards were less demanding and they now face even higher barriers. Does this create the risk that a high concentration of disadvantaged households will remain in public housing? Aside from quantitative measures about some socioeconomic variables describing families in conventional public housing, however, there is still little qualitative data about life in rehabbed family and senior developments. Since, taken together, these communities constitute a significant majority of the total number of units delivered by the Plan for Transformation, additional research about the outcomes for residents in these places should be undertaken.

Will the voucher holders continue to accumulate gains compared to those living in renovated family properties? Is it possible that renovation of family public housing could also instill some of the gains typical of more fully revitalized developments? In their study of the effects of welfare reform on Chicago families receiving TANF from 1999-2002 (just as the Plan began), Lewis and Sinha (2004) found "strong limits on income growth" (p. 158) and hypothesized that early income gains observed for participants would decline in subsequent years.

Beyond questions about income, other questions about long-term outcomes remain. Will residents remain lease compliant? Will access to institutional support affect residents' employment? Which services do residents actually use and which ones seem to have the greatest impact? Are there models of supportive housing that work well for CHA residents?

3. PLACES

Has the influx of voucher holders into Chicago neighborhoods had a negative impact on crime levels?

Neither Boston (2009) nor Hartley (2008) found an increase in crime in neighborhoods where Chicago public housing residents had relocated using Housing Choice Vouchers. Indeed, the demographic impact of this group of HCV holders (i.e., those HCV holders whose vouchers come as a result of moving away from public housing during the Plan for Transformation) in communities has been small, and the CHA reports that these HCV relocatees make up no more than 3 percent in any community. However, if all HCV holders are considered (both the ones used by 10/1/1999 households and the 31,000 vouchers used by others), voucher holders comprise as much as 10-15 percent of the total population in some Chicago communities (CHA, personal communication, May 25, 2010).

How well are existing public housing developments faring?

There is much evidence that the conditions in the already distressed public housing developments have deteriorated further since implementation of the Plan for Transformation has begun. High vacancy rates and an increased concentration of hard-to-house households have left the developments with an increasingly isolated and disadvantaged population.

Do the neighborhoods where CHA leaseholders live offer higher quality schools than those available prior to the Plan for Transformation?

Thus far, researchers have found little evidence of improvements in the schools serving children living in mixed-income developments. Jacob (2003) found that moving due to the demolition of public housing buildings had no impact on the academic achievement of younger children on a variety of outcome measures, including test scores, grades and retention. He further found movers were attending schools identical to those of a control group of students and, even when students did move to substantially better neighborhoods, they did not end up in significantly better schools. Moreover, Boston's draft report (2009) yielded negative findings about the quality of the elementary schools serving both the mixed-income neighborhoods and the neighborhoods accessed through use of vouchers. He found that, compared to the original public housing neighborhoods—both of these types of neighborhoods surprisingly had lower quality elementary schools. Looking forward, even if elementary schools improve near the redeveloped mixed-income communities, Pattillo (2007) holds that original poor public housing residents will also unlikely be the ultimate long-term primary beneficiaries of current educational reform initiatives in these newly constructed neighborhoods.

Mixed-income developments are the most visible expression of the Plan for Transformation and therefore merit special scrutiny. Perhaps because the completion dates for many of the mixed-income developments are still well into the future, as noted earlier, there is little definitive research on outcomes in mixed-income developments. Work on early outcomes from Joseph (2010) identifies some early successes, such as high levels of satisfaction from both groups about the physical redevelopment efforts. Yet the work also suggests that some of the anticipated outcomes, such as cross class interaction, are unlikely to occur in mixed-income developments (a finding that is consistent with what researchers in other cities have observed).

When does a lower neighborhood poverty rate become experientially significant?

There is an assumption in the literature that residing in lower poverty neighborhoods is beneficial for low-income people. However, there is little consensus about the precise income threshold level required for low-income residents to benefit from living in a higher income neighborhood. HUD developed criteria for defining "high poverty" and "low poverty" neighborhoods when devising the Moving to Opportunity (MTO) program in the early 1990s, identifying "high poverty" neighborhoods as census tracts with 40 percent or more households in poverty, and "low poverty" tracts as those with no more than 10 percent impoverished (Polikoff 2006, 264). Boston reports that, "families relocated to lower poverty neighborhoods when they relocated with vouchers or moved to a mixed-income development." By contrast (and not surprisingly), the neighborhood poverty level for families who went from one public housing unit to another public housing unit barely changed: from 46 percent poverty to 45 percent poverty. Families with HCVs went from 46.9 percent poverty neighborhoods to 26 percent poverty neighborhoods. Families moving into the new mixed-income community went from 48 percent poverty neighborhoods to 36.7 percent poverty (which is still close to the threshold for "high poverty"). In other words, despite moves in the direction of lower poverty neighborhoods, all categories of Plan for Transformation placements delivered residents to neighborhoods that were, on average, still closer to "high poverty" tracts than to "low poverty" ones.

Beyond this, there are further questions about how best to interpret the significance of "poverty deconcentration" that has been advanced by the Plan for Transformation. At base, the gains from deconcentrated poverty that go to larger numbers of families—those who leave public housing for other neighborhoods— are both modest (i.e., many still live in areas of high poverty) and inevitable because any new neighborhood that isn't public housing is likely to have a lower poverty rate. In 1999 public housing was located in the highest poverty neighborhoods in the city of Chicago. In short, it is doubtful whether it would actually be possible for residents to move to neighborhoods with higher levels of poverty than public housing neighborhoods. Any comparisons between poverty rates in 1999 public housing neighborhoods and poverty rates in 2007 post-public housing destination neighborhoods reveal little more than the obvious fact that a move from the city's highest poverty tracts to anywhere else represents an improvement. Moreover, while this is a statistically significant improvement, many question whether this kind of modest reduction in poverty leads to an experientially significant improvement in the lives of residents. For all the efforts to define an "opportunity" neighborhood, it remains to be seen whether there are particular thresholds of neighborhood poverty reduction that trigger other sorts of improvements in the lives of the least economically advantaged.

Galster (2009, 19) suggests that, "there is a substantial body of U.S. econometric literature suggesting that a variety of negative behavioral outcomes occur for residents when the neighborhood poverty rate exceeds a range of 15–20 percent." Most settings for CHA residents, after the Plan for Transformation as well as before it, exceed this threshold. It would be useful for researchers to replicate such studies for CHA-associated neighborhoods. Better still would be if research about poverty rate thresholds could be conducted in a way that includes experiential data, and not just aggregated econometric data.

What is the impact of the Plan for Transformation on the Chicago region?

There is not yet much research on the metropolitan impacts of the Plan. More ethnographic sorts of work is needed in communities on the South Side and in the south suburbs that have been most affected by the influx of former residents from CHA developments. The goal of the Gautreaux decision and of the Moving to Opportunity experiment was to move public housing residents out of poor inner city communities and into more affluent suburbs. Although there is some evidence that 10/1/1999 residents have moved to the South Side suburbs, the socioeconomic situation in these places likely represents little improvement from higher poverty neighborhoods within the city of Chicago. Boston's (2009) data show that some 10/1/1999 residents exited the CHA system with vouchers but the data do not show where these residents moved. A variety of questions about potential suburban destinations arise: Did any 10/1/1999 households move to lower poverty or affluent suburbs? If so, what was the process by which these residents located their new homes and how are these residents faring?

SOURCES FOR THIS PORTION OF THE MACARTHUR REPORT

Alexander, L. T., 2009. Stakeholder Participation in New Governance: Lessons from Chicago's Public Housing Reform Experiment. *Georgetown Journal on Poverty Law Policy.*

Boston, T. D. 2009. "Public Housing Transformation and Family Self-Sufficiency: A case study of Chicago and Atlanta Housing Authorities." Study prepared for the John D. and Catherine T. MacArthur Foundation. Draft version.

Buron, L. 2004. "An Improved Living Environment? Neighborhood Outcomes for HOPE VI Relocatees." *Urban Institute Metropolitan Housing and Communities Center Brief No. 3.*

Chicago Housing Authority. 2002. "Building New Communities: Building New Lives," brochure, The Chicago Housing Authority Plan for Transformation.

Chicago Housing Authority, The Partnership for New Communities and The Mayor's Office of Workforce Development. 2006. Opportunity Chicago. Thinking Strategically about Workforce Development for Chicago Public-Housing Residents.

Chicago Housing Authority. 2008b. FY 2008 Moving to Work Annual Plan, Plan for Transformation Year 9.

Cisneros, H. and Engdahl, L., eds. 2009. *From Despair to Hope: HOPE VI and the New Promise of Public Housing in America's Cities.* Washington, D.C.: Brookings Institution Press.

Galster, G. 2009. "Neighborhood Social Mix: Theory, Evidence, and Implications for Policy and Planning," Paper presented at the International Workshop on Planning For/With People, Israel Institute of Technology, Haifa, Israel, June.

Hartley, Daniel A. 2008. "The Effect of High Concentration Public Housing on Crime, Construction, and Home Prices: Evidence from Demolitions in Chicago," Job market paper. University of California, Berkeley.

Jacob, B. 2003. Public Housing, Housing Vouchers and Student Achievement: Evidence from Public Housing Demolitions in Chicago. *NBER Working Paper.*

Joseph, M.L. 2008. Early Resident Experiences at a New Mixed-Income Development in Chicago. *Journal of Urban Affairs* 30 (3): 229–57.

Lewis, D. and Sinha, V. 2007. "Moving Up and Moving Out? Economic and Residential Mobility." *Urban Affairs Review.*

Metropolitan Planning Council. 2008. Plan for Transformation Update. February.

National Opinion Research Center, University of Chicago. 2003. *Resident relocation survey methodology and results: Methodology and results.* National Opinion Research Center at the University of Chicago.

Pattillo. M. 2007. *Black on the Block: The Politics of Race and Class in the City.* Chicago: University of Chicago Press.

Popkin, S.J., Cunningham, M.K., and Burt, M. 2005. "Public Housing Transformation and the Hard to House." *Housing Policy Debate* 16 (1).

ACKNOWLEDGMENTS

This project is supported in part by an award from the National Endowment for the Arts. We'd also like to thank the Geraldine R. Dodge Foundation, the Joyce Foundation, the Illinois Program for Research in the Humanities at the University of Illinois at Urbana-Champaign, and the University of Illinois Research Board for their financial support.

The author would like to thank her friends and family for their love and encouragement throughout the production of *High Rise Stories*. Special thanks to Peter Orner for his faith in the idea of *High Rise Stories* from the very start, and for his patient counsel ever since. To Curtis Perry and Dianne Harris for their energizing votes of confidence. To Jamie Kalven, Alma Gottlieb, and Miles Harvey for their dedicated mentorship. To Barry Mayo, Matti Bunzl, Ari Weinzweig, Drea Hall, Carolyn Armenta Davis, Ellen Rozelle Turner, Sarah Ross, Ryan Griffis, Ned Schaub, and David Wright for fueling the book's progress at critical junctures. To my father Joe Petty for his clarity and calmness. To my sisters Jill and Miriam Petty for hearing me out and cheering me on. To my mother-in-law Madeline Murphy Rabb for setting a welcoming table at the end of many a long week. To my husband Maurice Rabb for his optimism and boundless mischief, and for reliable in-home tech support. And to my daughter Ella Esther for her giant hugs.

ART WORKS.
arts.gov

ABOUT THE EDITOR

AUDREY PETTY is an Associate Professor of English at the University of Illinois at Urbana-Champaign. A Ford Foundation grantee, her work has been featured in *Columbia*, *Storyquarterly*, and *Ninth*, among many others

The VOICE OF WITNESS SERIES

The Voice of Witness book series, published by McSweeney's, empowers those most closely affected by contemporary social injustice. Using oral history as a foundation, the series depicts human rights crises in the United States and around the world. *High Rise Stories* is the eleventh book in the series. The other titles are:

SURVIVING JUSTICE
America's Wrongfully Convicted and Exonerated
Edited by Lola Vollen and Dave Eggers
Foreword by Scott Turow

These oral histories prove that the problem of wrongful conviction is far-reaching and very real. Through a series of all-too-common circumstances—eyewitness misidentification, inept defense lawyers, coercive interrogation—the lives of these men and women of all different backgrounds were irreversibly disrupted. In *Surviving Justice*, thirteen exonerees describe their experiences—the events that led to their convictions, their years in prison, and the process of adjusting to their new lives outside.

VOICES FROM THE STORM
The People of New Orleans on Hurricane Katrina and Its Aftermath
Edited by Chris Ying and Lola Vollen

Voices from the Storm is a chronological account of the worst natural disaster in modern American history. Thirteen New Orleanians describe the days leading up to Hurricane Katrina, the storm itself, and the harrowing confusion of the days and months afterward. Their stories weave and intersect, ultimately creating an eye-opening portrait of courage in the face of terror, and of hope amid nearly complete devastation.

UNDERGROUND AMERICA
Narratives of Undocumented Lives
Edited by Peter Orner
Foreword by Luis Alberto Urrea

They arrive from around the world for countless reasons. Many come simply to make a living. Others are fleeing persecution in their native countries. But by living and working in the U.S. without legal status, millions of immigrants risk deportation and imprisonment. They live underground, with little protection from exploitation at the hands of human smugglers, employers, or law enforcement. *Underground America* presents the remarkable oral histories of men and women struggling to carve a life for themselves in the United States. In 2010, *Underground America* was translated into Spanish and released as *En las Sombras de Estados Unidos*.

OUT OF EXILE
The Abducted and Displaced People of Sudan
Edited by Craig Walzer
Additional interviews and an introduction by
Dave Eggers and Valentino Achak Deng

Millions of people have fled from conflicts and persecution in all parts of Sudan, and many thousands more have been enslaved as human spoils of war. In *Out of Exile*, refugees and abductees recount their escapes from the wars in Darfur and South Sudan, from political and religious persecution, and from abduction by militias. They tell of life before the war, and of the hope that they might someday find peace again.

HOPE DEFERRED
Narratives of Zimbabwean Lives
Edited by Peter Orner and Annie Holmes
Foreword by Brian Chikwava

The sixth volume in the Voice of Witness series presents the narratives of Zimbabweans whose lives have been affected by the country's political, economic, and human rights crises. This book asks the question: How did a country with so much promise—a stellar education system, a growing middle class of professionals, a sophisticated economic infrastructure, a liberal constitution, and an independent judiciary—go so wrong?

NOWHERE TO BE HOME
Narratives from Survivors of Burma's Military Regime
Edited by Maggie Lemere and Zoë West
Foreword by Mary Robinson

Decades of military oppression in Burma have led to the systematic destruction of thousands of ethnic-minority villages, a standing army with one of the world's highest numbers of child soldiers, and the displacement of millions of people. *Nowhere to Be Home* is an eye-opening collection of oral histories exposing the realities of life under military rule. In their own words, men and women from Burma describe their lives in the country that Human Rights Watch has called "the textbook example of a police state."

PATRIOT ACTS
Narratives of Post-9/11 Injustice
Compiled and edited by Alia Malek
Foreword by Karen Korematsu

Patriot Acts tells the stories of men and women who have been needlessly swept up in the War on Terror. In their own words, narrators recount personal experiences of the post-9/11 backlash that has deeply altered their lives and communities. *Patriot Acts* illuminates these experiences in a compelling collection of eighteen oral histories from men and women who have found themselves subject to a wide range of human and civil rights abuses—from rendition and torture, to workplace discrimination, bullying, FBI surveillance, and harassment.

INSIDE THIS PLACE, NOT OF IT
Narratives from Women's Prisons
Compiled and edited by Ayelet Waldman and Robin Levi
Foreword by Michelle Alexander

Inside This Place, Not of It reveals some of the most egregious human rights violations within women's prisons in the United States. In their own words, the thirteen narrators in this book recount their lives leading up to incarceration and their experiences inside—ranging from forced sterilization and shackling during childbirth, to physical and sexual abuse by prison staff. Together, their testimonies illustrate the harrowing struggles for survival that women in prison must endure.

THROWING STONES AT THE MOON
Narratives of Colombians Displaced by Violence
Compiled and edited by Sibylla Brodzinsky and Max Schoening
Foreword by Íngrid Betancourt

For nearly five decades, Colombia has been embroiled in internal armed conflict among guerrilla groups, paramilitary militias, and the country's own military. Civilians in Colombia face a range of abuses from all sides, including killings, disappearances, and rape—and more than four million have been forced to flee their homes. The oral histories in *Throwing Stones at the Moon* describe the most widespread of Colombia's human rights crises: forced displacement.

REFUGEE HOTEL
Compiled and edited by Juliet Linderman and Gabriele Stabile

Refugee Hotel is a groundbreaking collection of photography and interviews that documents the arrival of refugees in the United States. Evocative images are coupled with moving testimonies from people describing their first days in the U.S., the lives they've left behind, and the new communities they've since created.